Cinematicity in
Media History

Edited by Jeffrey Geiger and Karin Littau

EDINBURGH
University Press

© The chapters their several authors, 2013

Edinburgh University Press Ltd
22 George Square, Edinburgh EH8 9LF
www.euppublishing.com

Typeset in Garamond MT Pro by
Servis Filmsetting Ltd, Stockport, Cheshire,
and printed and bound in Great Britain by
CPI Group (UK) Ltd, Croydon CR0 4YY

A CIP record for this book is available from the British Library

ISBN 978 0 7486 7611 8 (hardback)
ISBN 978 0 7486 7612 5 (webready PDF)
ISBN 978 0 7486 7614 9 (epub)

The right of the contributors
to be identified as authors of this work
has been asserted in accordance with
the Copyright, Designs and Patents Act 1988
and the Copyright and Related Rights
Regulations 2003 (SI No. 2498).

Contents

Illustrations

Acknowledgements

In addition to our authors, there are a number of people we should thank for their helpful contributions to this collection. First, we'd like to express our appreciation to Kriss Ravetto-Biagioli and Martine Beugnet, for their support of the project, and to the editorial team at Edinburgh University Press, in particular Gillian Leslie, Jenny Peebles and Michelle Houston, for help and advice they've given over the course of producing the manuscript. We'd also like to thank the external readers of individual chapters for their scrupulous and constructive feedback, and the anonymous readers of our proposal, whose sensible advice contributed to making this a stronger and more balanced collection. Robert Weninger, former editor of *Comparative Critical Studies* and Richard Hibbitt, assistant editor, also provided detailed editorial support on many of the chapters included here. Laura Booth has provided further copy-editing support. Looking further back, we would like to thank the British Comparative Literature Association, under whose auspices the 'Cinematicity' conference was held at the University of Essex in 2007, and acknowledge the diverse and stimulating work of contributors at this event; their ideas continue to resonate in the current collection.

Chapters 1 to 3, Chapter 6 and Chapter 9 appeared in a special issue of *Comparative Critical Studies* 6.3 (October 2009), entitled 'Cinematicity' and a version of Chapter 4 appeared in a special issue of *e-Comparative Critical Studies*: Special Online Supplement 9.3 (October 2012).

Notes on the Contributors

NICO BAUMBACH is Assistant Professor at Columbia University School of the Arts. Publications include articles in *Comparative Critical Studies* and *New Review of Film and Television* and a chapter in *Critical Cinema: Beyond the Theory of Practice* (2010). He is currently working on two projects: a book on the writings on cinema by contemporary continental philosophers Alain Badiou, Jacques Rancière, Giorgio Agamben and Slavoj Žižek; and a study of Iranian filmmaker Abbas Kiarostami.

MARTINE BEUGNET is Professor in Visual Studies at the University of Paris 7 Diderot. She has written articles and essays on a wide range of contemporary cinema topics, and has published four books to date: *Sexualité, marginalité, contrôle: cinéma français contemporain* (2000), *Claire Denis* (2004), *Proust at the Movies* (2005, with Marion Schmid) and *Cinema and Sensation: French Film and the Art of Transgression* (2007, second issue 2012).

IAN CHRISTIE is a film and media historian. He has written and edited books on Powell and Pressburger, Russian cinema, Scorsese and Gilliam; and has contributed to many exhibitions and television programmes. He was Slade Professor of Fine Art at Cambridge University in 2006. A Fellow of the British Academy, he is Professor of Film and Media History at Birkbeck College, director of the London Screen Study Collection and vice-president of Europa Cinemas. Recent publications include: *Stories We Tell Ourselves: The Cultural Impact of British Film 1946–2006* (2009), *The Art of Film: John Box and Production Design* (2009) and *Audiences* (2012).

JEFFREY GEIGER is a Senior Lecturer at the University of Essex, where he founded the Centre for Film Studies in 2001. Along with *Cinematicity*, books include *Facing the Pacific: Polynesia and the U.S. Imperial Imagination* (2007), *American Documentary Film: Projecting the Nation* (2011) and the co-edited *Film Analysis: A Norton Reader* (2005, expanded edition 2013). His essays have appeared in many books, and in journals such as *Film International, Third Text, African American Review, Cinema Journal, PMLA* and the *TLS*.

TOM GUNNING is the Edwin A. and Betty L. Bergman Distinguished Service Professor in the Department on Cinema and Media at the University of Chicago. He is the author of *D. W. Griffith and the Origins of American Narrative Film* (1993) and *The Films of Fritz Lang: Allegories of Vision and Modernity* (2000), as well as numerous articles on early cinema, film history, avant-garde film, and cinema and modernism. In 2009, he was awarded an Andrew A. Mellon Distinguished Achievement Award, the first film scholar to receive one, and in 2010 he was elected to the American Academy of Arts and Sciences.

LEON GUREVITCH is the Director of the Culture and Context Programme, Marsden Research Scholar and Senior Lecturer at Victoria University of Wellington's School of Design. His current Marsden work is a major three-year project, funded by the New Zealand Royal Society to study digital image industry work cultures. As an active academic and photographer, he publishes both his images and writing. Recent publications have appeared in *Animation Journal, The Journal of Television and New Media, Senses of Cinema, The New Zealand Journal of Media Studies* and *The Journal of Popular Narrative Media*.

ANKE HENNIG is Research Fellow in the Collaborative Research Centre 626, 'Aesthetic Experience and the Dissolution of Artistic Limits', and teaches at the Peter Szondi Institute of Comparative Literature at the Freie Universität Berlin. She has published on Russian Formalism, the Russian avant-garde, theories of intermedia and more recently on the chronotopology of cinematic fiction and speculative poetics. She is the author of *Sowjetische Kinodramaturgie: Konfliktlinien zwischen Literatur und Film in der Sowjetunion der 1930er Jahre* (2010) and, with Armen Avanessian, co-author of *Präsens: Poetik eines Tempus* (2012) and she is co-editor of numerous collections, including *Jetzt und Dann: Zeiterfahrung in Film, Literatur und Philosophie* (2010).

KARIN LITTAU is Director of Research in the Department of Literature, Film, and Theatre Studies at the University of Essex, and serves on the Executive Committee of the British Comparative Literature Association. Her interests are book and film history, and comparative media. She is the author of *Theories of Reading: Books, Bodies, and Bibliomania* (2006; reprinted 2008), *The Routledge Concise History of Literature and Film* (forthcoming) and co-editor of two issues of *Comparative Critical Studies: Inventions: Literature and Science* (2005) and *Cinematicity* (2009). Recent publications include an article on cross-media for *Convergence* (2011) and on media philosophy in *New Takes in Film-Philosophy* (2011).

LEV MANOVICH is Professor at The Graduate Center, The City University of New York, a Director of the Software Studies Initiative and a Visiting Professor at the European Graduate School. He has been working with computer media as an artist, computer animator, designer and programmer since 1984, and he is the author of *Software Takes Command* (2013), *The Language of New Media* (2001), *Black Box – White Cube* (2005), *Soft Cinema* DVD (2005), *Metamediji* (2001) and *Tekstura: Russian Essays on Visual Culture* (1993). His artwork has been included in many international exhibitions, including a retrospective by the Institute of Contemporary Arts (ICA), London entitled *Lev Manovich: Adventures of Digital Cinema* (2002).

JOSS MARSH is Associate Professor of English at Indiana University, Bloomington. She is the author of *Word Crimes: Blasphemy, Culture, and Literature in 19th-Century England* (1998), and of essays on Dickens, Chaplin, the nineteenth-century novel and film, and Victorian visual culture. With her research partner David Francis, OBE, she has lectured widely on the magic lantern and has recreated actual lantern performances at, among others, the Cinemateca Portuguesa, the Academy of Motion Picture Arts and Sciences, The Museum of Modern Art (MoMA), the National Gallery of Art (DC) and the Vienna Art Museum/Film Archive.

KRISTIAN MOEN is Lecturer in Screen Studies in the Department of Drama: Theatre, Film, Television at the University of Bristol. His forthcoming monograph, *The Birth of Modern Fantasy: Fairy Tales and Film*, examines how fairy tales were used to negotiate modernity in nineteenth-century French theatre, early cinema and American cinema from the 1910s to the 1930s. He has published in *Screen*, *Early Popular Visual Culture*, and other journals.

KEITH B. WILLIAMS is Senior Lecturer in the Department of English at the University of Dundee, and Chair of the Scottish Word and Image Group, which has held annual conferences since 1994. His main research interest is in literature of the modern period and film. His books include *British Writers and the Media 1930–45* (1996) and *H. G. Wells, Modernity and the Movies* (2007) and a co-edited volume on *Rewriting the Thirties: Modernism & After* (1997). He is currently writing a monograph on *James Joyce and Cinematicity*.

Introduction: Cinematicity and Comparative Media

JEFFREY GEIGER AND KARIN LITTAU

Rapid changes in modern telecommunications technologies have heightened our awareness of the mediascape that we inhabit, prompting us to reflect more generally not merely on the fact, but on the usually hidden history, of media change. In a world where change has become the only constant, how does the perpetually new relate to the old? How does cinema, itself once a new medium, relate to what we now refer to as the New Media, or conversely, how did cinema as an emergent medium relate to its predecessors and contemporaries – eclipsing, challenging and transforming them in its wake? This collection sets out to examine these questions by focusing on the relations of cinema to other media, artworks and diverse forms of entertainment, demarcating their sometimes conjoined, sometimes separate, histories. *Cinematicity in Media History* thus seeks to make visible the complex ways in which media anticipate, interfere with and draw on one another, demonstrating how what we have called 'cinematicity' makes itself felt in practices of seeing, reading, writing and thinking *both* before and after the 'birth' of cinema.

CINEMA HISTORY AS MEDIA HISTORY

Cinematicity in Media History is premised on the idea that media inevitably bear one another's traces. Therefore, no medium may exhaustively be studied in isolation from others. Pivotal to this collection's enquiries are the interrelations between cinema, literature, painting and photography, not only to one another, but amid a host of other minor and major media: the magic lantern, the zoetrope, the flickbook, the iPhone and the computer. This collection, therefore, signals a commitment to the comparative study of media, which abandons what Henry Jenkins has called the compartmentalized approach of 'structuring the study of media around individual media', such as film, literature, painting, photography or digital culture.[1] Here intermediality becomes a useful concept for the environment in which this comparative labour is undertaken, since to study intermediality is to follow the intertwined histories and transformative relations between old and new, mechanical and electronic, analogue and digital, word-based and image-based media. Its scope ranges across history, technology and aesthetics. By plotting the elaborate ways in which media cross historical and cultural borders and, in the process, re-forge one another's boundaries, we gain crucial insights not only into the development of media, including cinema's niche in this broader media ecology, but also into the aesthetic possibilities of cross-media forms and the capacities of media insofar as they change the character and conditions of sensation. Intermediality has considerable currency in European and Canadian media theory,[2] mainly as an umbrella term for remediation, premediation and cross-media phenomena;[3] it also has ambitious, sometimes suggestively utopian (as in the influential work of Gene Youngblood), implications in Anglo-American media studies.[4] While we follow the history of the term 'cinematicity' below, we may say that we conceive of it as an instance of intermediality.

It should be obvious here that our concern is not with the medium-specific properties of cinema – that is, what makes cinema 'properly' cinematic. The formalist emphasis on what gives poetry its 'poeticity' or literature its 'literariness' (Jakobson), or what gives art its unique nature or identity as art (Greenberg)[5] relies on a notion of medial purity.[6] Rather, our concern is with what induces cinematicity in other media forms (such as literature, scriptwriting or aerial photography) and with what makes other media platforms (such as gaming, or watching a film on a miniature screen) 'cinematic'. As Berys Gaut describes it:

> [C]inema was never confined to photochemical images. The variety of the kinds of cinema has become obvious in the last fifteen years with the rise of digital cinema, both in its noninteractive and interactive forms; the latter encompasses a range of cases from videogames to digital interactive dramas to virtual reality displays.[7]

Furthermore, if blogs and other Internet usages are any indication, cinematicity is becoming an established point of reference – often in terms of describing the properties of gaming technologies. Sarah LeBoeuf, for example, uses cinematicity when referring to Pokémon 3DS, suggesting that 3D graphics and 'more cinematicity' would be an evolutionary step. Here, cinematicity would relate to the cinematic 'feel' of the game, a 'feel' that in fact has little to do with cinema in the traditional photochemical sense.[8] Hence, in the digital game we encounter a kind of 'mimetic trace' of the cinematic.[9] Equally, however, we find the presence of digital gaming technology in the very fabric of theatrical movies. Games borrow from films and films borrow from games[10] – a meshing that foregrounds how cinematicity perpetually leaves its traces in that which is not 'properly' traditional cinema, and in that which supposedly is.

By joining cinema (from its roots in the Greek *kinesis*, 'motion') to the suffixes -ic or -tic (from the French *-ique* and the Latin *-icus*, or 'pertaining to') and -ity (from the French *-ité* and the Latin *-itātem*, or 'the quality of'), we use the term 'cinematicity' to mark the cinematic trace: the close affinity to, and distance from, the photochemical realm of filmmaking and film exhibition that so many art forms, forms of entertainment, media and cultural expressions appear to manifest. In this sense, even the vast homage to photochemical and projected cinema called 'Film', produced by the artist Tacita Dean for the Tate Modern (London, UK) in 2011, was arguably marked by the interference and instabilities of cinematicity. That is, it did not just strive to capture an essence of film, it suggested the ways that cinema transmits across and is mutually influenced by other media.

Dean's installation was intended to mark the decline of celluloid by resurrecting it, and at the time she called anxiously for a swift rescue of the medium before film 'equipment, technology and experience is irreparably dismantled'.[11] Yet the 'Film' installation did not fully adhere to traditional cinematic modes. Displayed as it was in an art gallery, not in a theatre, and projected in pure silence onto a vertical, white, non-translucent slab instead of onto the shimmering and translucent movie screen, it arguably estranged the cinematic experience as much as it captured it. Dean's installation thus more closely resembled an instance of cinematicity than it was an artefact of 'pure' cinema. Cinematicity, then, relates to the qualities and traces of cinematic creation and perception: a mode of mind, method or experience that will surely endure beyond the life or death of celluloid.

If cinematicity can be found 'outside' cinema – on the pages of a Dickens novel, in the art gallery, on the iPhone screen or at the gaming console – it follows that using the term to reinforce media purity would falsify the context in which media operate, and would fallaciously determine the character of their emergence. Our point is not that '[i]n the beginning', as André Gaudreault has argued, 'cinema was so intermedial that it was *not even* cinema';[12] our argument is that all media, cinema included, are part of an ecology of intermedial borrowings, conjoinings and convergences. This does not mean that we cannot or should not specify what is cinematic about cinema. It does mean, however, that the very act of specifying what is specific about a given medium, like cinema, necessarily presupposes, or is parasitic upon, the comparison with another medium. Logically then, the reference to other media is a prerequisite in any definition of medium-specificity: A given medium's 'identity' can only be defined in a difference-relation to other media.[13] Mediality – including cinema's supposed cinematicity – can only be understood intermedially. All media (not just emerging media) are, therefore, in an intermediate state with reference to other media.

Our aim in putting this collection together has been to read film not just through the lens of cultural history but through that of media history, that is, to read the history of film retrospectively *as* media history, thereby extending the historical time span of our enquiry. Our contributors have not focused exclusively on the aesthetic or cultural impact of the film medium but have addressed cinematicity's constitutive role in shaping culture, its aesthetic outputs, inventions and technologies prior to and following from the emergence of cinema. Here, our thinking is perhaps closest to that of Thomas Elsaesser: 'So ubiquitous is the moving image in our urban environment that its impact cannot simply be located in individual films.' The same is true of cinematicity: '[C]inema is part of us, it seems, even when we are not at the movies.' It is precisely for this reason that 'we cannot go on thinking of film history as the history of films'.[14] As the title of this book suggests, we wanted this collection to reflect the varied roles and effects of cinematicity *in media history*. It is also worth stressing, as we discovered during the course of researching this project, that the term 'cinematicity' itself does not arise out of a vacuum, but has been employed (if unevenly) through the work of a number of scholars.

'CINEMATICITY' AND CINEMA STUDIES

When Ernest Betts, a regular writer for the avant-garde journal *Close Up*, invoked the relatively new term 'cinematic' in the 1920s, he admitted: 'This is a shocking word, but we must get used to it.'[15] And although Betts never goes so far as to mention the (probably more shocking) term 'cinematicity', his engagement with the implications of the 'cinematic' are worth quoting at length. Here might be the seeds of what we call cinematicity: namely, the perceptual frameworks that Betts refers to as 'mankind cast [. . .] in fluid images' and the 'cinematic mind'. Betts makes a striking comparison between an ancient sculpture and the cinematic:

> In Persia (the film will probably take you there for ninepence) you will see a great piece of sculpture cut into the rock high up in a cleft of the Black Rock Mountains. It is of Darius receiving the tributary kings. He stands with his handful of the conquered marching up to him, each cut in duplication of the next, and with such astonishing art that the figures appear to be moving. The Bisitun sculptures [aka the Behistun Inscription] have stood in this cleft for twenty-five centuries and the mind which conceived them and other such works embodying strong stylistic rhythms was manifestly a cinematic mind. (This is a shocking word, but we must get used to it.) We are rediscover-

ing now in a different medium the long-lost idea of the moving picture, of mankind cast not in stone, bronze, paint or print, but in fluid images.[16]

Betts finds the 'long lost' idea or trace of the cinematic in the illusory still/ moving poses of figures carved into the stone of Mount Behistun, now in modern-day Iran, at about 500 BC. In a double gesture, Betts proposes not only the cinematic of the 'actual' Behistun Inscription and the cinematic mind of its maker(s), but makes reference to the cinematic experience of its celluloid replica, encountered for ninepence in a movie theatre. In a third gesture, what is cut into stone, and still, appears in motion. Indeed, it is not just the maker who conceived the sculpture who has a 'cinematic mind', but the perceiver, Betts, too, is movie-minded: He, in effect, sees an old medium like sculpture through a mind-set 'moulded' by the new medium of film.

While rarely finding its way into dictionaries of cinema terms,[17] the word 'cinematicity' has more recently appeared in a number of guises, although its meaning is far from universally agreed upon and still appears to hold multiple and sometimes competing implications. When Stephen Heath used the term in 1981, he aligned cinematicity to the practice of reading film[18] along the traditions of 'pure cinema' (known in France as *cinéma pur*): an idealistic aesthetic theory and practice arising from French avant-garde filmmakers such as Germaine Dulac, where film's unique properties of art in motion are freed from 'outside' influences such as plot and theatrical staging. Here, cinematicity relates to the moving image's uniqueness and unity as an artistic and expressive medium. Heath thus refers to the 'aesthetic idea of pure cinematicity', which he critiques as operating 'on a line with the idea of "literarity" derived in literary criticism from Russian Formalism'.[19] Just as the Formalists argued for the study of the 'literariness' of literature in isolation from history and biography, the parallel in cinema – the concept of cinematicity – Heath argues, 'often become[s] a way of avoiding issues of ideology in its appeal to a technicist "structuralist poetics"'. The idea of cinematicity here therefore looks inward rather than outward, suggesting the opposite of reading cinema in terms of an expanded comparativism – that is, viewing cinema as intricately bound up in other heterogeneous media phenomena and modes of modern perception.

Indeed, cinematicity for Heath goes against a reading (that for him is imperative) of cinema as 'part of ideological systems in a capitalist mode of production', and as a collective effect across culture that is 'the achievement of a number of machines (institutions) which move, which *movie*, the individual as subject'.[20] Leaving aside Heath's intensive focus on the interpellative forces of ideology, the kernel of his argument – that cinema is not merely an object and does not simply appear, but actually acts on and in ('*movies*') the

subject – is suggestive, and in fact useful to advancing the concept of cinematicity that informs this collection, namely, cinematicity's constitutive role
in shaping the fibre of everyday life, and even how we think.

Writing in 1980, John M. Carroll also uses cinematicity in the more
restricted terms suggested by Heath, breaking down different elements of
film itself by opposing the idea of 'filmicity' to that of 'cinematicity'. Filmicity,
in this view, is related to film structure, or elements of narrative diegesis, and
the means of advancing the story, including editing, while cinematicity is
more explicitly aligned to the realm of 'film aesthetics'. Comparing Godard
to Warhol, and in particular drawing on the fact that Warhol's film *Empire
State Building* (aka *Empire*, 1964) – very unlike most of Godard's early films –
appears to have no cuts, Carroll argues that the Warhol film is 'unfilmic' due
to its lack of overt 'structure', but remains nonetheless 'cinematic'.[21] In this
sense, a film's cinematicity lies in its visual aesthetics and composition: in its
framing, lighting, *mise-en-scène* and so on. Interestingly, while Carroll focuses
on the absence of cutting, Warhol's minimization of movement – one of the
most profoundly 'pure' qualities in terms of pure cinema – does not enter into
his argument. Still, like Heath, Carroll invokes the term to indicate a concept
of cinema as encompassing unique, 'pure' aesthetic – 'cinematic' – effects.

The ways in which Christian Metz employs the term (*cinématographicité*) in
Language and Cinema comes closer to establishing cinematicity less as a quality
intrinsic or *proper* to cinema than as a descriptor of how the cinematic can
operate at more ephemeral and mobile levels. While Metz posits the properties of 'iconicity, mechanical duplication, and sequencing' as 'distinctive features of the material of expression proper to the image in the cinema which
is, in addition, *moving*', he notes that these are not cinema's *only* significant
features.[22] Moreover, while Metz's project is concerned with categorizing
different language systems and arriving at a definition of cinema's distinctive
signifying properties, the several systemic 'groups' or 'concentric circles' that
he posits and compares according to their 'degrees of cinematicity' (*degrés de
cinématographicité*) are insistently porous, overlapping and variable.[23] While the
cinema may belong for Metz to the groups or circles of language systems that
'rest upon the moving picture', *cinématographicité* itself becomes something
heterogeneous and mobile, and Metz locates it in precisely those art forms
and systems of representation (animated designs, photo novels, sequences of
still photographs and so on) that are not the cinema *per se*.

More recently (and this would include the essays in this volume), scholarship has been moving towards taking cinematicity out of the realms of pure
cinema to address what might be referred to as the 'impure' of cinema,[24]
reading the cinematic within an expanded comparative media studies. While
not refuting the notion that the traditional celluloid theatrical experience is in

many respects singular, the term 'cinematicity' indicates the complex ways in which the cinematic interacts with other media, and how its reverberations have been felt across culture and in a variety of cultural expressions. In such interdisciplinary and intermedial contexts, we find the term appearing in Susan Lord's 1994 article 'Love Machines: Prostitute/Hysteric/Automaton', where from a feminist standpoint Lord maps the nineteenth-century development of what she terms 'nascent cinematicity' in modernity's delineation of the woman and the female body.[25] This cinematicity is produced, she argues, 'through the tension between narrativity and fetishism; in other words, the forms or stagings (*mise-en-scène*) of desire produced through the movement of images in time and the stilling or petrification of such images'.[26] Her examples range from the 'sublime machine' of the female hysteric, a condition and trope captured, medicalized and studied in motion through serialized photography, to the nineteenth-century invention of the female android or automaton as the 'ultimate cinematic prosthesis'. Similarly, in Matilde Nardelli's work on the artist Bruno Munari, cinematicity appears as a set of qualities that, while related to cinema, do not, importantly, always directly arise from cinema in its historical or traditional apparatus. Hence, as in the expansive multimedia explorations of Munari, cinematicity can be located in objects and media that are not cinema.[27]

Taking this further into notions of the cinematic as spectral and embedded in culture and the psyche itself, cinematicity has been invoked as a means to reconsider conscious aspects of human perception, and the unconscious. In his 'Kino-I, Kino World: Notes on the Cinematic Mode of Production', Jonathan L. Beller rereads Lacan from a cinematic standpoint, and in so doing situates cinematicity at the heart of the unconscious itself: 'the unconscious of the unconscious is cinema'.[28] For Beller, Lacan's 'unconscious' resort to cinematic language in a description of the unconscious (the unconscious appears 'in the gap between words', or Beller argues, the 'cut') suggests that 'if psychoanalysis appears as a film theory of the imaginary, then psychoanalytic film criticism would be less like an inventory or an elaboration of psychoanalysis and more like the cipher of an archaeological discovery – the discovery of the cinematicity of the unconscious'.[29] Not unlike Friedrich Kittler then, Beller understands Lacan in the context of the 'conditions of mediality',[30] here cinematicity.

Such an 'unconscious' or spectral version of cinematicity might be seen appearing in Caetlin Benson's *Killer Tapes and Shattered Screens*, which includes the chapter, 'Going, Going, *Grindhouse*: Simulacral Cinematicity and Postcinematic Spectatorhip'. Here Benson locates in films such as Robert Rodriguez's *Grindhouse* (2007) a 'meta-subgenre [. . .] defined by the circumstances in which [it was] originally viewed', circumstances which the film metonymizes through simulating elements of the cinema experience, such as damage to the celluloid print, flecks of dust, scratches, colour distortion and even missing reels. For Benson, these mimetic traces invoke an 'aura' that she calls cinematicity, or the absent process and experience of theatrical exhibition. What these effects suggest is that 'cinema itself has become simulacral, a phantasm that no longer refers to any actual film culture but only conjures the cultural or economic capital of one'.[31] Twenty-first century cinematicity is therefore situated in the gap (or the 'cut', perhaps) between cinema and the post-celluloid cinematic world, where nothing remains 'purely' cinematic about cinema, and in its place appears a kind of simulacrum: the digital simulation of the materiality of celluloid.

It is, therefore, possible to break down the usages of the term into two broad, and perhaps broadly opposing, tendencies. The first, which might be seen as a more traditional use, employs cinematicity to suggest the cinematic properties that are unique to cinema itself. In this sense, cinematicity relates to film aesthetics, cinematography, theatrical projection and, if the discussion engages with 'non-cinematic' practices, to what the unique properties of cinema might bring to other art forms. But a second use of the word, which broadly aligns with our approach, stresses the ways that cinematicity might help express the sense of cinema as dynamic, interconnected and interrelated not only with those media it closely resembles, but with a broad range of art forms and expressive modes, even those that came before the watershed year of 1895 and that are likely to outlive the photochemical era of celluloid film projected to an audience in a movie theatre. So, true to the metamorphic nature of language, cinematicity develops and changes over the years, and now might encompass a wide array of scholarly approaches, from examining the phantasmagoric imaginations of writers and philosophers in the eighteenth century[32] to the changing modes of perception due to high-speed rail travel in the nineteenth century[33] to the holodeck imaginary of the future. And although we stress the idea of cinematicity *both* before and after 1895, the idea of expanding the cinematic away from a stress on purity towards considering its multiplicity has probably become most obvious with the emergence of digital technologies. Cinematicity, then, is that form of intermediality on which this collection concentrates, but its wider aim is to invite enquiries into further instances of intermediality, and thus to contribute towards the formation of a genuinely comparatist study of the media.

THE CONTRIBUTIONS

As we have been suggesting, some film purists might have us believe that sensory (and in particular, visual) perception was forever altered at a specific moment during the watershed year of 1895, when the Lumière Brothers debuted their *cinématographe*. Literary purists would pin the end of reading culture, and the beginnings of passive screen consumption, on this event. The idea of cinematicity is meant to serve as a potential corrective to these assumptions, extending the idea of the cinematic in terms of its traditional historical and perceptual frames: to go beyond the fetish of the *cinématographe* as the summa of what came before it and of what would follow, thereby 'challenging the idea that new technologies displace older systems with decisive suddenness'.[34] To this end we have included contributions on phenomena spanning from the nineteenth century to the present day, and ranging from optical toys to video consoles; from the popular French stage entertainment, the *féerie*, to the private consumption of watching movies on a mobile phone; from chronophotography to computer-generated imaging; from major media such as the computer or the book to minor, 'ephemeral' media such as the flipbook; from realists like Dickens to modernists like Joyce.

Following roughly a chronological order, this collection opens with three chapters that explore 'Cinematicity before Cinema'. In the first chapter, Joss Marsh suggests that visual culture in the nineteenth century cannot only be characterized by its fascination with what Tom Gunning calls, in Chapter Nine, 'technological exposure', but also with instruments of deception and illusion such as the magic lantern. Marsh recalls the primacy of this popular toy, educational tool and story-telling device, investigating the role of the lantern and in particular one of its techniques – the 'ancestor of the cinematic dissolve' – and its discreet manifestations in Victorian print cultures. The lantern dissolve both animated and was reflected in several key texts, ranging from the prominent (Charles Dickens) to the more obscure (James Anthony Froude). In her reading, Marsh charts the extensive cultural and creative impact that the lantern had on mainstream Victorian literary production, implying an inherent and often overlooked imbrication of the technological and the literary, the visual and the textual. As Marsh's analysis demonstrates, lantern, print and cinema bear the spectres of intermediality: It is 'by way of the magic lantern that cinema reveals itself as descended from Charles Dickens'.

If audiences were mesmerized by the 'dissolving views' and transformation scenes staged at diorama exhibitions and magic lantern shows in Victorian Britain, in nineteenth-century France, as Kristian Moen shows in Chapter Two, audiences were drawn to theatres to see the 'transformation views' of the *féerie*. Moen situates Georges Méliès's work within this tradition of the *féerie*, thus illustrating how through the use of elaborate spectacles cinema and theatre are entwined. Like its theatrical counterpart, the cinematic *féerie* is no less concerned with the trickery of 'transformation'. As Moen explains, such transformations come in a variety of guises: bodies, objects and settings transmorph, as if to indicate that the world itself is 'a place of mutability', is in flux. Whether in the form of theatrical plays, such as *Le Pied de mouton* (1806), luminous fountain displays at the Universal Exposition in Paris (1889) or the kaleidoscope, the 'so-called transformation view' of the *féerie* – used by Méliès as a term to categorize cinema itself – creates 'a vision of instability' that must be understood within the larger context of modernity's impact on visual perception.

Crystallizing the implications of Moen's argument, Ian Christie confronts the challenge of how to do media history head on, considering how 'inter-mediate' media live on, or are revived, in other media. This is not a model of media history according to the logic of the survival of the fittest, a Darwinian take, nor the teleological model associated with the linear medium of print[35] but, arguably, a cinematic model, and an early cinematic one at that. Media history here is not understood according to the language of later cinema, through the cut and the edit, nor the continuity principle, rather it works by dissolves and overlaps, in precisely the manner that many of the earliest films did. As Christie illustrates, the technologies of the kinetoscope, praxinoscope and filoscope are not 'stepping stones "towards" cinema proper', but they (co)exist in an 'ongoing ensemble, with frequent revivals and repurposings'. Thus Christie gives us an insight into the optical culture of the *fin-de-siècle*, foregrounding the cinematicity of ephemeral media.

The book's second part, 'Transitions: Early Cinema and Cinematicity', explores how cinema's 'always already' cultural and technological trace rapidly became central to modern life. Littau's chapter addresses the media-transitional period of the late nineteenth century and the early twentieth to show how aestho-physiological experiments in reading were linked to a variety of motion picture technologies. On the one hand, such technologies were used to measure reading speeds; on the other, they profoundly affected how readers began to perceive the printed word: no longer as static marks on the page but giving 'the impression of movement', which in turn was con-ceived 'in proportion' to how it *moved* the reader. By focusing on experiments by Vernon Lee, Gertrude Stein and Charlotte Perkins Gilman, and her story 'The Yellow Wall-Paper' – itself an experiment in phantasmagoric reading – she shows how reading during this period bore the traces of cinematicity; to the extent that in the 1930s 'movie-minded' writers like Robert Carlton Brown proposed 'reading machines', which would bring outmoded reading practices into line with modern cinema-viewing.

Perkins Gilman's allusions to optical media, both in her famous 1892 short story and in her subsequent writing on cinema, show just how much writers were plugged into the media culture of their day. Similarly, as Keith

Williams shows in Chapter Five, James Joyce's 'eye and imagination were already trained by the rich and diverse optical culture in which he grew up', even before cinema arrived. The cinematicity of Joyce's writings is not therefore just an after-effect of the *cinématographe*; rather, Joyce's 'visual literacy' and 'literary visuality' help explain 'his creative receptiveness to cinema' when it did arrive. As Williams's close readings of *A Portrait of the Artist as a Young Man* reveal, Joyce's novel presents us with a main protagonist whose perceiving and remembering consciousness is as variously evocative of the magic lantern as it is of chronophotography or cinema itself. It is this that makes the novel '*the* superlatively intermedial Modernist text'. Insofar as Joyce's fiction appears to extend the ancient principle of *ekphrasis* – verbal imitation of visual representations (paintings, sculpture, architecture and so on) – into this age of moving images, it should be seen as synergetic with key aspects of visual culture and technology that gave birth to cinematicity on screen.

It was with the Lumières' first film screenings that cinematicity, if not born, was first noticed. Nico Baumbach's chapter on the Lumières' film *Le Repas de Bébé* (*Baby's Meal*) (1895) takes as its starting point Georges Méliès's observation that it was through this film that he first registered the potential of cinema. But it is not the spectacular that Méliès notices, but the incidental detail of moving leaves in the background of the film. Baumbach thus homes in on this incidental detail to explore the significance it held for filmmakers, including D. W. Griffith. Baumbach addresses film's power to construct palpable, seemingly concrete, visual phenomena, although here he examines the transitory aesthetics of the 'wind in the trees'. Even amidst the dull silences of early actualities – what Gorky famously called the 'Kingdom of Shadows'[36] – the nostalgic image of lightly blowing leaves was conjured up by the likes of Griffith and Georges Sadoul as one of the hallmarks of cinematic 'magic'. Baumbach enriches the interest in what Gunning and André Gaudreault called the 'cinema of attractions' by suggesting, via detours into Kant, Benjamin and, notably, German Romantic poetry and Impressionist painting, that the inscription of the incidental could often be as powerful as the spectacular.

Part Three focuses on the era when the traditional experience of cinemagoing would become what Christie has called a 'universal pastime',[37] with chapters engaging with the role of cinematicity during the mid-twentieth century. Anke Hennig, in Chapter Seven, opens the discussion with an account of scriptwriting in the Soviet film culture of the 1930s. Her chapter locates an instance of cinematicity during this period in the political and aesthetic struggle to identify and establish the genre of the film script in relation to the literary arts from which it borrowed its medium, on the one hand, and the properly cinematic narrative it sought to embody in that medium, on the other. Taking Mikhail Bleiman as her main point of reference, she shows how his film script for *The Great Citizen* (1938) does not attempt to express the filmic by literary means, or to show the filmic in the literary, but rather to create a showing that remains inexpressible in the latter. Drawing on a range of contextual documentation, Hennig demonstrates how critics and avatars of the film script thus sought instances where the new genre (that they regarded as a 'fourth' genre alongside epic, drama and poetry) surpassed its literary precursors. On the basis of the historical vicissitudes of the film script, Hennig argues for the irreducibly multimedial basis of cinematicity.

Chapter Eight shifts ground from the Soviet Union to the United States during the same era. Here, Geiger explores interconnections between aerial perspectives and the moving image at a time when technological advances were producing a myriad of new ways of coming to terms with an increasingly globalized world. Aerial life was transforming social perceptions of space and terrain, and influencing how those spaces were managed and controlled. Along with the panorama, elevated and aerial views would therefore become central instruments in conceiving and grasping what Heidegger called the 'world picture'. The years between the wars also saw new pressures being placed on motion pictures to guide the public's political and moral sensibili-ties: to instil knowledge and understanding of citizenship, national belong-ing and one's place in the world at large. Focusing on the strategic uses of panoramic and elevated views and, especially with the coming of the Second World War, aerial photography, this chapter calls for a more dialectical reading of the role of cinematicity and the aerial view in modern perception, one that emphasizes how the aerial subject simultaneously can encompass seemingly opposed experiences of abstract distancing and emotional connec-tion, 'objective' overseeing and embodied feeling.

If aerial perspectives on the world provide an overseeing means to con-struct our place in it, Tom Gunning pursues the relentless immersion, at street level, of the urbanite in a city doubly composed of the seen and the unseen, image and shadow. Making evident what the city shares with the uneasy worldview of *film noir*, Gunning's essay casts light on the ways in which expe-riences of urban culture, modernity and the cinema are inextricably linked. This brings into play another aspect of cinematicity, namely that the city from the nineteenth century onwards had become what Gunning calls a 'hyper-visual zone' whose inhabitants were bombarded by an array of visual stimuli and partial impressions, as if preparing them for the onslaught of the moving pictures themselves. Beneath the visible façade of the city, as the detective figure who emerged in the literature of the period makes abundantly clear, also, however, lurk dark corners, dangerous places and invisible threats. It is here, Gunning argues, that the police's bull's eye lantern and the flash of the journalist's camera make visible what was invisible. Gunning's chapter thus shows us how in the urban milieu of *film noir*, cinematic representations of the city reveal through film styles and thematics how vision itself is shaped by social, historical and technological contexts.

The book's final part, 'Digital Cinematicity', takes the discussion forward, working to demonstrate how cinematicity flouts recent discussions concerning the 'death' of cinema, to survive in the digital age. Leon Gurevitch's chapter considers, beyond dichotomies of the ludic and narratalogical divide in games studies, the intersecting relationship between the 'cinematic' and game aesthetics. Rather than interrogate the implications of the predominance of photorealism in game aesthetics, Gurevitch asks why notions of the cinematic have often been, and continue to be, so important to commentators, games makers and players alike. His chapter not only problematizes the simplifications upon which the comparison between cinema and games has often rested, but asserts that notions of the 'cinematic' are now being redrawn by production techniques and consumption practices of the games industry, rather than the other way around. With special effects studios increasingly deploying game engines as pre-visualization tools, and motion capture, animation and compositing teams entering the cinema industry from games studios, the material practices and visual cultures that constitute the cinematic are being reconfigured. The issue, then, is not one of just how cinematic games have become, but of how the cinematicity of gaming is expanding notions of the cinematic.

If, as Gurevitch shows, material practices from one medium inflect another, so too do the technological platforms through which media are experienced. Thus, in response to the ubiquitous complaint that watching movies on a cell phone is 'uncinematic', Martine Beugnet investigates precisely the cinematicity particular to such devices. While, for instance, the tiny screen of an iPhone is paradigmatic of spectatorial habits in the digital age, it is equally and poignantly redolent of the kinetoscope's peephole apparatus prior to the emergence of the film theatre. Although the very antithesis, therefore, of the collective viewing practices of cinema audiences, the iPhone as a screening device envelops these practices within a broader and more individuated experience of cinematicity. Beugnet, therefore, proposes to leave the debate about 'proper' ways of screening films to one side, and to concentrate instead on the specific characteristics of watching films on very small screens and with sound-isolating devices. Drawing on haptic theories of visuality as well as the history and aesthetics of miniature art forms and the curio, the chapter examines issues of mobility, manipulability and distracted-versus-attentive viewing, before focusing on the effect of miniaturization on the film image itself.

Performing, as he calls it, Kino-Eye in reverse, Lev Manovich rounds out this collection with a discussion of his digital visualizations of Dziga Vertov's films. Manovich argues that Vertov's expressed desire for a 'graphic language' anticipates the recent work of a number of data visualization designers and artists who use computational analysis and computer graphics to visualize patterns in artistic works, including literary texts and films. Yet Manovich's work also explores how new visualization techniques can help us comprehend cinema differently, revealing patterns and dimensions that are hard or impossible to study through established film analysis methods. Like a digital counterpart to what Vertov theorized as the Kino-Eye, the digital photography and software applications Manovich manipulates collectively extend and transform the capacities of the human eye and its relation to film. In so doing, he in a sense reverses the tendency, noted by Gurevitch, to evaluate the cinematicity of the digital in hierarchical terms; here it is digital imaging that allows us to 'see cinema in new ways', revealing a whole new science and aesthetics of cinema in the data sets, maps, patterns and graphics that lie latent in the celluloid image.

This collection seeks to highlight how cinematicity is part of a longer and broader history of media than is suggested by the medium-specific history of film alone. Reflecting on these chapters, it has become abundantly clear to us that, as Elsaesser says, we must stop 'thinking of film history as the history of films'; but it is also striking indeed that none of our contributors any longer do. Instead, under the rubric of cinematicity, each follows the detailed twists and turns of one medium's involvement in others. If media histories ought no longer therefore to be written through the normative lens of monomediality, neither should it be forgotten that, by definition, media do not insensibly intermingle – behind our backs as it were – but rather do so in a manner that changes how we think about them, and how we think in general. As Aleida and Jan Assmann, echoing and developing a Nietzschean point, write:

> Everything that can be known, thought and said about the world is only knowable, thinkable, and sayable dependently upon the media that communicate this knowing. [. . .] It is not the language in which we think, but the media in which we communicate that model our world.[38]

The displacement recounted here of the centrality of language to our modelling of the world suggests a displacement of one medium by another. Yet a new medium always assumes functions presupposed to be specific to the old medium it supplants, and the sense of ourselves it supported. Accordingly if, as Nietzsche noted,[39] media act – via the sensoria they serve to complexify – on our thinking, the thinking this produces must also act in our thinking of these media. The writing of film history, media history, or any history, is never not touched by the media that shape our thinking. It is therefore our hope that this collection might provoke others not only to think further about cinematicity but to conceive of the myriad ways in which media act upon media, and on us, in the intermedial ecology we inhabit.

Notes

1. Henry Jenkins, 'From YouTube to YouNiversity', *Chronicle of Higher Education*, 16 February 2007, at: http://henryjenkins.org/2007/02/from_youtube_to_youniversity.html (accessed 23 June 2013). The model for comparative media studies is in part derived, according to Jenkins, from comparative literature. Conversely, comparative literature has recently called for an expanded notion of the discipline into comparative media studies. See Charles Bernheimer's report for the American Comparative Literature Association (ACLA), where he puts forward an expanded notion of literature as 'one discursive practice among many', arguing that an increasingly 'multimedia world' has made the term 'literature' inadequate to the task. In consequence, he proposes that 'comparative literature should include comparisons between media'. See *Comparative Literature in the Age of Multiculturalism*, ed. Charles Bernheimer (Baltimore, MD: Johns Hopkins University Press, 1995), pp. 15, 45. For a similar proposal, see Rey Chow, 'In the Name of Comparative Literature', in the same volume, *Comparative Literature in the Age of Multiculturalism*, especially pp. 115–16.

2. Intermediality was theorized in German scholarship in the 1980s as a counterpoint to intertextuality. An early formulation can be found in translation studies, a sub-branch of comparative literature; see Ernest Hess Lüttich, ed., *Text Tranfers: Probleme intermedialer Übersetzung* (Münster: Nodus, 1987). For a recent assessment of the state of the field, see Joachim Paech and J. Schröter, eds, *Intermedialität Analog / Digital. Theorien – Methoden – Analysen* (München: Wilhelm Fink, 2008). See also Jürgen Heinrichs and Yvonne Spielmann, eds, *Convergence* 8.4 (Winter, 2002), special issue on 'What is Intermedia'; and the Canadian journal *intermédialités: histoire et théorie des arts des lettres et des techniques*, at: http://cri.histart.umontreal.ca/cri/fr/intermedialites/ (accessed 2 January 2013).

3. See Jay David Bolter and Richard Grusin, *Remediation: Understanding New Media* (Cambridge, MA: The MIT Press, 1999); see also Grusin's essay 'Premediation' in *Criticism* 46.1 (Winter, 2004), 17–39; and Bolter's 'Remediation and the Language of New Media', where he suggests that 'remediation' is part of 'the larger project of intermediality', *Northern Lights* 5 (2007), 25–37 (p. 26).

4. See Gene Youngblood's important *Expanded Cinema*, intro. R. Buckminster Fuller (New York, NY: P. Dutton, 1970), especially Part Six, 'Intermedia'; Dick Higgins, 'Intermedia' (1981) in *Leonardo, the Journal of the International Society for the Arts, Sciences and Technology* 34.1 (2001), 49–54 (Higgins draws the term from Samuel T. Coleridge's 'intermedium'); and Higgins, *Horizons: The Poetics and Theory of the Intermedia* (Carbondale, IL: Southern Illinois University Press, 1984).

5. Roman Jakobson, 'What is Poetry', in Jakobson, *Selected Writings, Vol. III: Poetry of Grammar and Grammar of Poetry*, ed. Stephen Rudy (Berlin: Walter De Gruyter, 1981), pp. 740–50 (p. 750); Jakobson, quoted by Victor Ehrlich, *Russian Formalism* (Berlin: Walter De Gruyter, 1965), p. 172; Greenberg, 'Towards a Newer Laocoon' (1940), in John O'Brian, ed., *Clement Greenberg: The Collected Essays and Criticism* I (Chicago, IL: University of Chicago Press, 1986), pp. 23–37 (p. 32).

6. For a critique of media purity, see David Thorburn and Henry Jenkins, 'Introduction: Towards an Aesthetics of Transition', in D. Thorburn and H. Jenkins, eds, *Rethinking Media Change: The Aesthetics of Transition* (Cambridge, MA: The MIT Press, 2003), pp. 1–16 (especially p. 11).

7. Berys Gaut, *A Philosophy of Cinematic Art* (Cambridge: Cambridge University Press, 2010), p. 2.

8. Sarah LeBoeuf, 'Pokemon 3DS', http://www.gamesradar.com (accessed 1 January 2013). It should be noted that LeBoeuf suggests that 'more cinematicity' would be a technical advance for the game, although it would not necessarily improve it.

9. See Caetlin Benson, *Killer Tapes and Shattered Screens* (Berkeley, CA: University of California Press, 2013), p. 133, and below.

10. See also Jay David Bolter, 'Transference and Transparency: Digital Technology and the Remediation of Cinema', *Intermédialités* 6 (2005), 13–26 (p. 14).

11. Tacita Dean, 'Save Celluloid, for Art's Sake', *The Guardian*, 22 February 2011, at: http://www.guardian.co.uk/artanddesign/2011/feb/22/tacita-dean-16mm-film (accessed 23 June 2013).

12. André Gaudreault, 'Afterword (1998): Cinema, Between Literariness and Intermediality', in *From Plato to Lumière: Narration and Monstration in Literature and Cinema*, trans. Timothy Barnard, with Prefaces by Paul Ricoeur and Tom Gunning (Toronto: University of Toronto Press, 2009), pp. 151–64 (p. 156); italics in original.

13. Jens Schröter, 'Das ur-mediale Netzwerk und die (Neu-)Erfindung des Mediums im (digitalen) Modernismus. Ein Versuch', in Paech and Schröter, pp. 579–601 (p. 593). A similar point is made by André Gaudreault and Philippe Marion: 'A good understanding of a medium thus entails understanding its relationship to other media: it is through intermediality, through a concern with the intermedial, that a medium is understood.' See: 'The Cinema as a Model for the Genealogy of Media', *Convergence* 8.4 (2002), 12–18 (p. 15). See also William Uricchio's proposal for 'the intermedial redefinition of media' in the light of 'digital technology's implications for the media of photography, film, and television' in 'Historicizing Media in Transition', in Thorburn and Jenkins, pp. 23–38 (p. 31).

14. Thomas Elsaesser, 'The New Film History as Media Archaeology', *Cinémas: Journal of Film Studies* 4.2–3 (2004), 75–117 (pp. 76, 113).

15. Ernest Betts, *Heraclitus, or the Future of Films* (London: Kegan, Paul, Trench, Trubner, 1928), pp. 31–2.

16. *Ibid.*

17. The term has made it into very few guides to film terms, but is included

for example (as 'Cinematizität') on the 'Lexikon de Filmbegriffe' website, Christian-Albrechts University of Kiel, at: http://filmlexikon.uni-kiel.de/index. php (accessed 23 June 2013).

18. The terms 'cinema' and 'film' here are not being used interchangeably. When we refer to film we are suggesting the physical medium – celluloid and its related functions – itself. Cinema would refer to the whole realm of the film experience, including sound, projection and collective screening.

19. Stephen Heath, *Questions of Cinema* (Bloomington, IN: Indiana University Press, 1981), p. 8.

20. *Ibid.*; italics in original.

21. John M. Carroll, *Toward a Structural Psychology of Cinema* (The Hague: Mouton de Gruyter, 1980), pp. 69–70.

22. Christian Metz, *Language and Cinema* (The Hague: Mouton de Gruyter, 1974), p. 231; italics in original.

23. *Ibid.*, pp. 230–1.

24. For a similar embrace of media impurity, see Colin MacCabe, 'On Impurity: The Dialectics of Cinema and Literature', in Julian Murphet and Lydia Rainford, eds, *Literature and Visual Technologies: Writing After Cinema* (Houndmills: Palgrave Macmillan, 2003), pp. 15–28.

25. Susan Lord, 'Love Machines: Prostitute/Hysteric/Automaton', *Public: Art, Culture, Ideas* 10 (1994), 133–48 (p. 141).

26. *Ibid.*, p. 135.

27. Personal email exchange; also, Matilde Nardelli, 'Travelling Light: Cinematic Munari', lecture presented at the Estorick Collection of Modern and Italian Art on the occasion of the exhibition 'Bruno Munari: My Futurist Past', 27 October 2012. Nardelli also considers the 'cinematic' beyond the cinema apparatus in 'Leafing through Cinema', in Steven Allen and Laura Hubner, eds, *Framing Film* (Bristol: Intellect, 2012), pp. 127–47.

28. See 'Kino-I, Kino-World: Notes on the Cinematic Mode of Production', in Nicholas Mirzoeff, ed., *The Visual Culture Reader* (New York, NY: Routledge, 2002), pp. 60–85 (pp. 69–70).

29. *Ibid.*, p. 70.

30. See John Johnston's 'Introduction', pp. 2–26 (p. 24), to Friedrich A. Kittler, *Literature, Media, Information Systems: Essays*, ed. and intro. Johnston (Amsterdam: G&B Arts International, 1997), p. 134.

31. Benson, p. 133.

32. See Terry Castle, 'Phantasmagoria: Spectral Technology and the Metaphorics of Modern Reverie', *Critical Inquiry* 15 (1988), 26–61; Marina Warner, *Phantasmagoria: Spirit Visions, Metaphors, and Media into the Twenty-First Century* (Oxford: Oxford University Press, 2006); Stefan Andriopoulos, 'Kant's Magic Lantern: Historical Epistemology and Media Archaeology', *Representations* 115 (Summer, 2011), 42–70.

33. Wolfgang Schivelbusch, *The Railway Journey: The Industrialization of Time and Space in the 19th Century* (Leamington Spa: Berg, 1986 [1977]).

34. Thorburn and Jenkins, p. 2.

35. Marshall McLuhan associates print culture with linear thinking in *The Gutenberg Galaxy: The Making of Typographic Man* (London: Routledge & Kegan Paul, 1962).

36. Maxim Gorky, 'A Review of the Lumière Programme at the Nizhni-Novgorod Fair', trans. Leda Swan, in Jay Leyda, ed., *Kino: A History of the Russian and Soviet Film* (London: Allen and Unwin, 1960, repr. 1983), pp. 407–9 (p. 407).

37. Ian Christie, 'Cinematography and the Body', in Colin Blakemore and Sheila Jennett, eds, *The Oxford Companion to the Body* (Oxford: Oxford University Press, 2001), p. 158.

38. Aleida and Jan Assmann, 'Schrift – Kognition – Evolution', in E. A. Havelock, *Schriftlichkeit. Das griechische Alphabet als kulturelle Revolution*, eds and intro. A. and J. Assmann (Weinheim: VCH, Acta Humanoria, 1990), pp. 1–35 (p. 2); our translation.

39. As Nietzsche suggests with reference to the typewriter, 'our writing tools also work on our thoughts' ('Unser Schreibzeug arbeitet mit an unseren Gedanken'). See his letter, 'An Heinrich Köselitz in Venedig (Typoscript), [Genua] Ende Februar 1882', in Giorgio Colli and Mazzino Montinari, eds, *Briefwechsel. Kritische Gesamtausgabe*, III.1. Briefe von Nietzsche: 1880–1884 (Berlin: Walter de Gruyter, 1981), p. 172.

Part 1

Cinematicity before Cinema

Dickensian 'Dissolving Views': The Magic Lantern, Visual Story-telling and the Victorian Technological Imagination

JOSS MARSH

In the palmy years of the magic lantern, in England, from the 1860s to the 1890s, when perhaps twelve hundred lantern lecturers criss-crossed the country by railway and lantern companies splurged on studios, supplies and slide catalogues that were the size of bricks, lanternists cherished two dreams.[1]

The first (the focus of technical histories) was to make still images move – by all means possible: illusion and speed lines; panoramic 'sliders' that pushed across the beam of light; 'slipping' glasses; levers; ratchets and 'eccentrics'; and pulleys. Sometimes all of these methods were used at once. The second dream (a history that has barely begun to be told) was to tell stories in pictures, combining projected images with dramatic readings – not only fairy tales, *Arabian Nights*, Bible stories and *Robinson Crusoe*, but modern stories and stories written specially for the lantern – an extraordinary development, and a 'purely' and 'peculiarly' English one.[2] It depended both on technical developments – above all, the widespread employment, from the 1860s, of powerful limelight – and on broader cultural contexts, such as the rise and cachet of narrative paintings, which required Victorian viewers (as Henry James put it in 1877) to 'project [. . .] themselves into the story',[3] and the attraction of the lantern for temperance and missionary propaganda.[4]

This essay addresses that second dream, attempting to unravel, if possible, what knitted together the rise of lantern story-telling and what was perhaps the most significant development in the two hundred and fifty year history of the magic lantern. The lantern, of course, was the world's premier 'screen experience' and cinema's closest ancestor, whose importance – courtesy of colour, music and the spoken word (hand-painted slides, sing-songs, lecture-performances) – endured through the 1920s, well into the cinematic era.

The development I have in mind was not the phantasmagoria – the magic-lantern spectre show that fed on and commercialized the terrors of Revolutionary Paris. The phantasmagoria itself persisted through spirit photographs, macabre cabaret, the Grand Guignol, ghost shows and the horror film to the present day.[5] But its popularity peaked in Britain in about 1805, and it died out as a headlining popular entertainment in the 1830s. Yet it has dominated critical discussion at the expense of another, later, less glamorous development.[6]

This development was the 'dissolving view', the ancestor of the cinematic dissolve, whereby (roughly speaking) light was slowly stopped down on one lens and one image and brought up on another, with perfect registration, so that the second image slowly – almost magically – replaced the first on the illuminated screen.

There is disagreement about when and where 'dissolving views' origi-nated: The showman and pseudo-'scientist' 'Philidor' (later known as De Philipstahl) may have approximated the effect in a Dublin phantasmagoria of 1804; 'Monsieur Henry' featured what he variously called 'imperceptibly changing', 'magic' or 'dissolvent' 'views' of landscapes and buildings in February 1826.[7] But we do know that they were used shortly after by the painter and lanternist Henry Langdon Childe, who famously produced the landmark lantern stage effect of a ghost ship for the Adelphi Theatre's pro-duction of *The Flying Dutchman* in December 1826.[8] Childe became a creative mainstay of the Royal Polytechnic, the vibrant centre of Victorian multimedia culture (1838–76), where he was best known for his 'extravagant' lantern work.[9]

Childe's finale to a show of March 1827 included 'the eruption of Vesuvius, storm with shipwreck, mill scene with the effect of a rainbow' and '[Lord Byron's] Newstead Abbey [. . .] with moving swans!'.[10] (All of the subjects, except the last, became classics of the Victorian dissolving view repertoire.) Childe probably had a single lantern, and nothing more than his hand and a wad of fabric to wave in front of the lens to effect the transition from image to image; the effect was nevertheless reported to be 'truly aston-ishing'.[11] Dissolving views were an entertainment whose time had come: The audience that flocked to see the 'transformation' scenes of nineteenth-century pantomime and the transformative effects of Daguerre's Diorama was multiplied by the lantern's mechanical means.[12] And those means dramatically improved when, in the same year that the Diorama opened in London – 1823, Carpenter and Westley patented and began mass production of outline images. For, if a second image of a cottage or a country church could replace a first on screen with perfect registration, it became possible to produce such illusions as the transition from day to night or (one of Childe's most famous effects) from summer to winter. 'By the 1840s[,] dissolving views were considered the ultimate manifestation of the lanternist's art',[13] and dissolves were worked with two lanterns, placed side by side, or one on top of the other, while comb-like fan shutters, soft caps, iris diaphragms and tap dissolvers smoothed the transitions. Soon after, sophisticated 'bi-unial' and 'tri-unial' lanterns were invented.

The phantasmagoria had spawned works in which 'magic lanterns are used to deceive credulous would-be ghost-seers'.[14] For Carlyle and Paine, it was the image of choice for historic chaos and mass deception.

Victorian dissolving views, in contrast, brought the wonders of nature, Empire and science to respectable family audiences. The critical difference was the method of projection: Phantasmagoria lanternists worked from behind the screen, in total darkness, hidden from the audience, with 'pseudonecromantic' effect.[15] Limelight, and the front projection that it made possible, turned the lanternists who embraced the dissolving view into show-men-educators, expounding their marvels in full view of their much-enlarged audiences: Gibraltar by day and by night; Napoleon before and after Elba; the regions of the North Pole. Thus it was that the dissolving-view lantern-show became a Victorian metaphor for transformation, truth-telling and spiritual regeneration.

It may even be that the work that launched the Temperance movement into lantern propaganda, Cruikshank's *The Bottle* (1847), not only took 'primal inspiration' from the fear-inducing fantasy of the now-repudiated phantasmagoria, but specific instruction from the techniques of the uplifting dissolving view. For, in seven of Cruikshank's eight prints, the orientation of the drunkard's room (door on the left, hearth on the right, and so on) allows us more clearly to follow his metamorphosis from 'loving father to murderous maniac', as if we were dissolving from one image to the next.[16] Dissolving views made possible, even helped shape, a still newer kind of story than that drunkard's 'progress', however – a story that allowed travel through time and space. And it was Cruikshank's ex-collaborator who invented it: Charles Dickens.

Dickens fell in love with the lantern as a child. Mary Weller, the family's nursemaid, reported how 'little Charles' would come downstairs and say, 'Now, Mary, [. . .] we are going to have such a game', and then '[Cousin] George [. . .] would come in with his Magic Lantern'.[17] His work is saturated in lantern reference: Miss Havisham's 'ghostly reflection', for example, 'thrown large by the fire upon the ceiling and the wall'[18] and Genoa's 'extravagant reality' as phantasmagoria in the virtual-travel book *Pictures from Italy*.[19] Dickens's journals *Household Words* and *All the Year Round* give extended space to all of the 'optical discoveries' that had turned the modern mind into a 'wizard chamber of dissolving views'.[20] The lantern remained, throughout his career, a central image of transformation and multifariousness: 'I can't express how much I want [the London] streets', he confessed to John Forster, as he struggled with *Dombey and Son* in dull, idyllic Switzerland, in

1846. 'The toil and labour of writing, day after day, without that magic lantern [before me], is IMMENSE!'[21]

Dickens is the dominant literary source for later Victorian magic-lantern story-telling, uniquely important for lantern history, as he is for cinema. But while we have come to accept that cinema received its Dickensian inheritance in part from the nineteenth-century melodramatic stage, we have yet to learn that it is also by way of the magic lantern that cinema reveals itself as descended from Charles Dickens. Indeed, Dickens is 'cinematic' only and insofar as he responded to pre-cinematic technologies and popular entertainments.

What made him so attractive to lanternists? His works were in copyright – they could not be adapted with impunity. But his stories were adapted – sometimes legitimately, sometimes reworded – excruciatingly badly.

Part of the answer is critical commonplace: Dickens's imagination was profoundly visual; his works were illustrated; he had an unparalleled popular audience, created by serial publication. And, in giving public readings of his works, from 1853, Dickens himself had established a model for lantern performance of his stories.

Part of the answer is more complex. The lantern had inspired two of Dickens's most-loved stories. One was *A Christmas Carol* (1843); its illustrations, all light effects and ghostly superimpositions, were an open invitation to lanternists, and (when they began to tell stories) it quickly became a favourite. It was topped only by *Gabriel Grub*, one of the tales woven into *The Pickwick Papers* (1836), the story of a surly sexton, the prototype for Scrooge. The tale was granted a bravura production at the Royal Polytechnic in 1875, combining 'views and effects' with staged scenes, dramatic reading and intermittent carol-singing: It became a lodestar for later-century lantern story-telling.[22]

The *Carol* and *Gabriel Grub* became lanternist favourites not only for commercial, but for profoundly imaginative, reasons. For Gabriel's and Scrooge's Christmas-tide, changes of heart are directly inspired and made possible by the experience of the lantern show: The two misanthropes are '*show*[*n*] [. . .] *pictures*' by supernatural showmen – the Spirits of Christmas Past, Present and Yet-To-Come in *Carol* and a troupe of goblins in *Gabriel Grub*; both are transported through time and space by the visual magic of dissolving views.

Gabriel Grub openly displays its lantern inspiration. When Gabriel spends Christmas Eve digging a grave, he is seized upon by the King of the Goblins, who summons his minions, 'la[ys] hand upon [Gabriel's] collar, and s[inks] with him through the earth' – a grand effect at the Polytechnic, courtesy of a vertical panorama – to 'what appeared to be a large cavern'. (For clarity, in what follows all lantern-related terms are italicized.)

'And now', said the King, [. . .] '*show* the man of misery and gloom a few of *the pictures from our own great storehouse!*'

At which, like a theatrical curtain:

> [*A] thick cloud,* which obscured the remoter end of the cavern, *rolled gradually away, and disclosed,* [. . .] a small and scantily-furnished [. . .] apartment.

There follows an edifying visual story of family contentment in the face of adversity, presented in precise, almost technical lantern terms: The lantern inheritance of Dickens's work lives in techniques and metaphor, not in storyline or explicit reference. (Missing this, Fred Guida blankly concludes: 'There is no evidence to suggest that [Dickens] was in any way directly influenced by the magic lantern.')[23]

> A knock was heard at the door; [. . .] their father entered. [. . .]
> But *a change came upon the view, almost imperceptibly.*

Shifting slides takes time; the lanternist must focus.

> *The scene was altered* to a small bed-room, where the fairest and youngest child lay dying. [. . .]
> *Again the light cloud passed across the picture* …

It is as if a lanternist were fluttering his fingers before the lens, in the approved impromptu style of the dissolving view, or using his serrated fan shutter.

> *and again the subject changed.*

Shortly, of course, the parents die, too – but not before the spectator's conversion is achieved: It depends, unquestionably, on the transformative experience of the dissolving view.

> '*You*, a miserable man!' said the goblin. [. . .] '*Show him some more!*'
> At these words, the cloud was dispelled, and a rich and beautiful landscape was *disclosed to view.* [. . .]
> Many a time the cloud went and came, and many a lesson it taught to Gabriel Grub.[24]

A Christmas Carol is a far subtler tale – but it is no less lantern-derived. R. W. Paul found inspiration for a splendid dissolve in his inventive film version of 1901, not only in lantern versions, but in the first chapter of Dickens's text:[25]

> Now, it is a fact, that there was nothing at all particular about the knocker on the door [of Scrooge's house], except that it was very large. [. . .] [So] let any man explain to me, if he can, how it happened that Scrooge, having his key in the lock of the door, saw in the knocker [. . .] not a knocker, but

Marley's face.

Marley's face. [. . .]

As Scrooge looked fixedly at this phenomenon, it was a knocker again.[26]

And in the first Spirit we meet a figure in the style of the phantasmagoria, in which figures grew larger or smaller as the lantern 'tracked' towards or away from the screen: Christmas Past is 'like a child: yet not so like a child as like an old man, viewed through some supernatural medium, which gave him the appearance of having receded from the view, and being diminished to a child's proportions'. The 'medium' of the lantern produces no less 'supernatural' an effect: '[T]he figure [. . .] *fluctuate*[*s*] in its distinctness: being now a thing with one arm, now with one leg, now with twenty legs: of which *dissolving parts*, no *outline* would be visible in the dense gloom wherein they *melted away*' (68). 'I am the Ghost of Christmas Past', says the spirit; 'Rise! and walk with me!' (69). They 'passed through the wall', into a country lane, and thence (dissolving again) to a schoolroom. 'Good Heaven!' Scrooge cries; 'I was a boy here!' (69–70). It is the first moment that his heart is touched – and it is touched by the lantern-like effect of sudden movement through time and space.

The reality-effect, however, is just that – an effect. 'These are but shadows of the things that have been', the Spirit warns Scrooge; '[t]hey have no consciousness of us' (71).[27] But the disappointment finds lantern compensation. Old Scrooge watches his solitary child self 'intent upon his reading'. We jump forward to Christmas, and:

> Suddenly a man, in foreign garments: wonderfully real and distinct to look at: stood outside the window …
>
> 'Why, it's Ali Baba!' Scrooge exclaimed in ecstasy. 'It's dear old honest Ali Baba!' (72)

The supernatural slides move from one early nineteenth-century lantern-slide favourite to another (moments that became high-spots of lantern-slide *Carol* renditions), and old Scrooge cries again:

> 'There's the Parrot! [. . .] Poor Robin [*sic*] Crusoe', he called him [. . .] 'Poor Robin Crusoe, where have you been, Robin Crusoe?'

Then, with '*a rapidity of transition*' (a most self-consciously technical lantern term) that is 'very foreign to his usual character', Scrooge mutters, 'Poor boy!' and cries again. The Ghost '*waved its hand: saying as it did so, "Let us see another Christmas!"*' (72–3). The gesture suggests not only the lanternist's fluttering fingers, but assistants, behind the supernatural screen (79). He takes Scrooge to London, and to his young manhood: the ball at old Fezziwig's, where he was apprenticed, which now happens (as it were) all over again, in joyous present tense; the parlour of his fiancée's house, where she releases him from his engagement, and the pain of loss happens again, now, as if for the first time. Scrooge softens. The greatest '*effect*' (the word was common lanternists' parlance), however, is produced by the Spirit of Christmas Yet-To-Come: the sight of his own neglected grave, where Scrooge reads upon the stone 'his own name, EBENEZER SCROOGE' (124). And he makes his promise: 'I will honour Christmas in my heart . . . I will live in the past, present and future' (126). The promise honours the lesson of the magic lantern – and the dissolving views that have moved him magically through space and time.

In *A Christmas Carol* and *Gabriel Grub*, then, a nickel-and-dime entertainment, whose serious history is yet to be fully written, creatively enables the production of a new secular scripture; visual transformation produces spiritual conversion. A machine re-configures the human imagination – makes possible stories in which time can be stopped in its onward linear flow, can be rewound, and the past revisited with the freshness and conviction of cinematic flashbacks, seventy years before flashbacks came to be.

Dickens had wanted to 'strike a blow' at iniquitous social conditions in *Carol*. In a scarcely known ninety-page agnostic novella of 1847, by James Anthony Froude, the future historian and biographer of Carlyle, the blow told. 'The Lieutenant's Daughter' is driven (indeed lacerated) by Froude's recent loss of religious belief, by fury at the comforting faith in Divine Providence that underpinned Dickens's Christmas story – and by the imaginative experience of the magic lantern show that the 'Inimitable' had corralled into its service. Almost unknown to criticism, except for a passing reference to its 'audacious' 'obliquities of narrative method' by Kathleen Tillotson, 'The Lieutenant's Daughter' is overshadowed by a later novel (*The Nemesis of Faith*), which was publicly burnt at Oriel College, Oxford. The novella represents doubt, as Froude had experienced it, in writing (at Newman's request) a Life of St Neot of Ireland: as the volatile product of history's clash with myth; as textual instability. The tale is shot through by the kind of scientific and technological speculation that the lantern was so often used to illuminate for public edification.[28]

The story is simple melodrama: a fifteen-year-old governess, orphan Catherine Gray, is seduced by her employers' nephew and heir, an Oxford man hot for ideas like free love and universal philanthropy. When the affair comes to light, her employers throw her on the streets; Henry Carpenter, the nephew, takes her in, but quickly gets bored and absconds to London, strengthened in his desire to do the indecent thing by his uncle's threat of disinheritance. Catherine follows, and on the train to Paddington is befriended by an elderly woman, Miss Arthur, posing as Carpenter's 'friend' – a ruse to entrap her into a brothel. Miss Arthur blackmails Carpenter (one of her regulars) into writing a brush-off letter that will stun the girl into acquiescence in her own sexual degradation. The tale reaches a peak of capitalist brutality when the bawd discusses with her sister what to do with their new piece of meat: 'Lord William offers two hundred pounds . . . if it's quite fresh.'[29] Catherine is handed from man to man, 'till at last her haggard painted face was seen nightly in the theatre or the saloon' (250). When her 'cup of bitterness' is full, she crawls home to take poison on her parents' grave.

Pertinently, Catherine's story is preceded by a fourteen-page frame tale, in which our narrator voyages to Ireland, succumbs to fever, and, in a 'half delirium', is visited by a troupe of obliging genie-like demons. He asks to see their 'superior', and:

> [a] great curtain was stretched across the room, and on the surface of it, like a figure in a phantasmagoria, was hung the image I had summoned. What it was I cannot tell. [. . .] It was a meagre anatomy. [. . .] I begged for more light, [. . .] but [. . .] the more I had the light multiplied the feebler became the shadow. (200–1)[30]

This is the first level of magic-lantern reference in 'The Lieutenant's Daughter'. Lantern illumination here stands in for the 'lights' of science and Biblical criticism, which – in an ironic agnostic reversal of lantern reality – make the Devil more and more indistinct and unreal. The 'delirium' recasts, in up-to-date nineteenth-century terms, the 'deception' that Paine declared the Bible and the Christian priesthood had perpetuated on humankind, in his scandalous *Age of Reason* (1794), and the 'hallucination hypothesis' by which the most famous of the German 'higher critics', David Friedrich Strauss, accounted for belief in Christ's miracles, transfiguration, resurrection and ascension. (Froude corresponded with George Eliot, whose translation of Strauss's *Das Leben Jesu* was published in 1846.)

Both Paine and Strauss presented their cases in striking lantern terms. In Paine's account, the recent 'astonishing' 'exhibitions of ghosts or specters' in Paris – the 'mechanical and optical deceptions' of Robertson and his phantasmagore rivals – laid the foundation for a general argument against miracles.[31] In Strauss (among other pithy references), the presence or absence of the angel at the tomb becomes a 'phantasmagoric appearance, disappearance, and reappearance'.[32] If, for Dickens, as for lantern-toting missionaries like Dr Livingstone, the magic lantern was a Christian agent of hoped-for conversion and Damascene transformation,[33] for Paine and Strauss (as, later, for Thomas Hardy) the lantern experience actively encouraged scepticism by exposing the mechanics and potential for fakery in supernatural visions.[34] In Froude's 'The Lieutenant's Daughter', the *Christmas Carol* met *Das Leben Jesu* in the metaphorical projections of an illuminating machine.

For there is a second level of lantern reference in Froude's story of

Catherine: It is presented to the narrator as the main event of a lantern show that also includes glimpses of 'dead heroes', 'stately cities' (201), friends, relatives, and a 'second' and 'other' *'me'* going about daily business (202). '[O]ne of the genii arranged [her story] for me' (205); and one quick scene – in which fallen Catherine clings to her seducer's knees in a flaming saloon, 'pause[s]' before the narrator's eyes 'for a moment in *the shifting of the slides*' (251). The lantern thus provides the tale with a method of narration.

But the tale also provides the lantern with a description of its operation and psychological effect that not only tests (and proves) Castle's theory of the 'bizarre externaliz[ation]' of thought involved in the lantern metaphor,[35] but uncannily anticipates modern theoretical understandings of cinematic spectatorship: Catherine's story is simultaneously 'external, and independent of my power of willing' (199), a series of 'brilliant images', over which 'I had no power at all' (198), and 'a thing which befell me [. . .] internally', a 'phenomenon of mind' (196). These 'speculations [. . .] presented [. . .] in the form of a picture' (196) are a pre-cinematic lantern dream.

A third level of lantern reference in 'The Lieutenant's Daughter' is rooted in the narrator's sense of being 'haunt[ed] by Hooker's definition of time, as "the measure of the motion of the heavens"' (193), a material – and manipulable – phenomenon; indeed, the tale begins with a modernist fantasy of making time run backwards by launching a railway train 'in the same direction [as] the earth's motion and with double the velocity' (194–5). Like *A Christmas Carol* – and one reason for that story's attraction to cinema – it is steeped in the imaginative implications and anxieties of the 'railway mania' that altered space, time and vision in the 1840s: 'Back rolled the great wheels of time; whizzing by me so fast, the objects all melted into haze. [. . .] till I found myself on the platform of the Railway Station at Paddington' (221–2).

But the railway train is not the tale's only 'time machine'. The genii who show the narrator Catherine's story are lantern showmen who specialize in dissolving views – that, as we have seen, are temporal as well as optical effects. They produce their *pièce de resistance* when the narrator commands them: 'Go, reverse the order of the universe, and make time flow backwards' (202). The immediate effect is comic, as if we are watching mechanical slides worked backwards – a common lanternist trick, anticipating early cinema *trucs*, like the reverse projection of the Lumières' *Demolition of a Wall*: 'You saw the tea coiling up like a water-spout, [. . .] into the mouth of the pot' (203). But the ultimate effect is devastating. For the most startling innovation of this extraordinary little story is that *it is written backwards*.[36] Thus we dissolve from Catherine's suicide to her arrival at Paddington station, and from her degradation to Carpenter's 'exstatic' declarations of undying love and Catherine's innocent, mundane early history. The reversal of order, the 'shifting' backwards through the 'slides' of her life, whereby 'effects and causes [. . .] changed places' (203)*,* is the agnostic imagination's deliberately destabilized, lantern-lit blow at the linear narrative and fantasy of free will represented by the Bible. 'Think it over now,' says one of the genii; 'and see if you can tell when sin came in, and she began to deserve what fell upon her' (281).

That blow is enabled – visualized – by the magic lantern no less than the redemptive temporal fantasy of Dickens's *Christmas Carol.* And it is, finally, to that work, its author, and its lantern uplift, that Froude addresses himself.

The tale has had Dickens in its sights from the start: The local newspaper superintendent is 'hanging doubtingly between the last Pickwick and the least threadbare of his devotional sentiments', when a young clerk volunteers Catherine's suicide to fill a blank on the front page (216); the showmen-genii are parodies of the *Carol*'s spirits. However, the temporal reversal of Froude's tale destroys Dickens's comfortable morality and genial message; its lantern-inspired structural irony makes us ironic readers. And it dissolves not only time but closure, and certainty.

For at its end, the text has one last surprise. We read to the last page, discovering all (or so we think) about Catherine's early life: the death of her mother in childbirth, and – especially – the death of her father, which triggers the orphan child's downfall. Then the chief genie adds: 'I have another scene for you before we part.' And we are taken aback: Catherine, her husband (a naval officer), her two-year-old son and a clergyman file with a happy crowd from the church where her newborn baby has just been christened. The genie has offered us an alternative outcome of Catherine's life that depends on a different beginning. Only one tiny circumstance has changed. Like the Spirit of Christmas Yet-To-Come, the genie points the narrator towards a gravestone for the final revelation. It is Catherine's father's; the narrator read it earlier:

> 'The inscription, [the genie says] [. . .] read it'.
> I did so; it was the same, word and word the same, but with this one difference. The old man had outlived the date I had first read five summers; [. . .] and that was all; five links hung on upon the chain. (286)

The double ending is the final touch. Nor are we to know which ending is true. When the narrator asks, the genie responds: 'Come with me to the light, and I will show you.' The narrator crawls to his bedroom window, and finds himself awake. In what he sees, in the very last lines of the story, there is one last lantern reference, of a sort to blank out all pretension of 'meaning': '[M]y eyes were on the *white sheet* of the Atlantic, and the peaks of Achill were purpling in the rising sun' (287; italics added).

We have here, I think, something important: a Victorian taste of modern things to come, of fiction unchained from linear time, from the re-edited temporality of Fitzgerald's *This Side of Paradise* to the undifferentiated eternal-present-tense of Robbe-Grillet's *Jealousy*. We have, too, perhaps, a direct source for the suspended endings and back-to-front organization of texts like John Fowles's *The French Lieutenant's Woman* and Harold Pinter's *Betrayal*.[37] But we also have, as in the *Carol* and in *Gabriel Grub*, so extraordinary a level of response to the visual and temporal transformations of the magic lantern and its dissolving views, that we begin to understand how and why early and 'primitive' film called forth such a sophisticated and 'modern' response from its first audiences: It had been conditioned, previewed; imaginatively, as well as technologically, the lantern had gone before.

Notes

This essay is indebted to audiences at the Academy of Motion Picture Arts and Sciences (Beverly Hills), the Dickens Universe (Santa Cruz), the Cinemateca Portuguesa (Lisbon, Portugal) and the Museum of Modern Art (MoMA, New York), and to my lantern research and performance partner, David Francis, OBE.

1. This is David Francis's estimate of lecturer numbers. There were at least twenty-eight lantern and slide firms in London alone in the 1880s and 1890s. See Olive Cook, *Movement in Two Dimensions* (London: Hutchinson, 1963), p. 93.
2. Both references to Englishness, one from an 1855 French review of the Paris Exposition Universelle, the other by artist-illustrator Luke Fildes, from the 1860s, are quoted in Julia Thomas, *Pictorial Victorians* (Athens, OH: Ohio University Press, 2004), pp. 110, 63.
3. *Ibid.*, p. 118.
4. J. W. Kirton's famous temperance tale *Buy Your Own Cherries* (1862), for example, is known in at least four lantern versions, as well as a 1904 film by R. W. Paul (see below).
5. As Terry Castle puts it, in all of them, 'spectral technology' produces the ghosts we 'know' 'd[o] not exist'; see 'Phantasmagoria', *Critical Inquiry* 15.1 (Autumn, 1988), 26–61 (p. 30). See also, Mervyn Heard, *Phantasmagoria: The Secret Life of the Magic Lantern* (Hastings: The Projection Box, 2006), especially pp. 247–75, on the phenomenon's intermedia inheritances; Marina Warner, *Phantasmagoria: Spirit Visions, Metaphors, and Media into the Twenty-First Century* (Oxford: Oxford University Press, 2006), pp. 146–56; Erkki Huhtamo, 'Ghost Notes: Reading Mervyn Heard's *Phantasmagoria*', *Magic Lantern Gazette* 18 (2006), 10–17. Confusingly, the word 'phantasmagoria' was applied to shows and lanterns of all types later in the nineteenth century.
6. Cook spends only one page on the subject (pp. 95–6), and Laurent Mannoni devotes two paragraphs in *The Great Art of Light and Shadow*, trans. and ed. Richard Crangle (Exeter: University of Exeter Press, 1995, 2000), p. 157.

7. On M. Henry, see Heard, *Phantasmagoria*, pp. 198–203, and Edwin Dawes and Mervyn Heard, 'M. Henry's Dissolving Views', in Richard Crangle, Mervyn Heard and Ine van Dooren, eds, *Realms of Light* (London: Magic Lantern Society, 2005), pp. 159–62.

8. According to the *Dictionary of National Biography* (*DNB*) (1887) and the *Encyclopaedia Britannica* (1891), Childe may have produced prototype dissolving views sometime between 1807 and 1818.

9. Lester Smith, 'Entertainment and Amusement, Education and Instruction', in *Realms of Light*, pp. 138–45, see especially pp. 143, 141. Childe's 'dissolving views' were first given in 1841. Other attractions included persistence-of-vision machines and a giant projecting phenakistoscope.

10. Dawes and Heard, 'M. Henry's Dissolving Views', in *Realms of Light*, p. 162.

11. Playbill, Brighton Theatre Royal, 1833, quoted in David Robinson, 'New Magic Lantern Sensations of 1827', *New Magic Lantern Journal* 8.4 (December 1999), 14–15 (p. 15).

12. On pantomime transformation effects, see R. J. Broadbent, *A History of Pantomime* (London: Simpkin, Marshall, Hamilton, Kent & Co., 1901), pp. 172–86; on the Diorama, see Helmut and Alison Gernsheim, *L. J. M. Daguerre* (New York, NY: World Publishing Co., 1956), pp. 13–45.

13. Heard, 'Now You See It, Now You Don't: The Magician and the Magic Lantern', in *Realms of Light*, pp. 13–24 (p. 19).

14. Castle, 'Phantasmagoria', p. 39n.

15. *Ibid.*, p. 34.

16. Heard and Crangle, 'The Temperance Phantasmagoria', in *Realms of Light*, pp. 46–55, see especially pp. 52, 49.

17. Fred Guida, *A Christmas Carol and Its Adaptations* (Jefferson, NJ: McFarlane, 2000), p. 50.

18. *Great Expectations*, ed. Angus Calder (London: Penguin, 1985) p. 321. For further examples of Dickensian lantern references, see Stephen Bottomore, 'A Word Paints a Thousand Pictures', in *Realms of Light*, pp. 56–61.

19. *Pictures from Italy* (New York, NY: Bigelow, Brown and Co., 1868), p. 378.

20. Henry Morley and W. H. Wills, 'The Stereoscope', *Household Words*, 10 September 1853, p. 42.

21. Fred Kaplan, *Dickens: A Biography* (New York, NY: William Morrow, 1988), p. 208; emphasis in original.

22. See 'Optical and Mechanical Effects of the Lantern' by the famous dissolving-view artist Edmund H. Wilkie, Part Four, *Optical and Magic Lantern Journal* 9.15 (December 1898), p. 89. Commercial slides were standardized at 3¼″ x 3¼″, the Polytechnic's *Grub* slides were 12″ x 10″, allowing an unsurpassed level of detail.

23. Guida, *A Christmas Carol and Its Adaptations*, p. 50.

24. *Pickwick Papers*, ed. Robert L. Patten (London: Penguin, 1972, 1986), pp. 487–9. Interestingly, the lantern reading *Gabriel Grub; Or, The Story of the Sexton Who was Stolen by the Goblins* in fact edits and supplements the text to fit it for image-by-image presentation and to underline its lantern derivation.

25. Other lantern effects in Paul's *Scrooge* include superimpositions, double exposures and a black screen-within-the-screen (Scrooge's bedroom curtains) on which to present images of the past. The knocker dissolve features in York's twenty-four-slide 'Life Model': *Carol*, 1884 (David Francis collection).

26. *A Christmas Carol*, ed. Michael Slater (London: Penguin, 2003), pp. 54–5. Subsequent page references in text.

27. See Giambattista della Porta's *Magia naturalis*, or *Natural Magick*, 1589, on the foundational reality-effect of the *camera obscura*, 1658 edition (reprinted New York: Basic Books, 1957), p. 365.

28. Kathleen Tillotson, *Novels of the Eighteen-Forties* (Oxford: Oxford University Press, 1954, 1961), p. 62.

29. James Anthony Froude ('Zeta'), 'The Lieutenant's Daughter', *Shadows of the Clouds* (London: John Olliver, 1847), p. 229; subsequent page references in text.

30. The master-phantasmagore Étienne Gaspard Robertson made similar attempts to raise the devil in his youth, sacrificing a cock in his bedroom and commanding Lucifer to appear. '*Ici j'arrête le récit*', records his biographer, Françoise Lévie; '[j]e reviens légèrement en arrière. Comme pour un film dont on veut revoir le dernier raccord de montage. L'image défile à nouveau. Je vous vois tout éclaboussé de sang [. . .] Vous est extrêmement pale. [. . .] Puisque le diable refuse de collaborer avec vous, [. . .] vous aller l'inventer. Sous votre baguette, le cortège infernal prend forme, se met en roule vers la lumière.' Lévie, *Étienne Gaspard Robertson: la vie d'un fantasmagore* (Brussels: Les Éditions de Préambule, 1990), pp. 30–1. See also Étienne Gaspard Robertson, *Mémoires récréatifs, scientifiques et anecdotiques d'un physicien-aéronaute*, vol. 1: *La Fantasmagorie* (Langres: Café Clima Editeur, 1985 [1831]), pp. 95–110 ('*Premières idées de la fantasmagorie*'). The audiences of Philidor's lantern séances also reputedly begged him to raise the devil (Heard, *Phantasmagoria*, p. 67), as did those of the proto-phantasmagore Johann Schröpfer, who responded, tongue in cheek, with the image of a red demon with claws and tail, in the gown of a priest (Heard, p. 82).

31. Paine, *The Age of Reason*, ed. Philip S. Foner (Secaucus, NJ: Citadel, 1974), p. 94.

32. David Friedrich Strauss, *The Life of Jesus*, trans. George Eliot (London: Chapman, Bros., 1846, 4th edn), vol. 3, p. 317.

33. See David Livingstone, *Missionary Travels* (London: Ward, Lock & Co., 1857), pp. 259–60. See also Robert Louis Stevenson's *In the South Seas* (London: Chatto & Windus, 1918), which recounts this reaction to the lantern: 'Why then, . . . the Bible is true!', Stevenson is told by 'heathens' he has regaled with his lantern, 'we have seen the pictures' (p. 258). On the missionary lantern, see Paul Landau, 'The Illumination of Christ in the Kalahari Desert', *Representations* 45 (1994), 26–40.

34. See Jon Roberts's inaccurate but suggestive, brief discussion in 'Mortal Projections: Thomas Hardy's Dissolving Views of God', *Victorian Literature and Culture* 31 (2003), 43–66.

35. Castle, 'Phantasmagoria', p. 58.

36. Individual scenes are 'inverted' by the genii (Froude, 'Lieutenant's Daughter', p. 206).

37. Both 'The Lieutenant's Daughter' and *The French Lieutenant's Woman* are set in Exeter; both focus on female sexual degradation/emancipation. Pinter scripted Fowles's 1969 novel in 1981; Pinter's stage play *Betrayal* was staged in 1978 and was filmed in 1983.

CHAPTER 2

'Never Has One Seen Reality Enveloped in Such a Phantasmagoria': Watching Spectacular Transformations, 1860–89

KRISTIAN MOEN

In cinema's first decade, *féeries* such as *A Trip to the Moon* (Méliès, 1902) and *The Kingdom of the Fairies* (Méliès, 1903) were among the most popular films in the world.[1] With fantastic subject matter, elaborate spectacles, relatively lengthy running times, the use of colour and prominent trick effects, such films offered many different attractions. These films borrowed heavily from the narratives and spectacles of their stage antecedent, the theatrical *féerie*.[2] Roughly translatable as a 'fairy play', this type of theatrical show ran alongside melodramas and vaudevilles in the popular stages of nineteenth-century France, particularly in Paris.[3] As well as being an extension of this stage tradition, the cinematic *féerie* also extended a tradition of transformation. This is evident in the terms used to describe them; they were both '*féeries*' and a type of 'transformation view'.[4] Seen in this light, this important genre of early cinema can be drawn into a wider context of nineteenth-century visual culture in which the depiction of spectacular transformation had developed its own set of associations, specific sites and vernacular. While this discussion focuses on France, the taste for transformation was by no means exclusively national – for example, it was also evident in pantomime transformation scenes on the London stage and the international popularity (and production) of the cinematic *féerie*. However, this essay limits the scope mainly to French newspapers and periodicals in order to examine more closely specific examples of how such transformations were discussed. In particular, I focus on the revival of a popular theatrical *féerie*, *Le Pied de mouton*, in 1860 and the luminous fountains at the Universal Exposition of 1889 in Paris.

Examining the discourse surrounding visual transformations, I aim to draw out some of the implications of this use of spectacle. Rather than a secondary concern, spicing up a narrative or functioning as a discrete attraction, some accounts suggested that the depiction of mutability was a worthwhile sight on its own, filled with the potential to alter and enlarge perspectives. Such transformations were not limited to the metamorphosis of bodies or objects, but often presented the entire stage, or even world, as a place of

mutability. These spectacles would be linked to other aspects of the traditional arts or contemporary visual culture, indicating the breadth of appeal
that visual transformation held in the nineteenth century. It was not a fascination exclusive to this context, as early cinema's absorption and enlargement
of the taste for transformation indicates.

'A KALEIDOSCOPE IN MOVEMENT': THE FÉERIE IN THE EARLY 1860s

Reviews of theatrical *féeries* consistently indicated that spectacular sets, marvellous incidents and fantastic transformations were the integral features of
the genre. This is evident in some of the earliest discussions of *féeries*; for
example, the popular and influential *Le Pied de mouton* (1806) – sometimes
seen as the prototypical *féerie* – was described as 'remarkable for the variety
and the marvels of the incidents, the rapidity of its transformations, the bril-
liance and the multitude of the settings, and the precision with which so many
of its devices [*machines*] are played'.[5] The tale itself, of a young suitor and his
magical talisman (an enchanted lamb's foot), was secondary to its spectacle.
When *Le Pied de mouton* was revived as an extravagant production in 1860, a
similar refrain was heard. *L'Année littéraire et dramatique* described the play's
success as 'one of the greatest in the theatrical history of Paris', going on to
note that what made the play a real spectacle was

> entirely in the *mise en scène*, in the tricks and the marvels of the decor, in the
> ballets executed by rival troupes from diverse nations, in the bedazzlement of
> electric light, the showers of water and fire from magic fountains, in the land-
> scapes and the architectural splendours designed and composed by masters.[6]

Although a similar set of appeals had remained central to the *féerie* for more
than half a century, their deployment had changed. In *Le Figaro*, B. Jouvin
wrote:

> That which had so strongly enchanted our fathers would probably seem to us
> like an elementary and slightly naive *marvel*. The art of the painter-designer,
> of the costume designer, of the stagehand [*machiniste*], of the director, of the
> ballet director, was childlike on that date of 6 December 1806.[7]

Decades later, new technologies and an increased scope of spectacle had kept
the *féerie* up to date, helping to make it one of the most popular theatrical forms
– if not the most popular – in nineteenth-century Paris. With a similar emphasis on the visual design of settings, costumes and enchantment, *Rothomago* – a
major *féerie* staged two years later – was described as 'the counterpart to *Le
Pied de mouton*; it is the triumph, quite foreign to literature, of magnificent and
clever theatrical exhibitions, of tricks, of transformation views [*transformations
à vue*]'.[8] Using the phrase 'transformation views', employed decades later to

categorize a type of cinema, the review draws attention to the continuing centrality of spectacular images of mutability.

Two specific tropes were often used to create the effect of spectacular transformation in the theatrical *féerie*: *trucs*, which could be defined as 'any change of an object occurring before the eyes'[9]; and *changements à vue*, which enlarged the scope of the *truc* by transforming the stage itself through 'the rapid replacement of one decor by another before the spectator's eyes'.[10] In order to express the visual effect of such transformation, *féeries* were sometimes compared to kaleidoscopes. Describing the final scene of *Le Pied de mouton*, the apotheosis ending, the reviewer for *La Presse* told his readers to '[i]magine a monstrous kaleidoscope'.[11] Some reviews would refer to not only a single scene as kaleidoscopic, but to the play as a whole. Théophile Gautier, for example, wrote in his review of *Turlututu* (1858) that 'the stage, like a kaleidoscope that one turns, changes and recomposes perpetually'.[12] The comparisons to a kaleidoscope highlight the ways in which the *féerie* offered spectacular transformations that were, in some respects, akin to abstract figurations of colour and light in a state of ongoing movement. For Gautier, the effect of watching such spectacles could be exhausting and overwhelming. His review of *Rothomago* begins: 'The play hardly finished, and we are here leaning on a desk, beginning our review, our eyes still completely dazzled by this kaleidoscope of sets, of costumes and of tricks that we call the *féerie*.'[13] While being dazzled by such a 'kaleidoscope' might lead to a criticism of the play's lack of narrative or meaning, Gautier takes a much different tack: 'What does it matter? It's enough that the *tableaux* replace themselves rapidly and unravel ceaselessly in new decompositions.' Such a comment indicates just how central transformation was to the expectations and pleasures of the *féerie*.

The heightened role of spectacle was partly brought about by developments in stage technology and lighting. The theatre reviewer for *L'Année littéraire et dramatique* described how this should lead to a reconsideration of the ways in which authorship is valued, complaining that

> the theatres rich enough to go without talent require industry and applied science for their plays: they make themselves branches of Arts and Trades, of the Sorbonne, and largely exhibit engines and scientific experiments in the tricks. Gas, electricity and magnesium furnish them with streams of light which is enough for them; they inundate us with it.[14]

Louis Ulbach at *Le Temps* offered a different perspective on the intersection of industry and theatre. Referring to two of the most dazzling effects in *Aladin* (1863), he suggests that a Legion of Honour should not only be awarded to literary authors, but also to 'the great unknown artist who prepares these fabulous transformations, who creates an ingenious device [*machine*], with the aid of which a mushroom changes into a kiosk [. . .] and a ship suddenly transforms into a fantastic palace'.[15] Although marked by a rather exaggerated tone, both reviewers are gesturing towards the ways in which the production of spectacular transformation was crucial to the unfolding of these spectacles. They were, in some respects, authored by novel technologies.

LUMINOUS FOUNTAINS AND *LE PRINCE SOLEIL*

The discourse of transformation associated with the *féerie* would be used to describe other spectacles as well. One of the most prominent examples of this was in the descriptions of the extraordinary spectacle produced by the luminous fountains at the Universal Exposition of 1889 in Paris. Luminous fountains drew upon discoveries and developments in lighting technologies to display changing colours in streams and droplets of water that temporarily contained the light that had been shone on them. The science writer Louis Figuier wrote that 'the luminous fountains have been, along with the Eiffel tower, the great attraction of the Universal Exposition of 1889'.[16] Descriptions of these fountains would highlight their fantastic visions of colour and light in a state of ongoing transformation:

> The streams of coloured water projected themselves in showers of fire, falling back down in a rain of sparks; then, brusquely, the decor changed: from a golden yellow it became red, green or blue. Finally, these diverse tints transformed themselves, falling into one another, going from ruby and from emerald to the most delicate opaline nuances. It was a fairylike [*féerique*] spectacle.[17]

Employing the term 'decor', emphasizing the extraordinary transformations and using the trope 'fairylike', this account describes the luminous fountains in the same kind of language as was often used to describe the theatrical *féerie*. Sometimes these implicit links to the *féerie* were made directly; for example, one description of the luminous fountains begins: 'The hour advances and the night has arrived. The *féerie* is going to start, and nothing can describe it.'[18] The 'fairyland' created by the luminous fountains was a discursive extension of the stage *féerie*, a vision of instability and mutability.

Descriptions of how such luminous fountains were created sometimes evoked the changing conditions of authorship that had also been linked to the theatrical *féerie*. Describing the 'infinite variety' of colours in the illuminated streams of water, Louis Figuier noted how these are controlled by an operator like a painter at his palette or an organist at his instrument.[19] Offering a similar comparison, Eugène-Melchior de Vogüé described the engineer of the luminous fountains as 'a poet, a poet in action'.[20] Vogüé

Figure 2.1   *The Luminous Fountain of the Paris Exposition.*[21]

extended the implications of this comparison, suggesting that the luminous fountains offered an emergent visual language: '[W]hen the refined retina will distinguish, in the chromatic range of colours in movement, the vibrations that the ear perceives as sounds, there will be found perhaps a Chopin or a Liszt who will ravish souls with visual melodies.'[22] This manipulation of colour, light and instability might be, 'for the painter and the thinker, the occasion for thoughts, fecund experiences'.[23] Notably, Vogüé also drew attention to the labourers toiling at the bottom of the fountains: 'I watched them at the base of their underground passage, these brave labourers, readying the *féerie* in the heat and in the darkness.'[24] As a technology that produced visual transformation, the luminous fountains were drawn into the context of the *féerie*, helping refashion the relations between traditional arts and industry.

Some accounts suggested that the luminous fountains recast the world of the exposition itself by bathing it in a transformative light. For example, a discussion of the altered perspectives brought about by the luminous fountains provided the conclusion for a lengthy description of a visit to the Exposition in the *Atlantic Monthly*.[25] Near the end of the day, after having described numerous sights and spectacles at the Exposition, the reporter hurries out of the display of industrial might in the *Galerie des Machines*, writing, 'I nearly forgot that I was there for enjoyment, and made haste to get into the open air.'[26] Once outside, the Eiffel Tower at night becomes visible: 'Then the vulgarity of the crowd, the trivial details, the clap-trap, the pasteboard aspect of huge temporary structures, were lost in a vaster and more comprehensive impression, at once more real and more fantastic.'[27] The Eiffel Tower offers a more comforting and substantial sight, a respite from the onslaught of overwhelming or fleeting images characteristic of the Exposition. But rather than lingering on this view, the correspondent's attention quickly shifts from this emblem of modern stability to an emblem of instability – the luminous fountains: 'At a stated hour, the illumination of the fountains produced a marvelous transformation scene, beautiful enough for fairy-land.'[28] This spectacular image of transformation does more than offer a pleasing or astonishing sight; it seems to recast the environment into an enchanted world. Giving the impression of an intoxicated survey of a magical milieu, likely abetted by both physical fatigue and sensory overload, both the experience and the mode of writing open to fantastic possibilities; the correspondent now walks among the 'mysterious pavilions and strange gardens like Haroun Alraschid in search of adventure', seeing 'a transcendent grandeur' in the outlines of the buildings, belonging to 'precincts of enchantment'.[29] While this description partly evokes the ways in which electric lighting created the effect of an extraordinary new visual world, it also draws attention to how the luminous fountains themselves became a metonymy for such a world. The fountains offered an alternative to the display of industry at the Exposition, while still offering a spectacular vision of the modern world in the midst of transformation.

The notion that the play of light and the figuration of transformation could be situated within the modern world was dramatized in the most prominent *féerie* produced that year, *Le Prince Soleil*. It was heralded as an apt theatrical spectacle, 'a play for the Exposition'.[30] Two particular features may have contributed to this sense of the play's relevance to the Exposition. First, *Le Prince Soleil* presented a journey through different nations, offering a veiled commentary on contemporary political subjects. Francisque Sarcey, in *Le Temps*, characterized it as a 'scientific *féerie*, of which *Around the World in 80 Days* is the prototype'.[31] As a variation on the more traditional *féerie*, 'scientific' *féeries* offered contemporary iconography and subject matter, often replacing the onstage display of fantastic wonders with technological wonders. With a journey that took the play's hero – and the audience – on a voyage through Sweden, Portugal, the Indian Ocean and the empire of the Sun, *Le Prince Soleil* offered the international spectacle of the Universal Exposition in miniature, onstage. *Le Prince Soleil* also presented a visual correspondence with the Exposition's luminous fountains. Marcel Fouquier, in *La Nouvelle Revue*, wrote that 'it proceeds from *Around the World in 80 Days*, but with an interlude of classical féerie, truly staggering, and even more dazzling'.[32] Fouquier described this interlude as a variation on the spectacular fantasies of *Le Pied de mouton*, noting that it begins when the hero is shipwrecked on an island: 'Quite shaken by the incidents of his interrupted voyage, the prince imagines that he has been transported into the sun. He has hallucinations, and all that he thinks he sees, we see.'[33] He goes on to describe the interlude as 'an evanescent [*insaisissable*] enchantment on a foundation of fugitive light and fairylike [*féerique*] rays'. Rather than describing a single scene in terms that evoke the luminous fountains, Hector Pessard, writing for *Le Gaulois*, begins his review by describing the overall experience of watching the play in the terms of visual enchantment:

> I would never have believed that a human eye could contain so many things. [. . .] Imagine an immense crucible, in which a fusion of turquoises, amethysts, rubies, sapphires mix their streams of light with waves of liquid gold, fringed by a silver foam. [. . .] Conceive by a cerebral effort, the rainbow's glimmerings, the aurora borealis's brightness, the desert's white lights shining upon this fire of metals and gemstones. It's done? You have imagined, supposed, conceived? Well, you have an idea, but an imperfect idea, of the bedazzlements of only one of the tableaux of *Le Prince Soleil*.[34]

Using a similar language to describe both the scientific *féerie* and the luminous fountains, theatre reviewers and visitors to the Exposition presented an image of spectacular mutability within an increasingly contemporary frame.

CONCLUSION

Spectacular transformations were described in the popular press as an ongoing process, sometimes overwhelming and sometimes revivifying. These accounts suggested that the presentation of instability was itself worthy of wonder and contemplation. Such accounts also drew together different kinds of spectacles under the rubric of the *féerie*, as we have seen with the discourse surrounding both the kaleidoscope and, to a greater extent, the luminous fountains. Moreover, creating transformations was sometimes seen as akin to both authoring plays and presenting modern technologies. The extent to which early cinema could be placed within this framework becomes a subtext of Méliès's article on his filmmaking practice, 'Cinematographic Views', published in 1907. In the article, Méliès describes a chronology of film history as a development of different kinds of views, culminating in the appearance of his 'speciality', the cinematic *féerie* and the 'so-called transformation view'.[35] As well as situating such films as central to his own filmmaking practice, and to the history of cinema, Méliès draws specific connections between cinema and the theatrical *féerie* through references to fairy tales and fantasy. In its first sentence, the article refers to 'the thousand and one difficulties that professionals must surmount to produce the artistic, amusing, strange, or simply the natural subjects that have made the cinematograph such a craze all over the world'.[36] Evoking fairy tales by referring to 'the thousand and one difficulties', Méliès links the production of films to the telling of fantastic tales, but as a modern form of storytelling. Referring to cinema, he goes on to write that 'this marvellous instrument's popularity has only grown with every passing day until it has assumed prodigious proportions'.[37] Enlarging in size like an object in one of his trick films, the popularity of cinema is also situated in the language of fantasy. This rhetoric of fantasy even extends to his 'shooting studio', 'a quite faithful, small-scale likeness of a *théâtre de féerie*'.[38] Moreover, he writes that it was due to his apparent discovery of the substitution splice that he began making his first *féeries*.[39] These comments about film history, filmmaking, cinema's popularity, the staging of films and film editing all gesture towards an entwinement of the *féerie* and cinema itself. As well as situating cinema within a tradition of fairy tales and theatre, Méliès is situating cinema as yet another means to present spectacular transformation.

However, Méliès found the phrase 'transformation view' an unsuitable description, preferring the phrase 'fantastic view'. He wrote that 'if a certain number of these views in fact include scene changes, metamorphoses, or transformations, there are also a large number without transformations'.[40] The article goes on to list a range of different devices used within his films, such as 'prestidigitation, optics, photographic tricks, set design and theatrical machinery, the play of light, dissolves (*dissolving views* as the English have called them), and the entire arsenal of fantastic, magical compositions'. Distancing his films from a narrow definition of transformation, such a comment draws attention to cinema's use of a wealth of fantastic devices drawn from stagecraft and visual culture. Nevertheless, many of the devices he notes and his inclusion of cinema within the field of fantasy, particularly the *féerie*, indicates the extent to which transformation undergirded such films.

Méliès's discussion of the 'so-called transformation view' can also be seen as part of a larger interaction between theatre, visual culture and cinema. The presentation of spectacular mutability may have resonated with aspects of social, cultural and visual transformation. In an article from the early 1850s, Gautier suggested this link between a wider sphere and the depiction of transformation. He begins by criticizing the *Théâtre Français* for being too traditional to employ *changements à vue*, writing that '[l]ife is mobile and changes at each instant. It is therefore necessary that the theatre be mobile like it, for risk of only representing a philosophical abstraction.'[41] While this directly refers to the need for theatrical practice to change with the times, it also evokes a larger set of aesthetic and cultural concerns. Gautier's use of the phrase 'at each instant' to describe the changes in life corresponds to a trope that he often used to describe the scene changes in *féeries*.[42] In this respect, a theatre that employs the transformations of *changements à vue* spectacularly stages the transformations of life. Never settled, never static, a stage in a state of flux moves beyond a 'philosophical abstraction' or ideal form and begins to participate in mobility and instability. If cinema is drawn into this context as well, certain implications arise regarding how it might be approached as part of larger trends in visual culture. In the accounts I have been discussing, transformations were seen as a spectacular display of ongoing processes, an effect that tended to take away a sense of teleological aims or even of discrete events. Rather than expressing a desire for narratives or images that fix meaning, these accounts suggest that the presentation of instability was itself worthy of wonder and contemplation. And this instability was not simply linked to a modern experience of shock and chaos. For example, one description of the transformative light cast by the luminous fountains noted, '[n]ever has one seen reality enveloped in such a phantasmagoria. All the perspectives are changed and prodigiously enlarged; the beings themselves are as if transfigured, the groups of fountains resemble *tableaux vivants*'.[43] New perspectives and a newly animated world of marvels were generated by such displays of light, and would go on to be an important facet of how cinema would be discussed and understood.

Notes

1. See Richard Abel, *The Red Rooster Scare: Making Cinema American, 1900–1910* (Berkeley, CA: University of California Press, 1999).

2. André Gaudreault, for example, situates the *féerie* in the 'cultural series' of theatre. See his 'Méliès the Magician: The Magical Magic of the Magic Image', *Early Popular Visual Culture* 5.2 (July 2007), 167–74 (p. 172). See also Richard Abel, *The Ciné Goes to Town: French Cinema 1896–1914* (Berkeley, CA: University of California Press, 1994); Katherine Singer Kovács, 'George Méliès and the Féerie', in John L. Fell, ed., *Film Before Griffith* (Berkeley, CA: University of California Press, 1983), pp. 244–57.

3. See Paul Ginisty, *La féerie* (Paris: L. Michaud, 1910); Katherine Kovács, 'A History of the *Féerie* in France', *Theatre Quarterly* 29 (Spring, 1978), 29–38; Roxane Martin, *La Féerie romantique sur les scènes parisiennes, 1791–1864* (Paris: Honoré Champion, 2007).

4. Abel, *The Ciné Goes to Town*, p. 70.

5. Julien-Louis Geoffroy, 'Feuilleton du Journal de l'Empire', *Journal de l'Empire*, 11 December 1806.

6. *L'Année littéraire et dramatique*, 1861, p. 242.

7. B. Jouvin, 'Théâtres', *Le Figaro*, 13 September 1860; italics in original.

8. *L'Année littéraire et dramatique*, 1863, p. 233.

9. M. J. Moynet, *French Theatrical Production in the Nineteenth Century*, trans. Allan S. Jackson with M. Glen Wilson, ed. Marvin A. Carlson (New York, NY: State University of New York at Binghamton, 1976 [1873]), p. 66. This description is a standard definition, quoted in Kovács, 'A History of the *Féerie* in France', p. 37.

10. *Ibid.*

11. Paul de Saint-Victor, 'Théâtres', *La Presse*, 30 September 1860. Similarly, noting that many of the dazzling scenes and marvellous transformations in *Rothomago* have not been described, the reviewer for *La Presse* asks, 'But how can one analyse a kaleidoscope in movement?' (Paul de Saint-Victor, 'Théâtres', *La Presse*, 11 March 1862).

12. Théophile Gautier, 'Revue dramatique', *Le Moniteur Universel*, 18 January 1858.

13. Théophile Gautier, 'Revue dramatique', *Le Moniteur Universel*, 3 March 1862.

14. *L'Année littéraire et dramatique*, 1866, p. 195.

15. Louis Ulbach, 'Revue Théâtrale', *Le Temps*, 12 October 1863. In other reviews, Ulbach would develop this argument. For example, in a review of *Sept Châteaux du Diable*, he wrote, 'I reclaim the rights of authorship for the stagehands [*machinistes*], the set designers, the ballet directors and even the musicians' (Louis Ulbach, 'Revue Théâtrale', *Le Temps*, 26 September 1864).

16. Figuier, 'Arts Industriel', *L'Année scientifique et industrielle*, 1890, p. 381.

17. *Ibid.*, p. 388.

18. X., 'Fête de Nuit', *L'Exposition de Paris 1889*, 13 July 1889.

19. Figuier, p. 389.

20. Eugène-Melchior de Vogüé, 'À Travers L'Exposition', *Revue des Deux Mondes*, 15 July 1889, p. 449.

21. *Manufacturer and Builder* 21.11 (November 1889), p. 253.

22. Vogüé, p. 451.

23. *Ibid.*, p. 449.

24. *Ibid.*, p. 450.

25. 'Loitering Through the Paris Exposition', *Atlantic Monthly* 65 (March 1890), 360–74 (p. 371).

26. *Ibid.*, pp. 372–3.

27. *Ibid.*, p. 373.

28. *Ibid.*

29. *Ibid.*, p. 374.

30. Un monsieur de l'orchestre, 'La Soirée Théâtrale', *Le Figaro*, 12 July 1889.

31. Francisque Sarcey, 'Chronique Théâtrale', *Le Temps*, 22 July 1889.

32. Marcel Fouquier, 'Chronique du théâtre', *La Nouvelle Revue*, July 1889, p. 582.

33. *Ibid.*, p. 583.

34. Hector Pessard, 'Les Premières', *Le Gaulois*, 12 July 1889.

35. Georges Méliès, 'Cinematographic Views' (1907), trans. Stuart Liebman, in *French Film Theory and Criticism. A History/Anthology, Vol. 1: 1907–1939*, ed. Richard Abel (Princeton, NJ: Princeton University Press, 1988), pp. 36–9.

36. *Ibid.*, p. 35.

37. *Ibid.*, p. 36.

38. *Ibid.*, p. 39.

39. *Ibid.*, p. 44.

40. *Ibid.*, p. 38.

41. Gautier, *La Presse*, 16 June 1851.

42. For example, in a review of *Les Pilules du diable* (1839), Gautier wrote that '[w]hat's charming in this type of play is the immense voyage that we make with our eyes without budging from the seat. – At each instant, the theatre changes' (*La Presse*, 18 February 1839).

43. X. 'Fête de Nuit', p. 154.

CHAPTER 3

Moving-picture Media and Modernity:
Taking Intermediate and Ephemeral Forms Seriously

IAN CHRISTIE

> Somewhere between live media and dead media is ephemeral media, some-
> thing that might deserve a passing comment, if only to contrast it to the really
> dead stuff.
>
> Stefan Jones, 'Dead Medium: Children's Dead Media'[1]

In 1994, I was working on a television series and book, *The Last Machine*,
subtitled 'early cinema and the birth of the modern world', which tried among
other things to locate moving pictures in a wider cultural and technological
field than was normal at the time.[2] But in wanting to rescue this history from
a merely technicist or 'pioneer' account, based on inventions and scientific
principles, there was a danger of going too far in the opposite direction,
paying excessive attention to ancestry and context. To say, as others did at
this time of celebrating the centenary of cinema, that late nineteenth-century
culture was '"cinematic" before the fact', so that 'the emergence of cinema
was both inevitable and redundant', does not actually explain very much,
even if it provides a capacious platform for the exploration of retrospectively
'cinematic' qualities in other media.[3] The original rallying cry of the new historians of early cinema had been 'against teleology': rejecting a selective account
of the early period that identified 'primitive' techniques and forms as pointing
towards the achievement of true cinema, in favour of an unprejudiced survey
of all early forms of film in order to identify the full range of intermedial influences and connections from which the institution of cinema would emerge.

In the same year as *The Last Machine*, Tom Gunning published one of his
key papers on this same theme, 'The Whole Town's Gawking', with a subtitle
coincidentally similar to mine, 'Early Cinema and the Visual Experience of
Modernity'.[4] In this sequel to his influential earlier paper on 'the cinema of
attractions',[5] Gunning began by restating the case against the *telos* of narrative,
before suggesting that 'attractions' not only open up the study of distinctive
forms of reception and exhibition of early cinema, but also provide 'the key
for exploring what a primarily German tradition describes as "modernity"'.[6]
And from this he moved beyond the historiography of early cinema itself to

consider environmental and psychological features of the world in which the first films were made and seen.

It was such claims, by Gunning, myself and others, that led David Bordwell to question this equation between the characteristic forms of moving pictures and modernity in his historiographic study *On the History of Film Style*.[7] For Bordwell, this amounts to a claim that the nature of human perception itself changed 'at some point between 1850 and 1920', which he terms the 'history of vision' or 'vision-in-modernity' thesis, and proceeds to interrogate by asking what independent criteria there could be to confirm such a shift. But despite such scepticism, it must be admitted that the attractions-modernity thesis has become something like received opinion.[8] The 'pull' of this equation is understandable in a culture that has fetishized 'modernity' and made 'Modernism' its correlate, even if Bordwell's critique of the explanatory value of 'modernity' remains hard to answer on his terms. What I want to do here is backtrack from this apparent impasse, and consider some other implications of disavowing the teleological inevitability of cinema. Certainly, it is clear that the mass viewing of projected narratives became a major leisure activity for an increasing number of twentieth-century citizens around the world. But it is also becoming clear that many factors over and above the visual organization of these narratives contributed to this outcome – economic, social and psychological factors that 'delivered' the mass audience, which then subjected early moving pictures to modification by means of customer feedback. These are the lessons of spectator-based approaches to cinema history.[9]

Another consequence of rejecting teleology is to call into question the 'succession' thesis, whereby optical toys 'led to' the first viewing apparatuses, which were then superseded by projected pictures.[10] If the history of modern media tells us anything, it is surely that very few if any of these media have ever died out. On the contrary, they have existed in an ongoing ensemble, with frequent revivals and re-purposings, and of course technological upgrades. So instead of a succession model, we need some other way of conceptualizing what I am calling the ensemble of visual media. And if we succeed in this, we might also want to confront the edifice that 'modernity' has become – questioning its explanatory, or even its descriptive value.

DEAD MEDIA?

There is a website devoted to commemorating 'dead media'.[11] Ironically, this has become something of a dead medium in its own right, having been created in the late 1990s and since abandoned to float in cyberspace. Two apparently contradictory propositions lay behind this quixotic initiative. One is the claim that few media ever truly 'die': Instead they 'jostle around' and often reposition themselves in relation to a newer medium; or they may shrink back into a 'protective niche'. But the same manifesto also noted that many media forms have proved temporary, and in effect died, and the website was intended to gather information about these as a collective endeavour. The primary impulse behind its accumulated archive of 'working notes' was clearly the meta-history of media that began to emerge in the 1960s, originally inspired in large part by Marshall McLuhan and later by Friedrich Kittler, but now boasting its own eclectic history of speculation and even its own folklore.[12] Another impulse, perhaps equally strong, was the alliance that has grown up between specialist antiquarians and internet enthusiasts, making the web a vast archive of personal collections and research about these – and of course a global marketplace for collector-scholars of every kind of apparatus and ephemera. Thanks to such intensive activity, there are few kinds of collectible artefact that lack visibility on the web, and it is surely this burgeoning virtual presence that has boosted awareness of 'dead media' beyond anything previously achieved by traditional museum displays.[13]

Such displays were invariably chronological and supported an implicitly teleological account of how optical toys and devices 'led to' the climactic achievement of photographic moving pictures in the early 1890s.[14] What was readily apparent, however, was that the successful pioneers of moving pictures – Thomas Edison, the Lumière brothers, Birt Acres and Robert Paul – had little involvement with such 'pre-cinema' devices. Their skills were essentially mechanical and/or photographic, even if their machines exploited various principles involved in other optical devices. Moreover, much of what subsequently consolidated the appeal of moving pictures came from quite different cultural sources: from the variety theatre and the lantern lecture. So the idea of a genealogy or a chain of invention could hardly be proved – and perhaps was never intended as an explanatory argument, but rather more of a presentational convenience for organizing a selection of otherwise heterogeneous material. For the sheer profusion of devices and entertainments that could be drawn into even a loose association was vast, as has become apparent in the different kinds of presentation that have emerged since the late 1990s. In the displays mounted by the Bill Douglas Centre (in situ and online), the Filmoteca Española and other museums, and in the Getty Museum's 'Devices of Wonder' exhibition and the touring exhibitions based on Werner Nekes's collection (also on DVD), there has been a sharply diminishing concern with placing these devices in relation to the institution of cinema, and a corresponding interest in displaying their diversity and intrinsic appeal.[15]

This may correspond to a wider shift towards a 'new antiquarianism', which values historic items of many kinds for their individuality, and for their rarity, rather than as precursors of modern instances. The Internet has undoubtedly facilitated access to this history, and allowed a closer engagement with individual objects than traditional glass-case static display, but paradoxically it is no substitute for being able to 'use' such devices either manually or optically.

The 'deadness' of such media, together with their quaint names and rarity, may appeal to the self-styled 'necronauts' of the website, but the key research issues are to revise the taxonomy of such media, and to determine the extent of their contemporary appeal and the significance of their diverse lifespans. Ever since McLuhan provocatively expanded the range of what might be considered a 'medium' to include modes of transport, power sources and tools, we have become accustomed to considering a wide range of technologies and forms as media – and to McLuhanesque claims about their psychological and social influence.[16] But such claims normally relate to the major media that shape an era – print, telegraphy, photography, cinema, broadcasting – and have little to say about minor media. If it is implausible that a minor recreational device or 'medium' should exert wide influence, what can we say about the significance of such products? If they do not determine or shape a culture, are they symptomatic of aspirations or widely shared interests? Might they point to what Noel Burch called a 'collective drive'?[17] And deserve rescuing from a cinematic version of what the historian E. P. Thompson called 'the enormous condescension of posterity'?[18]

THREE 'DEAD' MEDIA

I want to consider here three examples of what might normally be termed 'ephemeral media' (or perhaps 'intermediate technology'), and explore the implications of taking these seriously *as* media forms: not as stepping stones 'towards' cinema proper, but as devices that were developed, launched and marketed – all apparently with some success – during the same period of fascination with kinetic images that saw projected pictures emerge.

The first of these is the Praxinoscope, patented in 1877 in France by Émile Reynaud.[19] This was a development of two earlier optical toys, the Phenakistiscope, launched in 1833 by Joseph Plateau; and the Zoetrope, which was developed from the Phenakistiscope by William Horner in 1835, and often known in Britain by the less classicized name of 'wheel of life'. Both of these were effectively means of viewing a series of sequential images so that these would merge into a single, apparently moving, figure. The Phenakistiscope was in the form of a flat disc, viewed through another slotted disc, while the Zoetrope was a cylinder with perforated slots, which could be viewed by more than one spectator. Reynaud retained the cylinder

Nouveau praxinoscope à projection de M. Reynaud.

Figure 3.1   *Reynaud's Projecting Praxinoscope.*[20]

and introduced a mirror and a central candle, making his device a self-contained table top means of viewing animated pictures. He would go on to create two main variations on this device: the Praxinoscope-Théâtre in 1879, with a second strip of images that provided a changeable static background to the performing figure, framed by a miniature proscenium; and then a Projecting Praxinoscope, capable of throwing its images onto a wall (Figure 3.1).[21] In 1888, Reynaud devised the Théâtre Optique, using a belt of images passed before a lantern, and exhibited it at the following year's Exposition Universelle, where the Lumière brothers and Edison may well have seen it. The Théâtre Optique was eventually installed at Paris's famous waxworks and palace of curiosities, the Musée Grevin, in 1892, where Reynaud performed under the title 'Pantomimes Lumineuses' and steadily added new subjects over the subsequent eight years.

All of this is now relatively well known, and has become part of the familiar 'story of moving pictures', first mentioned in passing by Bardèche and Brasillach in 1935 and then firmly inserted into the lineage of moving pictures in the mid-1960s.[22] The shape of Reynaud's story is also very familiar: how he battled against the success of the Lumière Cinématographe after 1896, but was eventually forced out of his Musée Grevin residency in 1900, and later destroyed much of his apparatus in despair, before dying in poverty in 1918 – a martyr to the mechanization of spectacle that the Cinématographe inaugurated. The problem here, I suggest, is partly one of an overdetermined narrative, buttressed by anxieties over industrialization and its impact on the artisanal. Reynaud has become more important as an emblematic figure – prefiguring the tragic story of Méliès, forced into obscurity and poverty during the teens and twenties – than as the creator of a highly successful series of devices. In fact the Praxinoscope received awards at both the 1879 and 1889 expositions and its box lid boasted of 100,000 sold, while the Théâtre Optique was seen by 500,000 spectators during its eight years at the Musée Grevin.[23]

To modern eyes, the Praxinoscope seems so limited in what it offered – no more than a few seconds of moving image – that it can only be regarded as a toy, with the implication that it is therefore *only* distracting or diverting. And yet, the optical toy had inherited the tradition of the 'philosophical toy' of the eighteenth century and the twentieth, whose purpose was by no means merely to entertain children.[24] These 'toys' of the Enlightenment were in effect demonstration apparatuses, revealing the principles of 'natural magic', that is to say of anatomy and physics. Their successors were increasingly aimed at children and marketed as 'educational' in an era when self-improvement was paramount. But it was Baudelaire – otherwise hardly a follower of Samuel Smiles's doctrine of useful knowledge – who observed in the 'Morale du joujou' that such devices as the Phenakistiscope would develop in the child 'a taste for marvellous and surprising effects' – as had indeed happened to him, after he received a Phenakistiscope at the age of twelve:

> Each little figure [on a strip of twenty] benefits from nineteen others. On a circle, she turns, and the speed makes her invisible; in the mirror, seen through the turning window, she appears immobile, carrying out all the movements distributed across the twenty figures. The number of pictures that can be created in this way is infinite.[25]

Like Robert Louis Stevenson's later account of the charm and suggestiveness of the toy theatre, this communicates an experience that we can no longer have.[26] And the Praxinoscope seems to have belonged to that same tradition, offering a table-top world of remediated popular entertainment – through the many printed strips available for it of clowns, jugglers, fairy tales, children playing – in an elegant form that was also, incidentally, a demonstration of the persistence of vision. To subordinate it to the *telos* of cinema is to abstract it from a context in which it marked a real and lasting achievement, well suited to both the market and the *mentalité* of its era. The Théâtre Optique was indeed superseded by the Cinématographe and other public moving-picture

Figure 3.2   *Edison's Kinetoscope.*

shows, but the Praxinoscope was arguably followed by the 'toy projector', a
domestic version of the public film show, and in fact continued to be sold
widely well into the cinema era.[27]

The second device I want to discuss is the Kinetoscope (Figure 3.2),[28] patented in March 1893 by Thomas Edison, and probably much better known to
almost everyone with even a passing knowledge of cinema history. For much

of the twentieth century, the Kinetoscope seemed to belong firmly to the category of primitive forerunners, part of the vast lumber room of 'pre-cinema' devices that preceded the real thing. But now that the 'real thing' has itself splintered into so many different forms of delivery, from giant IMAX screens to mobile phone displays, we can perhaps look afresh at the Kinetoscope and appreciate what an important achievement it marked in its own right. For three years, from 1894 to 1896, this was widely hailed as the marvel of the age. It was not yet the forerunner of projected pictures, which only existed fitfully in the workshops and dreams of a few scattered experimenters. It *was* moving pictures, and remained the benchmark when projection first appeared. Many 'first encounter' reports of projected pictures invoked the familiar Kinetoscope experience to explain that this was the same, only now thrown on a screen – that of course linked it with the already even more familiar magic lantern experience.

Like other devices that exploited scientific principles and new technologies, it still enjoyed an ambiguous status, part 'demonstration' and part novelty, waiting to see if there was a market. Edison spoke of his doubts that it had a commercial future in some early interviews,[29] and the fact that he did not seek patent protection beyond the United States has often been interpreted as being due to his lack of belief in the Kinetoscope's market potential. However, since he had already spent many years and much staff time on it, another explanation is that he would have realized that some of its features would not be patentable abroad, where other moving-picture devices already used perforated translucent strips and intermittent illumination.[30]

Whatever the reservations about its potential or parentage, the Kinetoscope made its commercial debut in a special 'parlour', or arcade, on Broadway on 14 April 1894. With ten machines, each offering a different subject, the Holland Brothers' venture proved an immediate success, leading them to open similar parlours in Chicago and San Francisco within six weeks. Unlike much of the subsequent history of moving pictures, the economics of this first phase of exhibition are largely known. The Hollands paid $300 for each machine to the Kinetoscope Company, which in turn bought them for $200 from Edison. Against this relatively high outlay, and the high cost of viewing – 5 cents for less than 30 seconds – they apparently grossed an average of $1,400 per month for the first year, which translates into an average of 1,000 customers per day.[31] Other companies sprang up to open Kinetoscope shows in many cities around the world – one of which was London, where the first parlour opened on Oxford Street on 17 October. Before long, there would be as many as six venues in London.[32]

No doubt, what drew such crowds at the beginning was literally novelty – to be able to see 'life' in action, through the addition of movement to normal 'still' photography. Edison had worked hard to establish his name as a brand, promising endless new marvels, and was already associated with the lifelike recording of sound.[33] But the choice of subjects photographed for the first Kinetoscope loops was also shrewd. Six of the ten were variety acts of the kind that might be seen on the vaudeville or music hall stage (two featuring Ena Bertholdi, a British-born contortionist; a *Highland Dance*; Sandow the strongman posing; trapeze and wrestling acts). Two were genre scenes, *Blacksmiths* and *Horse Shoeing*, which might have been the subject of photographs or prints, but were now in natural motion. *Barber Shop* was a physical comedy, a cartoon subject brought to life; and *Cock Fight* was a sporting scene, albeit of a sport that was then banned in both the US and Britain.[34] Their main purpose was of course to demonstrate movement, but they also offered a varied bill of attractions, based on the variety theatre, while also gesturing in other potential directions.

Discovering who attended the Kinetoscope parlours is inevitably more speculative. Anecdotes recorded in newspapers during 1894 and 1895 turned on how rapidly word of this wonder had spread and the impact it had on the unsuspecting. A Syracuse newspaper declared in December 1894 that 'everyone knows that the kinetoscope is the device by which a prize-fight, a family row, skirt dancer [. . .] can be reproduced pictorially'.[35] And a March 1895 account of the first encounter is already patronizing the inexperienced:

> The expression on the customer's face undergoes a swift change… He gazes at the picture in rapt amazement, as if he expected the figures in it to speak. Before he recovers from his surprise the vivid scene is blotted out in a snap.
>
> He lifts his astonished eyes from the picture, and looking up exclaims: 'By gosh, I've allus heard tell that them livin pictures was great'.[36]

Accounts would also vie to convey its life-likeness, as exemplified by the anecdote of a boxer watching the Corbett–Courtney fight on a Kinetoscope on Broadway and bragging that, on the basis of what he'd seen, he 'could punch [Corbett's] head off'.[37] However, one of the few available photographs of a parlour with people present, from San Francisco, shows two women at the back of the row of machines, where three men pose stiffly (probably the proprietors). And in a promotional illustration of the period, published in New York, a fashionable lady is placed prominently in the foreground. An advertisement from Bradford in December 1894 spoke of

> expressions of astonishment at the wonders which the instruments reveal. It is undoubtedly the duty of everyone who is interested in the progress of events, of who wishes to be thoroughly 'up-to-date', to visit this scene of attraction. Not that the Kinetoscope, any more than the phonograph, is exclusively of scientific interest. It is also a means of entertainment.[38]

All of this circumstantial evidence points to the Kinetoscope attracting, or at least intending to attract, a mixed clientele of men and women, and also underlines the 'improving' or educational dimension of displays of new technology at this time.

Edison's original large Kinetograph camera required a stable mounting and electrical supply, with strong lighting of its subjects and a black background to provide the maximum contrast between brightly lit performers and black drapes, producing 'the singular distinctness of the kineto strips' described by Edison's assistant W. K. L. Dickson, which ensured that these remained legible when viewed in the Kinetoscope. These factors may not have wholly determined what Dickson and his colleagues chose to film. But their choices *did* serve to attract the first audiences. And what happened next was something like a rehearsal of the course of cinema itself, all compressed into less than eighteen months. Soon after the first variety subjects came multi-part pictures, with a boxing match specially staged for the Kinetograph in June, so that it could be shown, round by round, on a row of Kinetoscopes. Next, a range of dancers offering ever more alluring images of the scantily dressed female body; and by December, the grand finale of a full-scale Broadway musical, Hoyt's *The Milk White Flag*, with 'thirty-four persons in costume'. During the next year, the repertoire would broaden even more dramatically, as independent manufacturers entered the field outside the United States and also became producers of films for their Kinetoscopes. The largest body of these are the Paul-Acres films, but others were active as well, even if their efforts are now lost.[39]

Mainstream cinema history has traditionally assigned the Kinetoscope to a minor and transient role in the development of moving pictures, but this is to fall into the trap of thinking that media evolve sequentially, with each replacing its predecessor. We should not forget that all the films first shown on screens, other than those of the Lumières, were originally made for Kinetoscope use; and that almost all of the first generation of moving picture makers and spectators began with the Kinetoscope. Less obviously, it has left its own cultural trace in such classics as H. G. Wells's 'The Time Machine' and Marcel Proust's *A la recherche du temps perdu* and in many lesser-known works.[40] Nor did it simply disappear in early 1896, when the first screen projection began in Europe. Again the traces are scant, but there is evidence that Kinetoscopes continued to be operated until the end of the decade; and its direct descendant, the robust Mutoscope, using single cards instead of a filmstrip, would continue to provide popular entertainment well beyond the middle of the twentieth century.

We may say that, from a non-teleological point of view, projected moving pictures were a hybrid of two existing types of optical entertainment – the long-established magic lantern and the recent moving-picture Kinetoscope device. But the Kinetoscope was also imbricated in two other systems. It belonged to the tradition of optical toys, like the Praxinoscope, with the added attraction of using electricity for both motion and illumination. And as a coin-operated machine – at least in some markets – it belonged to a new form of retailing-cum-entertainment. The single viewer paying for a brief glimpse of 'living pictures' fitted well with a new business model, as automatic vending and gambling machines began to make their appearance on both sides of the Atlantic. Being part of this new wave of mechanization no doubt contributed to its popularity.

The first such machine is usually credited to an English publisher and bookseller, Richard Carlisle, who began selling postcards automatically in London in the 1880s. Near the end of the decade, the Adams Gum Company installed machines to sell its Tutti-Frutti chewing gum across the New York subway system and Charles Fey in San Francisco produced the first Liberty Bell gambling machine, with a lever to spin its three drums. By 1891, Sittman and Pitt's similar machines were common in New York bars, suggesting a kind of forerunner of the Kinetoscope parlour, with its brief bursts of kinetic excitement. In Germany in 1892, Ottomar Anschütz's electric 'Schnellseher' (literally 'Rapid Viewer') showed images on a celluloid disk and was coin-operated. All of the new American devices used nickels, which presumably guided the Edison laboratory's decision that the Kinetoscope should take the same coin. And the link between early moving pictures and automated confectionery sales would continue. The British pioneer (and Paul's temporary partner) Birt Acres was hired in 1895 by the German chocolate company Ludwig Stollwerck to make films for its Kinetoscope parlours;[41] while in 1897 another American gum company would introduce animated figures as an extra attraction on its vending machines, as if acknowledging Edison's success.

But the Kinetoscope was not only part of the latest thing in vending: it was also a precursor of what would soon be known as 'automatic' or 'electric vaudeville', a condensation of the variety theatre or vaudeville experience, realized in an amusement arcade. One of the most famous amusement arcade proprietors was Marcus Loew, the future cinema magnate – that again, of course, draws us into the fast-forward effect of teleological history. Yes, Loew saw the writing on the wall – or screen – and moved into cinema; but the amusement arcade survived, and flourished, later to become the seed-bed of video gaming. So rather than a succession model, we have here a network or rhizome model. What we do not need – as Tom Gunning said in his 1994 article – is a biological schema, and certainly not a Darwinian one of survival of the fittest.

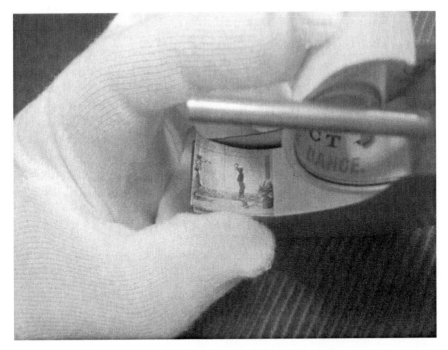

Figure 3.3 *Filoscope (courtesy of the Bill Douglas Centre, University of Exeter).*

And so I come to my third and final instance of an apparently ephemeral medium or form: the Filoscope (Figure 3.3). This follows the pattern we have already seen in the Phenakistiscope-to-Praxinoscope series. It is a commodified and improved version of the traditional flipbook or flickbook, with a batch of printed sequential photographs in a metal casing, moved by means of a lever. To the moving picture or optical toy historian, this belongs in the series of devices that includes the Lumières' Kinora and Herman Casler's Mutoscope – all using the product of the film camera as a basis for a paper-based moving picture experience, derived from the earlier drawn images of the flipbook.

This new improved flipbook was patented by Henry Short, who had played a momentous part in moving image history in Britain, first by introducing the Kinetoscope entrepreneurs Georgiades and Trajedis to Robert Paul in 1894; and then by introducing Paul to Birt Acres, which led to the development of the first successful moving picture camera in Britain, producing films for the Kinetoscope. Short also took the first major foreign series of films for Paul, in Spain and Portugal, in 1897. These achievements have naturally rather overshadowed his invention of the Filoscope, launched in 1898, and of the three devices discussed here, this probably had the least impact, despite being marketed by the grandly named Anglo-French Filoscope Company. In fact, according to the historian of flipbooks, Pascal Fouché, Short's invention was only one of a forest of similar devices launched between the 1880s and 1900s, with another British patent granted only months before his, in 1897.[42]

What Fouché's researches point to, from the media historian's perspective, is a relationship between two sequential forms – the book and the moving image. Rather than see Short's Filoscope and its contemporaries as curiosities, or mere by-products of film, we ought to take a longer view and recognize that there is a very long interaction between one of the most successful and durable forms of portable entertainment – the book – and the moving image, in its various forms of support, from cardboard and celluloid to digital displays on plasma and light emitting diode (LED) screens. And thanks to modern optical-to-digital technology, we can use the surviving Filoscopes to re-create otherwise lost films originated on celluloid by Robert Paul – in an operation that has some parallels to archaeology.[43]

What then is 'the moral of these toys', to paraphrase Baudelaire? For repentant film scholars or born-again media historians, it is of course very simply that we need to get out more; to look at more kinds of apparatuses and learn from those who do this more professionally – namely instrument historians. It is also that we need to be aware of other histories, not merely in an opportunistic way, but engaging seriously with the history of the book, of science and technology, of recreation and of the domestic interior. And crucially, that we need to be prepared to renounce finally the grandiose vision of André Bazin's 'myth of total cinema', in which he suggested that all the pioneers of moving pictures were striving towards a complete simulacrum of the visible world, recognizing this as, precisely, a myth rather than a history or a blueprint.[44] What we called 'cinema' was never unitary, but always hybrid. It was never 'achieved', or indeed 'classical', but existed in a constant state of development and flux; and it always belonged to a long history of what Laurent Mannoni has persuasively called 'deceptive art' (in his contribution to the catalogue for *Eyes, Lies and Illusions*, the magnificent exhibition drawn from Werner Nekes's collection). Looking at the devices lovingly collected, first by Will Day and Henri Langlois, then by John and William Barnes, Bill Douglas and Peter Jewell, we can begin to appreciate the vastness, beauty and complexity of the art of illusion. We might agree with Mannoni that this should be regarded as 'an autonomous current of aesthetic and technical questing', but not one divorced from wider tendencies. The Praxinoscope, the Kinetoscope and the Filoscope could be regarded as symptoms of Burch's 'collective drive', not initially 'to extend the "conquest of nature" by triumphing over death through an Ersatz of life itself',[45] but to satisfy social and economic motives. Two of these were the instrumentalization of leisure, especially for children, and the commodification of time.

As the distinctive patterns of middle-class society emerged during the nineteenth century, childhood increasingly came to be seen as a period of instruction and formation for adult life. In Britain, Thomas Arnold of Rugby School initiated a reform of the public school curriculum, introducing elements of science, history and modern languages into a previously classical domain.[46] Science made slow progress within the school system, but the traditional retailers of technical toys, opticians, began to add to their range of steam engines, magic lanterns and building blocks, such novelties as the Kaleidoscope and the Zoetrope and their successors.[47] A key feature of these instructive new toys was that they would also appeal to adults, fostering a bond between parent and child. So an advertisement for the Praxinoscope states that 'this instrument provides an interesting recreation for adults which is also attractive to children', while the most famous illustration of the Praxinoscope-Théâtre in use shows an older male and a young girl, both fascinated by its display.[48] Time, as Alice is rudely reminded in Lewis Carroll's *Through the Looking Glass*, 'is worth a thousand pounds a minute'.[49]

BACK TO 'MODERNITY'

Finally, does this have any bearing on 'modernity' and Bordwell's critique of the 'history of vision' and other 'culturalists' theses? Certainly he was right to question the idea of a single experience of modernity, which a crude invocation of the 'cinema of attractions' might imply. What the actual spectatorial experience of *c.* 1897–1917 offered was an irregular series of shifts and conflicts within the field of projected entertainment – and it was this very heterogeneity that constitutes a part of the experience of 'modernity' reflected in the rise of cinema, as Virginia Woolf recorded in her retrospect on the experience of early cinema.[50] Cinema, as it emerged, could embrace an extremely diverse range of kinds of entertainment, from short slapstick comedies, through actualities about the 'wonders of the world' (a genre that has been consistently ignored, yet remained present in cinema programming until, probably, the 1960s) to emerging forms of immersive drama. Sometimes these emerging forms of long drama included 'internal' diversity, as in Griffith's *Intolerance* (1916), Thomas Ince's *Civilisation* (1916) and Cecil B. DeMille's flashback and parallel stories (in the 1923 *The Ten Commandments*, which is very different from its 'unified' 1956 version). But their spectators were in any case living in a world that included much more visual and affective novelty than cinema – where the cinema experience was embedded in a whole culture of optical and visual forms: stereoscopes, comics, fan magazines, picture postcards, cigarette cards – a mass of 'ephemera' that continued unabated. Some of these had preceded cinema, but came to refract it; others, like the Filoscope and Mutoscope, stemmed from it, and continued in parallel. These testify to a persistence of novelty, of a taste for visual distraction that 'normalized' cinema, however successful in other respects, did not satisfy. The dominant history of cinema that is still widely reproduced not only ignored the variety of spectatorship and exhibition, but also concentrated almost exclusively on the normalized film experience, dismissing such 'distractions' as colour inserts, 3D glasses, trailers and posters.[51]

Bordwell is right to say that culturalist/modernity arguments do not challenge, or explain, the *stylistic* history of what became cinema, which is largely a history of filmmakers 'replicating, amplifying, or synthesizing schemas' that enable them to pursue their commercial and artistic goals.[52] But many would argue that the modernity hypothesis operates at a different level – initially referring to the turn-of-the-century bricolage that includes early screened moving pictures, and later to the avant-garde assault on precisely those synthesized schemas that had become narrative cinema – Léger's celebrated 'revenge of the poets and painters' on conventional cinema.[53]

But another reason for the apparent impasse between Bordwell and the advocates of the 'history of vision/modernity' thesis surely stems from confining attention to the normalized mainstream of cinema, which did indeed allow a critical mass of filmmakers and film viewers to pursue apparently convergent goals. A history of cinema focused on the evolution of narrative form and style works to minimize, if not completely erase, 'extraneous' aspects of cinema going and moving-image consumption. Yet we know that such factors were an intrinsic part of 'cinema', often looming much larger than the experience of the 'film itself', which is arguably a retrospective construct made possible by the non-theatrical technologies of 16 mm, video and digital that have been central to academic film study. Equally, it is now apparent that the received history of cinema largely ignored the procession of novelties that characterized cinema, such as the addition of live and recorded sound, colour, widescreen and super-size formats, and 3D, which continue to this day. And of course the theatrical model also suppressed recognition of the continuity of domestic and portable forms (miniature formats, television, recorders, handheld devices).

Yuri Tsivian has argued persuasively against attempts to unify the histories of cinema and film around single organizing concepts or substances, proposing instead that these are, respectively, a 'multiple, nonunifiable' object and process.[54] The 'nonunifiable process' must surely be expanded and revised to include the many moving image cognates, of which I have considered just three, and also to counteract that 'enormous condescension' that cinema effectively directed towards ephemeral and minor media. In an age of rapidly proliferating media, many of which may prove much more ephemeral than the flipbook, it is surely time not just to resist teleology, but to deepen and democratize our media history.

Notes

1. <http://www.deadmedia.org/notes/0/004.html> (accessed 24 June 2013).
2. The five-part television series, presented by Terry Gilliam and co-produced by the British Film Institute (BFI) and Illuminations, with VPRO Netherlands, was transmitted on BBC2 in 1995. The related book was Ian Christie, *The Last Machine: Early Cinema and the Birth of the Modern World* (London: BBC Educational Projects/British Film Institute, 1994).
3. The phrases come from the 'Introduction' to such a wide-ranging survey: *Cinema and the Invention of Modern Life*, eds Leo Charney and Vanessa R. Schwartz (Berkeley, CA: University of California Press, 1995), p. 1.
4. Tom Gunning, 'The Whole Town's Gawking: Early Cinema and the Visual Experience of Modernity', *Yale Journal of Criticism* 7.2 (1994), 189–201.
5. Gunning's widely quoted 'The Cinema of Attractions: Early Film, Its Spectator and the Avant-Garde' first appeared in *Wide Angle* 8.3–4 (Fall, 1986), 63–70; and is most easily found in *Early Cinema: Space, Frame, Narrative*, eds Thomas Elsaesser and Adam Barker (London: British Film Institute, 1990), pp. 56–62.
6. Gunning, 'The Whole Town's Gawking', p. 192.
7. David Bordwell, *On the History of Film Style* (Cambridge, MA: Harvard University Press, 1997), pp. 125–7, 144–9.
8. See, for instance, the recent discussion of its influence in *The Cinema of Attractions Reloaded*, ed. Wanda Strauven (Amsterdam: Amsterdam University Press, 2007).
9. As examples of recent spectator-based work, see Luke McKernan, '"Only the Screen was Silent …": Memories of Children's Cinemagoing in London before the First World War', *Film Studies* 10 (Spring, 2007), 1–20; also *Going to the Movies: Hollywood and the Social Experience of Cinema*, eds Richard Maltby, Melvyn Stokes and Robert C. Allen (Exeter: Exeter University Press, 2007).
10. While this was a mainstay of earlier histories of film, it also reappears in one of the key texts of the 'new film history', Noel Burch, *Life to Those Shadows*, trans. Ben Brewster (London: British Film Institute, 1990), p. 9.
11. The Dead Media Project, at: <http://www.deadmedia.org/index.html> (accessed 24 June 2013). From internal evidence, this appears to have been created largely between 1999 and 2001.
12. The catalyst of much modern 'media theory' was Marshall McLuhan, especially in his *Understanding Media: The Extensions of Man* (London: Routledge, 1964). Friedrich Kittler, a German media theorist, has also become increasingly influential, especially since the translation of his 1986 *Gramophone, Film, Typewriter* (Stanford, CA: Stanford University Press, 1999). The science-fiction writer William Gibson and others have fostered a genre often known as 'cyberpunk', in which media theory, new technology and social dislocation come together:

examples are the novel by Gibson, *Neuromancer* (1984), and Ridley Scott's film *Blade Runner* (1982).

13. Indeed there has been a reduction of these, at least in the UK, with the closing of the British Film Institute's Museum of the Moving Image (1988–9), and the move of the Science Museum pre-cinema display from London to Bradford in 2005, as well as the sale of the Barnes Collection to Turin.

14. This was the pattern of the Early Photography section of the Science Museum in London and of the British Film Institute's Museum of the Moving Image. It is an account that has been labelled 'the Basic Story' by Bordwell in his *History of Film Style*, Chapter 2.

15. The Bill Douglas Centre for the History of Cinema and Popular Culture at the University of Exeter houses the Bill Douglas/Peter Jewell Collection; see <http://www.exeter.ac.uk/bdc/> (accessed 24 June 2013). The Filmoteca Española in Madrid offers an interactive display of pre-cinema and early cinema devices. The Getty Museum exhibition *Devices of Wonder* (2001) maintains a website that allows dynamic investigation of various devices; see <http://www.getty.edu/art/exhibitions/devices/flash/> (accessed 24 June 2013). Werner Nekes's magnificent collection of pre-cinema media is regularly exhibited around the world, and is also accessible on a set of DVDs under the title *Medien Magica*; details at: <http://www.c3.hu/perspektiva/nekesen.html> (accessed 24 June 2013). For the catalogue of an exhibition drawn from the Nekes collection, see *Eyes, Lies and Illusions* (London: Hayward Gallery, 2005), eds Laurent Mannoni, Werner Nekes and Marina Warner.

16. McLuhan acknowledged that an important source of his claims about media 'influence' was the work of the economic historian Harold Innis, as in his studies *Empire and Communications* (Oxford: Clarendon Press, 1950) and *The Bias of Communication* (Toronto: University of Toronto Press, 1951).

17. 'The fantasy of a class became the fantasy of a culture: to extend the "conquest of nature" by triumphing over death through an Ersatz of life itself.' See Burch, *Life to those Shadows*, p. 7.

18. E. P. Thompson, *The Making of the English Working Class* (Harmondsworth: Penguin, 1968), p. 16.

19. On Reynaud's life and inventions, see Dominique Auzel, *Émile Reynaud et l'image s'anima* (Paris: Editions du May, 1992).

20. From *La Nature. Revue des Sciences* 10.2 (1882), p. 357.

21. Both of these enhancements seem to have appeared in 1878 and 1879, together with a 'toy Praxinoscope' (*Praxinoscope-jouet*) and an electrical version of the Praxinoscope-Théâtre, with a motor to rotate the drum and an electrical bulb. See Auzel, *Émile Reynaud*, pp. 99, 42–46.

22. Maurice Bardèche and Robert Brasillach, *Histoire du cinéma* (Paris: Denoël et Steele, 1935). The first book in England to do so appears to have been Olive Cook, *Movement in Two Dimensions* (London: Hutchinson, 1963); followed by the English translation of C. W. Ceram, *Archaeology of the Cinema* (London: Thames and Hudson, 1965). Interestingly, Terry Ramsaye's popular history, *A Million and*

One Nights (New York, NY: Simon and Schuster, 1926) made only passing – and confused – reference to Reynaud (p. 40).

23. Auzel, *Émile Reynaud*, p. 75.

24. On the 'philosophical toy', see Christie, 'Toys, Instruments, Machines: Why the Hardware Matters', in James Lyons and John Plunkett, eds, *Multimedia Histories: From the Magic Lantern to the Internet* (Exeter: University of Exeter Press, 2007), pp. 3–17.

25. Baudelaire compared the Phenakistiscope to the better-known Stereoscope, describing its simulation of movement, performed with 'a fantastic precision', as 'equally marvellous'; see '*Morale du joujou*', in Charles Baudelaire *Œuvres Complètes, Vol. 3: L'Art Romantique* (Paris: Calmann-Lévy, 1924), p. 146.

26. R. L. Stevenson, 'A Penny Plain and Twopence Coloured', in *Memories and Portraits* (London: Chatto & Windus, 1887), pp. 103–9.

27. Auzel reproduces pages from the catalogues of the department stores Au Bon Marché and Le Printemps, showing in 1902 the Praxinoscope on sale alongside a toy version of the Cinématographe, and a plagiarized version in 1905.

28. From *La Nature. Revue des Sciences* 22.2 (1894), p. 324.

29. 'I do not see there's anything to be made out of it. I have been largely influenced by sentiment in the prosecution of this design', 'Thomas A. Edison. His Latest Invention', *Newark Daily Advocate*, 9 April 1894.

30. Reynaud's Théâtre Optique and Marey's Photogun for instance; the intermittent illumination principle had already been used by Ottomar Anschütz in his Tachyscope of 1887.

31. $1,400 gross revenue = 28,000 viewings at 5¢ or *c.* 1,000 per day per month.

32. On the career of the Kinetoscope in London, see John Barnes, *The Beginnings of the Cinema in England 1894–1901*, vol. 1: 1894–1896 (Exeter: Exeter University Press, 1998, revised edition), pp. 1–20.

33. His 1894 catalogue was named 'Edison's Latest Wonders'.

34. Cock fighting was banned in Britain in 1849 and is illegal in most US states.

35. *Syracuse Daily Standard*, 25 December 1894, p. 3.

36. *Middletown Daily Argus*, 20 March 1895, p. 7, reprinted from the *Atlanta Constitution*.

37. *Coshocton Democratic Standard* (Ohio), 21 December 1894, reprinted from the *New York Herald*.

38. 'The Wonders of the Kinetoscope', *Bradford Daily Argus*, 20 December 1894, p. 3. Quoted by Richard Brown, 'The Kinetoscope in Yorkshire', in Simon Popple and Vanessa Toulmin, eds, *Visual Delights: Essays on the Popular and Projected Image in the Nineteenth Century* (Trowbridge: Flicks Books, 2000), pp. 112–13.

39. Although most accounts of the Kinetoscope concentrate on well-documented instances of exhibition in major cities of the United States, in London and in Melbourne and Sydney, there remains to be researched a wider history of its spread to many smaller communities, as described in Brown's pioneering study of Yorkshire.

40. Wells's description of how the Traveller appears and disappears seems to be

based on experience of the Kinetoscope. See H. G. Wells, 'The Time Machine' (1895). Proust's novel contains innumerable references to various optical devices, ranging from the magic lantern to the Bioscope (a popular name for moving pictures); see, for example, the opening pages of *Swann's Way* (*Du côté de chez Swann*, 1913), with mention of a Kaleidoscope (p. 2), Bioscope (p. 6), magic lantern (pp. 9–10), *Remembrance of Things Past*, trans. C. K. Scott Moncrieff (London: Chatto & Windus, 1925). See also, for example, Jack London, 'Two Gold Bricks', *The Owl* 3.2 (September 1897), and *Martin Eden* (New York, NY: Macmillan, 1909).

41. Martin Loiperdinger, 'Ludwig Stollwerck, Birt Acres and the Distribution of the Lumière Cinématographe in Germany', in Roland Cosandey and François Albera, eds, *Images Across Borders, 1896–1918: Internationality in World Cinema* (Lausanne: Payot, 1995), pp. 167–77.

42. Pascal Fouché, FLIPBOOK.info, at: <http://www.flipbook.info/index_en.php> (accessed 24 June 2013).

43. Three early films known only from their Filoscope versions are included in the compilation *R. W. Paul: The Collected Films 1895–1908*, British Film Institute BFIVD642, 2007, namely *Westminster Bridge, Andalusian Dance* (filmed by Henry Short) and *Chirgwin the White-Eyed Kaffir* (all 1896).

44. André Bazin, 'The Myth of Total Cinema' (1946), in *What Is Cinema?*, vol. 1, ed. and trans. Hugh Gray (Berkeley, CA: University of California Press, 1967), pp. 17–22.

45. Burch, *Life to Those Shadows*, p. 7.

46. Richard D. Altick, *Victorian People and Ideas* (New York, NY: Norton, 1973), p. 252.

47. Hampshire Museum Childhood Collection, at: <http://www3.hants.gov.uk/museum/childhood-collections/toys.htm> (accessed 24 June 2013).

48. Auzel, *Émile Reynaud*, pp. 41, 43. The illustration first appeared in *La Nature* in 1881.

49. Lewis Carroll, *Through the Looking Glass* (1897), in Martin Gardner, ed., *The Annotated Alice* (Harmondsworth: Penguin, 1965), p. 217.

50. Writing in 1926, Woolf recalled above all the discontinuous experience of early film shows, with unrelated scenes following in rapid succession; see 'The Cinema', in Rachel Bowlby, ed., *The Crowded Dance of Modern Life* (London: Penguin, 1993), pp. 54–8.

51. Wanda Strauven rescues and discusses a speculation by Thomas Elsaesser on the 'perversions' of cinema in her article 'S/M', in Jaap Kooijman, Patricia Pisters and Strauven, eds, *Mind the Screen: Media Concepts According to Thomas Elsaesser* (Amsterdam: Amsterdam University Press, 2008), pp. 276–87.

52. Bordwell, *Film Style*, p. 154.

53. Fernand Léger, 'Autour du *Ballet Mécanique*' (1924–1925), in Léger, *Fonctions de la peinture* (Paris: Gallimard, 1997), pp. 133–9.

54. Yuri Tsivian, '"What is Cinema?" An Agnostic Answer', *Critical Inquiry* 34.4 (2008), 754–76 (p. 775).

Part 2

Transitions:
Early Cinema and Cinematicity

CHAPTER 4

Reading in the Age of Edison: The Cinematicity of 'The Yellow Wall-Paper'

KARIN LITTAU

Arguably, there have been three 'revolutions' that altered how the written word was consumed. Historians of the book have demonstrated how transitions from scroll to codex, codex to print, and print to hypertext, have transformed reading in the West. Little, however, has been said about another media 'revolution' that is just as significant for the history of reading, and that occurred when animated and projected images first began to rival the print medium. The focus of this chapter will be on the media-transitional period of the late nineteenth century and the early twentieth to ask what difference the cinematograph and its precursor media, such as the magic lantern, zoetrope and phenakistiscope, made to the culture of reading, including its practices and habits. Drawing on periodical writings from science-, literary- and professional film journals, reading experiments by Gertrude Stein, Vernon Lee, and Charlotte Perkins Gilman, and her story 'The Yellow Wall-Paper' – itself an experiment in phantasmagoric reading – I show how reading during this period was repeatedly represented, or addressed, through the lens of visual technologies; to the extent that in the 1930s 'movie-minded' writers like Robert Carlton Brown proposed 'reading machines', which would bring outmoded reading practices into line with modern film-viewing.

To this end, I take seriously Bertolt Brecht's claim from 1931 that 'the film viewer reads stories differently. But the person who writes stories is for his part also a film viewer.'[1] Made in the context of a discussion of the ways in which old media are affected by the arrival of new ones, and cannot exist alongside them unchanged, Brecht's claim is an early acknowledgement of how media compete and adapt to one another. It is also one of the first articulations of intermediality, that is, the idea that media bear one another's traces, and are impoverished if they are therefore treated in isolation from one another. In another, little-noticed, piece from 1925 on Robert Louis Stevenson's 1889 novel *The Master of Ballantrae*, Brecht qualifies the point by stressing how mistaken it is to assume that cinema alone was responsible for 'filmic optics' since this was already operative in Stevenson's novel-writing.

It is 'ridiculous to claim that cinematic technology introduced a new visual perspective into literature', because 'filmic optics existed on this continent before the cinema itself'.[2] What Brecht calls 'filmic optics', and what this volume has called 'cinematicity', is therefore not specific to cinema: It neither has to wait for the arrival of cinema, nor is it an essential property of the cinema. What is specific to the phenomena of cinematicity, to which Brecht draws our attention, is the conjunction of movement and vision regardless of the medium in which these figure.

It is precisely this characteristic that first excluded cinema from the 'proper' arts for poets such as Ezra Pound, who draws attention to the idea of cinema as kinesis in an essay for *New Age* magazine in 1918, against the notion that 'art is a stasis'. The assumption that the true artist 'tries to make something which can stay still' so that it will 'stand a long and lively inspection',[3] suggests that looking at a painting or sculpture, or reading a poem, is marked by prolonged contemplation. Film, by contrast, is a technology that makes it difficult to procure the necessary moment of tranquility because it bombards viewers with the quick succession of moving images. Whereas static art forms, Pound implies, involve the active use of mind, a kinetic art like cinema, and in common with the experience of modernity more generally, is experienced as an 'assault' on 'every one of the senses' – a mode of consumption to which Siegfried Kracauer and Walter Benjamin have famously referred as 'distraction'.[4] Qualitative difference between contemplation and distraction, used here to distinguish art from non-art (Pound), old media from newer ones (Kracauer, Benjamin), blurs into a quantitative difference: New technologies, to rephrase Lewis Mumford, only know one speed – faster.[5] My question then is this: If movement, or its correlative velocity, is a condition of modernity, and of cinematicity more specifically, in what respects does this condition also affect the reader?

The fear that cinema would diminish 'the joy of reading' was widespread in literary circles in the first decades after its invention.[6] Even the editor-in-chief of the professional film journal *Lichtbild-Bühne* thought in 1910 that '[t]hings will get much worse as cinemas increase in number. The "see-sickness" will spare no one. We will end by forgetting how to read.'[7] The issue for psychologists was not that their contemporaries would forget how to read, but that they would be too inattentive to remember what they had read. In an age of heightened nerves, reading became an issue linked to attention span. Motion picture technologies played a crucial part in testing attention span and measuring reading speeds, but also in rethinking reading, modernizing it, and re-imagining the future of reading. As I shall demonstrate, there is a profound technological, conceptual and physiological continuum constantly being re-engineered between old media and emerging media. Cinematicity is a principal player in this re-engineering, especially in the period spanning from the 1870s to the 1930s. Accordingly, this chapter pursues two strands of enquiry: the sensory overstimulation associated with nineteenth-century print and visual media, and the 'cross-stimulation' between media, whereby the characteristics of one medium are 'remediated' by another not just as content or form, but as perceptual-physiological engines.

SPEED-READING, 24X A SECOND

The October 1877 issue of *Popular Science Monthly* drew attention to 'the invasion of the region of aesthetics by natural science'.[8] This remark was made in the context of a review of Grant Allen's *Physiological Aesthetics*. Allen, who became a well-known science writer and was later to become a prolific novelist, declared: 'The object of the present work is to elucidate physiologically the nature of our Aesthetic Feelings.'[9] While we may be tempted to read 'aesthetic' here in its pre-Kantian mode, that is, as referring to sense experience, this was not how it was understood by Allen's contemporaries. For instance, one reviewer commented that he had made 'a valuable attempt to add to the physiological foundations of art'.[10] Grant Allen's project ties in with a number of mid- and late nineteenth century studies in 'Aestho-Physiology', to borrow a term coined by Herbert Spencer, the philosopher to whom Allen's book is dedicated.[11] I am thinking here of Hermann von Helmholtz's treatise on physiological optics,[12] Edmund Huey's work on the psychology and physiology of reading,[13] Vernon Lee's notes on her and her friend Clementina Anstruther-Thomson's bodily responses to art,[14] and Gertrude Stein's attention span experiments that she and Leon M. Solomons carried out on reading subjects.[15]

But why was aestho-physiology so important in this period? And why is it becoming popular again now?[16] I think the answers have to do with an 'intensification of nervous stimulation', which the sociologist Georg Simmel famously equates in 1903 with the experience of modernity.[17] Aestho-physiological concerns are a response to the pressures of an accelerated, technologized modern life, felt so acutely in the decades leading up to the fin de siècle (and revisited at the cusp of our own millennium). As Friedrich Nietzsche sensed in 1888, modern life bombards us with an 'abundance of disparate impressions', making it impossible for us to take anything in 'deeply, or to "digest" anything', to absorb anything but in fragments.[18] This, of course, also affects the conditions of reading. Where reading had once been a fever (such as the famous Werther-fever), as easily caught as any contagious disease, by the mid-nineteenth century reading comes to be experienced as a shock to the nervous system,[19] linked to information overload, sensory assault and what one critic in 1889 referred to as 'mental overcharge'.[20]

In part, this has to do with the sheer number of books that flood the literary market place after the invention of pulp in about 1860, which enabled more books to be printed, and more cheaply. As C. H. Butterworth complains in 1870, books on 'poetry, history, fiction succeed and overwhelm one another with such alarming rapidity, that the man who stops for a moment to take breath and reflect, is lost'. [21] This remark finds an uncanny echo in Kracauer's description of cinematic experience decades later: '[T]he stimulations of the senses succeed each other with such rapidity that there is no room left for even the slightest contemplation to squeeze in between them.'[22] Sensory assault is also, however, associated with fiction itself. The 'sensations excited by fiction', George Clarke explains in 1898, 'are superior in rapidity of succession to those of real life'.[23] Clarke is writing three years after the Lumière Brothers' exhibition of the *cinématographe* and seems to capture in his description of reading a key aspect of the film medium, namely the rapidity with which images succeed one another on the screen. It is as if nineteenth-century print culture provided a training ground for the machine art par excellence, the movies.

Quantitative increases in book production clearly had qualitative cultural effects: overload in material and sensory terms. If the reader was to keep up with an ever-increasing bulk of printed matter, then accelerated comprehension was a prerequisite. Given this context, it is hardly surprising that the 1880s and 1890s saw, as Nicholas Dames shows in *The Physiology of the Novel*, the birth of the 'speed reader'. Capable of adapting to a 'culture of acceleration', the speed-reader is a product of the 'industrialization of the reading act'.[24] Reading too much and too quickly became a concern not least because skimming necessarily entails reading fleetingly and in bits.[25] In consequence, it was inattentive reading that caught the attention of literary critics and scientists alike, spawning a field of study we might call 'experimental aesthetics'.

Physiological psychologists developed a variety of devices to measure attention- and reaction-time thresholds, among them, tachistoscopes, kymographs, horpterscopes and chronographs. James McKeen Cattell, for instance, who was interested in calculating the rapidity of thought, developed an apparatus that could both display text and measure the reading subject's reaction times to it. This so-called gravity chronometer became the prototype of the tachistoscope – 'the fundamental tool' according to Dames 'for determining not simply visual acuity, but also neural speed in general'; it also served generations of researchers in the field of modern speed-reading pedagogy.[26] Such devices – that were developed in conjunction with Eadweard Muybridge's mechanically operated shutters for his animal locomotion photography – were not deployed merely to measure reaction time during reading, but also to manage, and crucially increase, reading speeds and attentiveness. The idea that proto-cinematic machinery could be used in managing visual stimuli more effectively and efficiently also tallies with Hugo Münsterberg's deployment of film in the laboratory to train subjects to deal 'with the rapid, visually oriented tasks demanded by modern industry and commerce'. As Laura Marcus has pointed out, the ways in which film motion can train the eye and brain to be attentive is for Münsterberg 'essential for the successful management of modern life, with its unprecedented speed and motion'.[27]

Clearly then, there was an attempt to get the reader up to speed with the emerging film spectator: to process visual cues in the form of written marks as quickly as one might 'read' images in motion, to take them in at a glance. Edmund Huey's suggestion, based on tests that he had carried out in 1899, to redesign Western typography, was geared towards this task. A change to the materiality of the page, its typefaces and layouts, would enable, he argued, easier legibility, so as to speed up the reading process, even enhance skimming.[28] Arguably then, Huey, Cattell and others in the field sought means by which to adapt the reader's body – kinetically – to machine speeds. Such 'motor readiness' was entirely compatible, as Jonathan Crary points out, with the 'then-new patterns of production and spectacular consumption'.[29]

DISTRACTED READING

Others who engaged in experimental aesthetics in the 1890s were artists like Stein. Together with Solomons, she examined the limits of readers' attention spans by conducting experiments on Radcliffe and Harvard students in the Harvard Laboratory; then under the supervision of Münsterberg, whose interests in film and psychology – that culminated in *The Photoplay: A Psychological Study* (1916), one of the first major studies on cinema as an art form to be written – are by no means irrelevant in the context of these experiments. This is how Stein and Solomons describe the experiment on 'automatic reading':

> The subject reads in a low voice, and preferably something comparatively uninteresting, while the operator reads to him an interesting story. If he does not go insane during the first few trials he will quickly learn to concentrate his attention fully on what is being read to him, yet go on reading just the same. The reading becomes completely unconscious for periods of as much as a page. [. . .] [H]e is conscious of a confused murmur heard all the time – the sound of his voice – but it bears about the same relation to his consciousness as the murmur of the stream, beside which one reads on a summer day – a general background of sound, not belonging to anything in particular.[30]

For another experiment on 'automatic writing at dictation', they devised this scenario: '[T]he person writing read aloud while the person dictating listened to the reading'. This particular experiment revealed that 'at interesting parts of the story, we would have the curious phenomenon of one person unconsciously dictating sentences which the other unconsciously wrote down; both persons meanwhile being absorbed in some thrilling story'.[31]

These experiments overload the subject with sensory stimuli so as to test his or her powers of concentration. Again and again the tests demonstrate that distracted reading is unlike 'hermeneutic reading'.[32] Whereas hermeneutic reading seeks to understand the fragment in relation to the whole, the subjects of these experiments read in bits: their reading interrupted by others reading. The mechanics of reading turn out to be a form of mechanical, automated and atomized reading: a reading acted out by the body, vocal cords and lips, but without self-consciousness, or with a split consciousness. It is a reading that knows the mechanics of reading, but reads without remembering – not unlike 'the "temps perdu" which Helmholtz defined as the body's reaction-time, separating motor activity from apperception',[33] nor unlike the manner in which one image supplants or erases another in cinematic experience.

Stein and Solomons are thus experimenting on the structures of apperception, or self-consciousness, to find out whether or not the unity presumed to attach to this structure can, in reading, be riven without a concomitant destruction of conscious experience. In this respect, the experiments are an attempt to realize in reading that capacity for which Stein later praised cinema, namely 'its dual ability to focus and fragment attention through the continuous supplanting or erasing of one image by another'.[34] The experiment is also an attempt to realize in reading the synesthesia of cinematic experience.[35] In other words, it is an attempt to induce that aspect of cinematicity Stein notes and praises, in the context of reading. It is unlikely that Stein was familiar with cinema at the time of publishing the results of her work with Solomons on 'Normal Motor Automatism' in September 1896. Nevertheless, when Stein reflects in the 1930s on *The Making of Americans*, which was first published in 1903, she highlights its cinematicity:

> I was doing what the cinema was doing [. . .] I of course did not think of it in terms of the cinema, in fact I doubt whether at that time I had ever seen a cinema but, and I cannot repeat this too often any one is of one's period and this our period was undoubtedly the period of the cinema and series production. And each of us in our own way are bound to express what the world in which we are living is doing.[36]

Crucially, as Stein acknowledges here, cinematicity was in the air, whether one had or had not seen motion picture technology in the flesh.

MOVING PAINTINGS

Experimental aesthetics, albeit not confined to the laboratory but taken out into the galleries and churches of Europe, is what Lee (a confessed admirer of Münsterberg's work)[37] and her friend Anstruther-Thomson undertook when they conducted experiments on themselves in the 1890s. The purpose of these self-observations was to record their responses to art. Of particular interest to them were the 'kinaesthetic processes' by which 'bodily sensations' accompany 'visual perception'.[38] This is how Anstruther-Thomson describes her findings in a diary note:

> 'Movement' in a work of art is intelligible to every one when it is the picture or statue of a living human being which is shown in movement, because living human beings do move.
>
> But there is another sort of movement in art – the movement of *lines*; that is, movement which appears to us to be taking place in *in*animate things, like ornamental patterns and like hanging draperies – passive things that can't possibly be imagined as really moving.
>
> Now, how do these things show movement? They do it by lines which call up in *us* an impulse to move [. . .] these movements are called up in us by lines which swing to one side or the other side, and by lines which lift upwards or press downwards, because we, in looking at them, have a quite involuntary impulse to imitate them by movements of our own bodies.[39]

It is not just lines and patterns that *move* our bodies. Colour, too, stimulates the eye; even our nostrils and throat are affected, causing altered rates of breathing.[40] From these recorded responses, it is clear that aesthetic experience is not exclusively cognitive but also physical, not reducibly a matter of judgement, but of physical continuity of the body from which these effects issue with the body in which they are registered. The same is true of our engagement with a work of literature, which according to Lee 'produc[es] patterns of action and reaction in our mind, our nerve tracks – who knows? in our muscles and heartbeats and breathing'.[41] These experiments recount in detail physical responses to works of art, leading Lee to the conviction that 'it ought to be possible to invent some graphic apparatus which should register any bodily alterations' during moments of intense 'aesthetic attention'.[42] What we can see here is the confluence of aesthetics, physiology and technology. That this confluence is significantly shaped by cinematicity is as evident in their descriptions of painting, sculpture and architecture as it is in Lee's description of literature. Drawing on their methodology for studying fine art, Lee states with reference to literature: 'A page of literature, whatever its subject-matter, gives us the impression of movement in proportion as it makes *us* move: not forwards merely, but in every direction.'[43] Key here are her references to movement in still objects. Experimental aesthetics of this kind, therefore, provide a rich resource for examining how media technologies alter our perceptions: Lee is looking at an old technology (print) through the lens of a new technology (moving pictures).

If kinematics proved that motionlessness is a 'physical impossibility',[44] and medicine found that 'the eyeball hardly ceases motion for an instant',[45] in aestho-physiological terms this meant that no picture, painting, sculpture, or page in a book is ever without motion either. This is how Lynda Nead sums up the scientific and aesthetic implications of the trickery by which even inanimate objects, such as those described by Lee and Anstruther-Thomson, are now perceived to be in motion:

> [P]sychological aesthetics proposed a new scientific model of looking which was embodied and kinetic. Incessant ocular movement and associated muscular adjustments in the body created an effect of motion of images and objects even when there was none. The eyes deceived and the illusions that were the subject of psychological research also constituted the founding principles of motion pictures.[46]

It is the last sentence of Nead's thesis that is crucial because it suggests that aesthetics as much as medicine is haunted by the spectre of cinematicity. While illusions, deceptions and trickery are the stuff of cinema and pre-cinema, so too is movement. To conceive of the entire apparatus of perception according to the logic of motion picture technology means that mediality is imbricated in the very fabric of thinking: We cannot think outside the media environment we inhabit, and this environment shapes every aspect of our thinking.[47] To recall Stein's words once more: '[A]ny one is of one's period and this our period was undoubtedly the period of the cinema.' We can draw two preliminary conclusions here: Media are perceptual manipulators, and no medium is insulated from the effects of and on others.

WORDS IN MOTION

There is another, more concrete, way in which cinematicity informed the culture of reading. The sheer barrage of images in motion intensified the strain on the eyes (even more than book-reading had done). This is certainly the quasi-medical and pathologizing argument that emerges in the first two decades after the invention of the cinematograph, especially by critics who fear that 'Edison [is] the new Gutenberg',[48] and that cinema might break the monopoly of the book as the dominant medium. Dr Campbell, for instance, warns in 1907 of 'an irritation of the retina caused by the confusion of images', and Konrad Lange, professor of aesthetics, blames the cinematograph in 1912 for 'promoting short-sightedness and nervousness'.[49] Others, by contrast, emphasize the positive role that moving image technologies might play in combatting eye fatigue caused by speed-reading; among them, Huey, who, in a chapter entitled 'The Future of Reading and Printing' (1908), puts it like this:

> Indeed there are those who [. . .] predict the displacement of much of reading, *in toto*, by some more direct means of recording and communicating. Just as the telegrapher's message was at first universally read from the tape, by the eye, but has come to be read far more expeditiously by the ear; so, it is argued, writing and reading may be short-circuited, and an author may talk his thought directly into some sort of graphophone-film book which will render it again to listeners, at will.[50]

A similar scenario is imagined by the French journalist and bibliophile Octave Uzanne in 1894 – a year after visiting Edison at his Laboratories in West Orange. In an article entitled 'The End of Books' he suggests that the author of the future will record his/her work on a phonograph and illustrate it with a kinetograph. Both inventions of Edison's would be used to listen to 'the marvellous adventures which the flexible tube will conduct to ears dilated with interest', while '[s]cenes described in works of fiction and romances of adventure', would be 'projected upon large white screens in our own homes' (Figure 4.1). The convergence between the two media – the kinetograph and the phonograph – would bring relief to the 'enervated condition' of the reader, his or her weary eyes, and tensed body.[51]

While Uzanne imagines a world where newer media have displaced the older medium of the book, and where the reader has been usurped by the listener-cum-spectator, an altogether different scenario is envisaged by the American avant-garde writer Robert Carlton Brown. A precursor of the Concrete poetry movement, Brown wants to do away with 'the existing medievalism of the BOOK',[52] but not the reader. In lieu of the book he proposes 'a word-conveyer': '[R]eading will have to be done by machine; microscopic type on a movable tape running beneath a slot equipped with a magnifying glass and brought up to life size before the reader's birdlike eye.'[53] Like Apollinaire, Brown is interested in the optical art of writing, and like Gertrude Stein – who admired his machine aesthetics – he is interested in ridding language of worn-out words and the fluff of superfluous ones. Brown's reading machine, and the kind of telegraphic, jump-cut literature that he envisages for it, is designed, according to Craig Saper, 'to shift reading away from cognition towards optics.'[54] Literature is to be absorbed 'optically' not aurally[55] – a point echoed in George Kent's poem 'RE . . . READIES' where he suggests that the reading machine will be a 'silencer of words . . . thoughts will go right into the head . . . heart . . . stomach'.[56]

The Romance of the Future.
(With Kinetoscopic Illustrations.)

Figure 4.1   '*The Romance of the Future (With Kinetoscopic Illustrations)' by Albert Robida,* Scribner's Magazine *16.2 (August 1894), p. 230.*

Rather than providing relief from eye-strain, Brown seeks to modernize reading, so as to bring outmoded reading practices in line with 'the speed of the day'.[57] What he wants is:

> A simple reading machine which I can carry or move around, attach to any old electric light plug and read hundred thousand word novels in ten minutes if I want to, and I want to. A machine as handy as a portable phonograph, typewriter or radio, compact, minute, operated by electricity, the printing done microscopically by the new photographic process on a transparent tough tissue roll which carries the entire content of a book and yet is no bigger than a typewriter ribbon, a roll like a miniature serpentine that can be put in a pill box.[58]

This machine, Brown calls the 'readies': 'The word "readies" suggests to me a moving type spectacle, reading at the speed-rate of the present day with the aid of a machine, a method of enjoying literature in a manner as up to date as the lively talkies.'[59] In other words, Brown seeks to bring reading practices in line with modern film-viewing, and the state of the modern nervous system. It is apt to mention here that Brown wrote and published his manifesto in the German spa town of Bad-Ems – during a rest cure. Thus far, we have discussed the manners in which reading was reimagined in terms of what we have called 'cinematicity', consisting in the transfer of technologies of motion into the domain of print. We now turn to an explicitly literary attempt to realize this transfer.

THE MOVIE-MINDED READER: CHARLOTTE PERKINS GILMAN

Gilman's 'The Yellow Wall-Paper', written in 1890[60] and first published in 1892,[61] is a story about a rest cure by an author who famously was prescribed such a cure. It is also a story about seeing and reading. As Kate Flint has reminded us: '"[D]emanding" reading was one of the crucial things to be banned for those "hysteric", nervous, or depressed patients prescribed the rest "cure".'[62] Thus, Gilman's narrator – in the absence of reading material in the form of books – hones in on the wallpaper instead.

The story has been interpreted in myriad ways: as a story about gendered reading (Lanser); an exploration of misreading (Kolodny); a tale about unreadability, that is, indecipherability of the wallpaper (Jacobus); an exemplification of the somatic effects of reading (Thrailkill); an expression of 'Gilman's anxiety about the cultural power of yellow journalism' (Edelstein); a literalization of arsenic poisoning from wallpaper paste (Thomas); and as a cautionary tale about nineteenth-century reading practices, especially reading addiction (Hochman).[63] Indeed, as Catherine J. Golden puts it, 'little in the text has escaped the critic's gaze'.[64] What I want to suggest is that one crucial aspect of this story has so far been overlooked, namely that in alluding to a range of optical media, it bears the traces of cinematicity. 'The Yellow Wall-Paper' is not just a story about reading marks on paper but also about reading pictures in motion.

Although Gilman wrote the story five years before a group of specta-tors paid to see movies at the Grand Café in Paris, and four years before Thomas Alva Edison opened his first kinetoscope parlour, where films could be watched on an individual basis by peering into a coin-operated peep-box, devices for animating pictures were of course conceived well before the 1890s. It is the immediate years before Gilman wrote her story that in film-historical terms are of interest here. According to Edison's co-worker, William Kennedy Laurie Dickson, it was as early as 1887 that his employer 'disclosed' to him 'his favorite scheme of joining his phonograph to pictures taken photographically with a device like the *Zoetrope*',[65] a recollection con-firmed by Edison himself:

> In the year 1887, the idea occurred to me that it was possible to devise an instrument which should do for the eye what the phonograph does for the ear. [. . .] This idea, the germ of which came from the little toy called Zoetrope, and the work of Muybridge, Marié [*sic*], and others.[66]

That Edison had been thinking along these lines is also evident from the wording of the caveat (which is an initial draft) for a patent he filed on 17 October 1888:

> I am experimenting upon an instrument which does for the eye what the pho-nograph does for the ear, which is the recording and reproduction of things in motion, and in such a form as to be both cheap, practical and convenient. This apparatus I call a Kinetoscope 'moving view'.[67]

Edison met both the English photographer Muybridge who lived in California and the French physiologist Étienne-Jules Marey, the former in West Orange in 1888, the latter in Paris in 1889. In all likelihood, he was therefore familiar with their respective inventions: Muybridge's zoopraxiscope, a combina-tion of a magic lantern and a phenakistiscope or 'spinning picture disc', through which he projected moving pictures as early as 1880, and Marey's chronophotography, a new means by which to capture successive pictures on film.[68]

I have not uncovered any positive evidence that Gilman knew of Edison's ideas about moving pictures. This said, as a keen reader of science journals – in 1877 she was given by her father a run of *Popular Science Monthly*, a magazine she considered 'valuable'[69] – she would have come across the numerous mentions of Edison's inventions; she might also have been familiar with *Science: A Weekly Journal of Scientific Progress*, which Edison started with John Michels, a former contributor to *Popular Science Monthly*.[70] More to the point, Gilman's retrospective account of optical toys demonstrates an active interest on her part in the pre-history of cinema. Thus, in 1926, when writing in praise of, and in 'recognition of the true importance of the motion pictures', she says: 'More than one of our great inventions appeared at first as but a toy or curiosity.'[71] Clearly, she had optical toys and curiosities like the zoetrope in mind. Here, she also makes a pedagogic case for the 'need' for 'public libraries of motion pictures', on the basis that film upstages the medium of print on one important front: '[I]t takes from literature an essential message and conveys it farther and faster and to more people than books.'[72] In another article on cinema, she asks 'who has time to read, and who likes to read'.[73] This is how she explains the advantages of the new medium:

> Reading has to be learned, which takes time; to practice reading requires not only access to books, but leisure and liking to read. In the marvellous condensation of the motion picture a volume may be shown in an hour, to millions at once, to all ages, classes and races.[74]

Film's virtue is that it is more speedy and efficient in getting its message across, an observation that would have chimed with Huey, Uzanne and even Brown. One of the reasons why Gilman is so positive about film has undoubtedly to do with her own reading history. Having been an eager reader before her breakdown, afterwards she finds that she

> could read nothing – instant exhaustion preventing. As years passed there was some gain in this line; if a story was short and interesting and I was feeling pretty well I could read a little while. Once when well over forty I made a test, taking a simple book on a subject I was interested in [. . .] I read for half an hour with ease; the next half-hour was harder, but I kept on. At the end I could not understand a word of it. / That surely is a plain instance of what I mean when I say my mind is weak. It is precisely that, weak. It cannot hold attention.[75]

It is not my intention to draw parallels between the author of the short story and its narrator. Rather, I want to suggest that reading in the age of Edison had made attention-span into an issue such that, as we have already seen, widespread empirical testing, not least by Gilman on herself, was the result. Furthermore, as we know from experiments by Cattell and Münsterberg, remedies for attenuated attention-spans were routinely cast in relation to the emergence of proto-cinematic media or cinema itself. It follows that in this media-transitional period reading and viewing are indissociably linked, one putting the other to the test, so to speak.

'THE OPTIC HORROR': READING THE YELLOW WALL-PAPER

Although Gilman's wallpaper is not the *papier peint panoramique*, of which
Giuliana Bruno says that it 'paved the way to the invention of film',[76] its 'florid
arabesque' (175) patterning nevertheless raises the spectre of cinematicity via
Edgar Allan Poe's Gothic tale 'Ligeia' (1838). Poe's narrator, upon entering a
room, finds himself 'surrounded by an endless succession of ghastly forms'.
These 'arabesque figures' create a 'phantasmagoric effect [which] was vastly
heightened by the artificial introduction of a strong continual current of wind
behind the draperies – giving a hideous and uneasy animation to the whole'.[77]
Gilman's narrator too experiences the phantasmagoric effects of her wall
coverings. The intertextual reference to the Poe story is therefore also an
intermedial reference to the phantasmagoric effects of one of cinema's most
prominent precursors, the magic lantern. In this respect, both stories belong
to an emerging cinematic imagination.

The tendency to read the yellow wallpaper metaphorically as text, or as
'palimpsest, a parchment written upon, erased, and written upon again',[78]
belongs to a bibliographic imagination. In our account the story is not about
reading as 'an exercise in scriptographically or typographically induced
verbal hallucination, whereby linguistic signs [are] commuted into sounds
and images',[79] since the paper on the wall is not a text with words but consists of shifting patterns. It is a story about a woman who tries to read the
strange phantasmagoric projections that the light casts against the wall of her
chamber, and to which she refers on more than one occasion. 'There is one
marked peculiarity about this paper,' she tells us, 'a thing nobody seems to
notice but myself, and that is that it changes as the light changes' (176). It is
as if a magic lantern has projected eerie shapes and the shadowy outlines of a
woman onto the walls of her room. She also points out that 'in twilight, can-
dlelight, lamplight, and worst of all by moonlight, it becomes bars!' (176). The
woman and her shadowy double seem to be trapped in Plato's cave. Like the
prisoners in Plato's allegory, the narrator no longer wants to leave her room;
she prefers the flicker of images to the sunlight outside. Even as a child, she
confesses that, awake at night, she would 'get more entertainment and terror
out of blank walls [. . .] than most children find in a toystore' (170).

When she examines the 'florid arabesque' patterning of her wallpaper,
and notes that she had never seen 'so much expression in an inanimate thing
before' (170), her reaction is not unlike Vernon Lee's, who also experiences
the motion and velocity of an inanimate object when looking at the 'ara-
besques of the ceiling' of a Simone Martini painting in the Uffizi Gallery in
Florence and who also has a physical reaction to what she sees.[80] Like Lee,
Gilman's narrator is looking at an old medium through the eyes of a new

medium. This is why still images turn into moving images in both of their accounts. The narrator's reference to the wallpaper's 'delirium tremens' quality (172), reminiscent of the psychedelic and mesmerizing patterns of the phenakistiscope, exhaust her. She cannot follow the pattern of the paper, because it perpetually 'turns a back-somersault' (175), just like an animation strip inside the drum of a zoetrope. Mental exhaustion finds its outlet in bodily exertion: She ends up crawling around the room, 'round and round and round – it makes me dizzy!' (178). Round and round and round: the spinning of a zoetrope.

Gilman's story seems to suggest that there has occurred a displacement of word by image. Writing has been banned from her room, increasingly instead she watches images – images, moreover, which are not still but animated. The narrator's insistence that 'the paper *did* move' (174; italics in original), unhinged as it seems, is in effect a foreshadowing of a shift in cultures. Put differently, the story reflects on a period of media transition: from paper and ink to shapes projected by light sources, from 'dead paper' as she refers to her diary (166) to animated paper walls. This is why the narrator refers to her experience of the wallpaper as an 'optic horror' (172). What she has discovered is that the hallucinatory power of reading, which allows us to read between the lines in books and dream images from the words inscribed on pages, has been supplanted by the cinema of the wallpaper, which renders the hallucination visible. For Gilman's protagonist, 'the monopoly of writing was over': not because her husband forbade her to write, but 'from the moment that moving images could be transferred onto paper without any literary description or any help from a painter's hand'.[81] Walter Benjamin's insight that 'every epoch sees in images the epoch which is to succeed it',[82] is also Gilman's: Her narrator sees in the wallpaper – precisely because it moves – the shape of things to come.

Gilman's text is not merely narrating a character's fate, but also that of reading insofar as it is affected by the motion, resistance to depth, speed and successivity of the moving picture. Her 'expressive inanimate' echoes precisely the names and effects of the early devices for the realization of moving pictures – the zoetropes, bioscopes and vitascopes along with the moving figures of the dead that seem to furnish the magic lantern with its necromantic content. That marked paper should move and so place the reader in a kinetic-visual environment in which the practices and conventions of reading yield not meaning but confusion, makes Gilman's 'The Yellow Wall-Paper' into a literary attempt to realize cinematicity in a medium increasingly set against incipient cinema, with its spectator as the pathological double of the reader, as the work's contemporaneous experiments show. Moreover, the structuring presence, albeit largely invisible, of the technologies of the moving image in the story reveal the imbrication of media one in another. Such intermediality as we have seen exemplified in the phenomena of cinematicity, therefore, draws attention both to the technological and physiological continuum that channels and forms aesthesis, and to the non-isolability of the media realized within it. Why else would paper *move*?

Notes

1. Bertolt Brecht, 'The Three Penny Trial: A Sociological Experiment', trans. Lance W. Garmer, in Richard W. McCormick and Alison Guenther-Pal, eds, *German Essays on Film* (New York, NY, and London: Continuum, 2004), pp. 111–32 (p. 113).
2. *Bertolt Brecht on Film & Radio*, ed. and trans. Marc Silverman (London: Methuen, 2000), p. 8 (translation modified).
3. Ezra Pound (published under the name B. H. Dias), 'Art Notes', *The New Age: A Weekly Review of Politics, Literature, and Art* XXIII.22 (26 September 1918), 352.
4. Siegfried Kracauer, 'Cult of Distraction: On Berlin's Picture Palaces', trans. Thomas Y. Levin, *New German Critique* 40 (Winter, 1987), 91– 6 (p. 92); Walter Benjamin, 'The Work of Art in the Age of Mechanical Reproduction', in Hannah Arendt, ed. and intro., *Illuminations*, trans. Harry Zohn (London: Fontana, 1973), pp. 219–53 (p. 241).
5. Lewis Mumford, *Art and Technics*, with a new introduction by Casey Nelson Blake (New York, NY: Columbia University Press, 2000), p. 106.
6. See, for instance, Joseph August Lux, 'Über den Einfluß des Kinos auf Literatur und Buchhandel' (1914), in Anton Kaes, ed., *Kino-Debatte. Texte zum Verhältnis von Literatur und Film 1909–1929* (Tübingen: Max Niemayer, 1978), pp. 93–6 (p. 93). Apart from this anthology of early writings on cinema edited by Kaes, see also his article 'Literary Intellectuals and the Cinema: Charting a Controversy (1909-1929)', *New German Critique* 40 (Winter, 1987), 7–34.
7. Quoted by Robert Jütte, *A History of the Senses: From Antiquity to Cyberspace* (Cambridge: Polity, 2005), pp. 300–1.
8. Quoted in *The Popular Science Monthly* XI (October 1877), p. 760. For a discussion of this quote, Allen's book, and Vernon Lee's theorizing of aesthetic feeling, see Carolyn Burdett, '"The Subjective Inside Us Can Turn into the Objective Outside": Vernon Lee's Psychological Aesthetics', *Interdisciplinary Studies in the Long Nineteenth Century* 12 (2011), at: <http://19.bbk.ac.uk/index.php/19/article/view/610/712> (accessed 8 July 2011).
9. Grant Allen, *Physiological Aesthetics* (London: Henry S. King & Co., 1877), p. 1.
10. *The Popular Science Monthly*, p. 760.
11. Herbert Spencer, 'Aestho-Physiology', *Principles of Psychology,* vol. 1 (New York, NY: D. Appleton and Company, 1897, 3rd edn), pp. 97–128.
12. Hermann von Helmholtz, *Handbuch der Physiologischen Optik* (Leipzig: Leopold Voss, 1867); English translation of the 1909 German, *Treatise on Physiological*

Optics, 3 vols, ed. and trans. James P. C. Southall (Menasha, WI: Optical Society of America, 1924–5).

13. Edmund B. Huey, 'On the Psychology and Physiology of Reading: I', *American Journal of Psychology* 11.3 (1900), 283–302; 'On the Psychology and Physiology of Reading: II', *American Journal of Psychology* 12.3 (1901), 292–312.

14. Vernon Lee and Clementina Anstruther-Thomson, *Beauty and Ugliness, and Other Studies in Psychological Aesthetics* (London: John Lane, 1912).

15. Leon M. Solomons and Gertrude Stein, 'Normal Motor Automatism', *Psychological Review* 3.5 (September 1896), 492–512.

16. See Friedrich A. Kittler, *Discourse Networks 1800/1900*, trans. Michael Metteer, with Chris Cullen, Foreword by David E. Wellbery (Stanford, CA: Stanford University Press, 1990), and *Gramophone, Film, Typewriter*, trans and intro. Geoffrey Winthrop-Young and Michael Wutz (Stanford, CA: Stanford University Press, 1999); Jonathan Crary, *Suspensions of Perception: Attention, Spectacle, and Modern Culture* (Cambridge, MA: The MIT Press, 1999); Lynda Nead, *The Haunted Gallery: Painting, Photography, Film c. 1900* (New Haven, CT, and London: Yale University Press, 2007); Nicholas Dames, *The Physiology of the Novel: Reading, Neural Science, & the Form of Victorian Fiction* (Oxford: Oxford University Press, 2007).

17. Georg Simmel, 'The Metropolis and Mental Life' (1903), trans. Hans Gert, in David Frisby and Mike Featherstone, eds, *Simmel on Culture* (London: Sage, 1997), pp. 174–85 (p. 175).

18. Friedrich Nietzsche, *The Will to Power*, ed. Walter Kaufmann, trans. Kaufmann and R. J. Hollingdale (New York, NY: Vintage, 1968), p. 47.

19. Jane Wood makes a similar point in *Passion and Pathology in Victorian Fiction* (Oxford: Oxford University Press, 2001): 'As early as 1807, Thomas Trotter unhesitatingly confirmed that "nervous disorders have now taken the place of fevers, and may be justly reckoned two thirds of the whole, with which civilized society is afflicted"' (3). See also my discussion of reading-fever and its links to the so-called 'cinema-fever' in *Theories of Reading: Books, Bodies, and Bibliomania* (Cambridge: Polity, 2006), especially pp. 39–42 and pp. 50–2.

20. Benjamin Ward Richardson, 'The Health of Mind', *Longman's Magazine* XIV. LXXX (1889), 145–63. According to Richardson, '[i]f too sudden and extreme an impression be made on the mind, there is commonly a start or convulsive movement. That is overcharge, the surplus of vibration cast from the mental into the muscular organisation' (p. 162).

21. C. H. Butterworth, 'Overfeeding', *Victoria Magazine* 14 (November to April 1870), 500–4 (p. 501).

22. Kracauer, 'Cult of Distraction', p. 94.

23. George Clarke, 'The Novel-Reading Habit', *Arena* 19 (May 1898), 670–9 (p. 671), quoted in Barbara Hochman, 'The Reading Habit and "The Yellow Wallpaper"', *American Literature* 74.1 (March 2002), 89–110 (p. 98).

24. Dames, *The Physiology of the Novel*, pp. 208, 222.

25. Concerns about reading fleetingly and in bits were widely expressed already in the eighteenth century in debates about so-called 'reading addiction'. As Johann

Gottfried Hoche in Germany in 1794 diagnoses this *malaise*: 'One reads every-thing in a higgledy-piggledy fashion without aim, one savours nothing and devours everything, nothing is put in its proper order, and everything is read fleetingly and just as fleetingly then forgotten, which with some of course is a useful thing.' See Rudolf Schenda, *Volk ohne Buch: Studien zur Sozialgeschichte der populären Lesestoffe 1770–1910* (Frankfurt: Klostermann, 1970), p. 60.

26. Dames, *The Physiology of the Novel*, p. 214.
27. Laura Marcus, *The Tenth Muse: Writing about Cinema in the Modernist Period* (Oxford: Oxford University Press), p. 211.
28. Huey, 'On the Psychology and Physiology of Reading: I', p. 284; for a discussion of Huey's proposals see Dames, *The Physiology of the Novel*, pp. 220–1.
29. Crary, *Suspensions of Perception*, p. 309.
30. Solomons and Stein, 'Normal Motor Automatism', pp. 503–4.
31. *Ibid.*, p. 505.
32. Kittler goes even further, suggesting that Solomon and Stein's experiment in automatic reading was 'made as if to dismiss hermeneutic reading'; see *Discourse Networks*, p. 226.
33. Tim Armstrong makes this point with reference to Stein's automatic writing in *Modernism, Technology, and the Body* (Cambridge: Cambridge University Press, 1998), p. 199.
34. For this quote and a discussion of Stein in relation to Chaplin and Man Ray, see Susan McCabe, *Cinematic Modernism: Modernist Poetry and Film* (Cambridge: Cambridge University Press, 2005), pp. 56–92 (p. 57).
35. We should remember here that Solomons and Stein's experiments were under-taken at a time when the exhibition context of film was not that of the darkened auditorium, but that of the fairground, which afforded a film-going experience closer to distraction than absorption.
36. See Gertrude Stein, *Look At Me Now And Here I Am: Selected Works 1911–1945*, ed. Patricia Meyerowitz (London: Peter Owen, 2004), pp. 104–5.
37. For references to his work, including an appendix to his work, in *Beauty and Ugliness*, see pp. 144–7.
38. Lee, 'Conclusion [1911]', in *Beauty and Ugliness*, pp. 351–65 (especially pp. 356–8).
39. Anstruther-Thomson, *Art and Man: Essays and Fragment*, ed. and with an intro-duction by Vernon Lee (London: John Lane, 1924), p. 117; italics in original. The book is based on previously unpublished material by Anstruther-Thomson, both original and done in collaboration with Lee in the 1890s, and was posthumously edited by Lee.
40. According to Anstruther-Thomson 'we seem to *inhale colour*'; see *Beauty and Ugliness*, p. 204 (an observation that is also pertinent to Perkins Gilman's narra-tor, who repeatedly refers to the smell of the yellow wallpaper).
41. Vernon Lee, *The Handling of Words and Other Studies in Literary Psychology* (London: John Lane, 1923), p. 69.
42. Lee and Anstruther-Thomson, *Beauty and Ugliness*, pp. 137–8.
43. Lee, *The Handling of Words*, p. 232.

44. Nead, *The Haunted Gallery*, p. 41.

45. B. Joy Jeffries, *The Eye in Health and Disease* (Boston, MA: Alexander Moore, 1871), p. 77, quoted by Nead, *ibid.*, p. 30.

46. Nead, *ibid.*, p. 41.

47. This is the logic Kittler derives from Marshall McLuhan when he writes, 'Media determine our situation' in *Gramophone, Film, Typewriter*, p. xxxix.

48. See Adolf Behne, 'Die Stellung des Publikums zur modernen deutschen Literatur [1926]', in Anton Kaes, ed., *Kino-Debatte*, pp. 160–3 (p. 162). For a discussion of early responses to cinema, see also Sabine Hake, *The Cinema's Third Machine: Writing on Film in Germany, 1907–1933* (Lincoln, NE: University of Nebraska Press, 1993), pp. 3-104.

49. Dr Campbell is quoted in Lynn Kirby, 'Male Hysteria and Early Cinema', *Camera Obscura* 17 (December 1988), 113–31, (p. 115); Konrad Lange is quoted in Heide Schlüpmann, *Unheimlichkeit des Blicks. Das Drama des frühen deutschen Kinos* (Frankfurt: Stroemfeld/Roter Stern, 1990), p. 203.

50. Edmund B. Huey, *The Psychology and Pedagogy of Reading* (New York, NY: Macmillan, 1921 [1908]), p. 429.

51. Octave Uzanne, 'The End of Books [with illustrations by Albert Robida]', *Scribner's Magazine* 16.2 (August 1894), 221–32 (pp. 227, 229, 224). Uzanne also envisages that '[l]ibraries will be transformed into phonographotecks' (p. 225) and bibliophiles will become 'phonographiles' (p. 226). For a discussion of Uzanne's article see Priscilla Coit Murphy, 'Books are Dead, Long live Books', in David Thorburn and Henry Jenkins, eds, *Rethinking Media Change: The Aesthetics of Transition* (Cambridge, MA: The MIT Press, 2003), pp. 81–93.

52. Robert Carlton Brown, *The Readies* (Bad Ems: Roving Eye Press, 1930), p. 27; in the facsimile, ed. Ben Allen with a transcript and 'Afterword' by Craig Saper (Rice University, Houston, TX: Connexions, 2010), see p. 62. This edition is available online at: <http://cnx.org/content/col10962/1.1/> (accessed 24 August 2010).

53. Brown, *The Readies*, p. 13 (facsimile p. 34); for an example of the reading machine, see Saper's simulation at: <http://www.readies.org/> (accessed 27 January 2013).

54. Saper, 'Afterword', pp. 115–22 (p. 117).

55. Brown, *The Readies*, p. 30 (facsimile p. 68).

56. Quoted by Michael North, 'Words in Motion: The Movies, the Readies, and "the Revolution of the Word"', *Modernism/Modernity* 9.2 (April 2002), 205–23 (pp. 215–16).

57. Brown, *The Readies*, p. 37 (facsimile p. 82).

58. *Ibid.*, p. 28 (facsimile p. 64).

59. *Ibid.*, p. 27 (facsimile p. 62).

60. In a letter to Martha Luther Lane, dated 27 July 1890, Gilman writes that her husband Walter had read 'The Yellow Wallpaper' no less than '<u>four</u> times, and thinks it the most ghastly tale he ever read'; see Charlotte Perkins Gilman, *'The Yellow Wall-Paper' and the History of its Publication and Reception*, compiled and ed.

Julie Bates Dock (University Park: Pennsylvania State University Press, 1998), p. 90; underlining in original.

61. Charlotte Perkins Gilman, *The Yellow Wall-Paper, Herland, and Selected Writings*, ed. and intro. by Denise D. Knight (London: Penguin, 1999), pp. 166–82. This edition of the story is taken from the original publication in *New England Magazine* 5 (January 1892), 647–56. All subsequent page references to the story appear in the main text.

62. Kate Flint, *The Woman Reader 1837–1914* (Oxford: Clarendon Press, 1993), p. 60.

63. Susan Lanser, 'Feminist Criticism, "The Yellow Wallpaper", and the Politics of Color in America', in Christina Gilmartin, Sharlene Hesse-Biber and Robin Lydenberg, eds, *Feminist Approaches to Theory and Methodology: An Interdisciplinary Reader* (New York, NY, and Oxford: Oxford University Press, 1999), pp. 195–214 (p. 197); Annette Kolodny, 'A Map of Rereading: Gender and the Interpretation of Literary Texts', in Elaine Showalter, ed., *The New Feminist Criticism* (London: Virago, 1985), pp. 46–62 (p. 54); Mary Jacobus, *Reading Woman: Essays on Feminist Criticism* (London: Methuen, 1986), p. 245; Jane F. Thrailkill, *Affecting Fictions: Mind, Body, and Emotion in American Literary Realism* (Cambridge, MA: Harvard University Press, 2007), pp. 134, 145; Sari Edelstein, 'Charlotte Perkins Gilman and the Yellow Newspaper', *Legacy* 24.1 (2007), 72–92 (p. 74); Heather Kirk Thomas, '"[A] kind of debased Romanesque with Delirium Tremens": Late-Victorian Wall Coverings and Charlotte Perkins Gilman's "The Yellow Wallpaper"', in Catherine J. Golden and Joanna Schneider Zangrando, eds, *The Mixed Legacy of Charlotte Perkins Gilman* (London: Associated University Presses, 2000), pp. 189–206 (p. 196); Barbara Hochman, 'The Reading Habit and "The Yellow Wallpaper"', p. 102.

64. Catherine J. Golden, *Images of the Woman Reader in Victorian and American Fiction* (Gainesville, FL: University Press of Florida, 2004), p. 193.

65. W. K. Laurie Dickson, 'A Brief History of the Kinetograph, the Kinetoscope and the Kineto-phonograph', *Journal of the Society of Motion Picture Engineers* 21 (1933), repr. in *A Technological History of Motion Pictures and Television*, ed. Raymond Fielding (Berkeley and Los Angeles, CA: University of California Press, 1979), pp. 9–16 (p. 9).

66. Foreword by Edison, in W. K. L. Dickson and Antonia Dickson, *History of the Kinetograph, Kinetoscope and Kineto-Phonograph*, facsimile edition (New York, NY: The Museum of Modern Art, 2000 [1895]), p. 3.

67. Edison Caveat No. 110, Handwritten Draft reproduced in Harold G. Bowen, 'Thomas Alva Edison's Early Motion-Picture Experiments', in Raymond Fielding, ed., *A Technological History of Motion Pictures*, pp. 90–6 (p. 92).

68. See Laurent Mannoni, *The Great Art of Light and Shadow: Archeology of the Cinema*, ed. and trans. Richard Crangle, intro. Tom Gunning, with a preface by David Robinson (Exeter: Exeter University Press, 2000), pp. 312, 320.

69. Gilman, *The Living of Charlotte Perkins Gilman: An Autobiography by Charlotte Perkins Gilman*, intro. Ann J. Lane (Madison, WI: University of Wisconsin Press, 1990 [1935]), p. 36.

70. See Neil Baldwin, *Edison: Inventing the Century* (Chicago, IL: Chicago University Press), p. 120.

71. Gilman, 'Public Library Motion Pictures', *The Annals of the American Academy* CXXVIII (November 1926), 143–5 (p. 143).

72. *Ibid.*, pp. 145, 144.

73. Gilman, 'Mind-Stretching [1925]', in Antonia Lant, ed., with Ingrid Periz, *Red Velvet Seat: Women's Writing on the First Fifty Years of Cinema* (London: Verso, 2006), pp. 285–91 (p. 287).

74. Gilman, 'Public Library Motion Pictures', p. 145.

75. Gilman, *The Living of Charlotte Perkins Gilman*, pp. 99–100.

76. Giuliana Bruno, *Atlas of Emotion: Journeys in Art, Architecture, and Film* (London and New York, NY: Verso, 2002), p. 166.

77. Poe, 'Ligeia', in *The Fall of the House of Usher and Other Writings* (London: Penguin, 2003), pp. 62–78 (p. 72).

78. Golden, *Images of the Woman Reader*, p. 195.

79. I am borrowing these words from Winthrop-Young and Wutz, the translators of Kittler's *Gramophone, Film, Typewriter*, p. xxiv. They make this point about Kittler's differentiation between a culture based on books and reading circa 1800 and a culture circa 1900, where the hallucinations or dreams produced by words can now be technologically reproduced on the screen.

80. See Lee, *Beauty and Ugliness*, pp. 294–5; as Nead explains in *The Haunted Gallery*, the 'velocity of the painting produces in Lee a state of hyperaesthesia, causing her to become highly sensitive to her surroundings' – 'practically hallucinatory' (p. 40).

81. Friedrich Kittler, *Optical Media*, trans. Anthony Enns and intro. John Durham Peters (Cambridge: Polity Press, 2010), p. 112.

82. Walter Benjamin, *Charles Baudelaire: A Lyric Poet in the Era of High Capitalism*, trans. Harry Zohn (London: Verso, 1973), p. 159.

CHAPTER 5

Time and Motion Studies: Joycean Cinematicity in A Portrait of the Artist as a Young Man

KEITH B. WILLIAMS

The Irish writer James Joyce (1882–1941), widely regarded as the most 'cinematic' among modernist writers, came to be deemed ahead of the game even by filmmakers, such as Sergei M. Eisenstein, who advocated in the 1930s that *Ulysses* (1922) be treated as a creative template for the progress of cinema itself.[1] However, as historicization of the symbiosis between Dickens's fiction and moving magic lantern techniques confirms, increasing reciprocity between 'visual literacy' and 'literary visuality' in the nineteenth century helps explain Joyce's extraordinary creative receptiveness to cinema when it finally arrived. Like his 'low-modern' elder, H. G. Wells, Joyce was instrumental in extending the classical principle of *ekphrasis* – verbal imitation of visual modes such as painting, sculpture or architecture so that audiences may 'visualize' them without seeing them directly – into the simulacral age of moving photographic images, by playing on and extending aspects of the common visual imaginary of his time.[2] This chapter suggests that we can explain the extraordinary parallelism with film evident in Joyce's fiction only by exploring how his eye and imagination were already trained by the rich and diverse optical culture he grew up within, which predated, but also led to film itself. Joyce's work highlights the period's emergent 'cinematicity', but also registers that its culmination in 1895's cinematograph has complex roots in both scientific analysis and forms of visual entertainment through moving images and projection. This pre-filmic cinematicity comprised optical toys, shadowgraphy, magic lanternism, panoramas, dioramas, rapid photography and peepshows based on Edison's Kinestoscope. Their attractions and techniques are referenced in Joyce's fiction and their effects emulated and explored in its pages, with *ekphrastic* cinematicity or imagistic movement surpassing contemporary writers.

In this context, the innovative modernist form of Joyce's quasi-autobiographical Bildungsroman, *A Portrait of the Artist as a Young Man* (henceforth, *Portrait*), arguably derives from speculations about representing developing consciousness framed in visually dynamic terms in Joyce's earliest and shortest version of the fiction, his 1904 unpublished autobiographical sketch, 'A Portrait of the Artist' (henceforth, 'A Portrait'). Its proposed experimental method was finally achieved in the published novel (serialized 1914–15). If *Portrait* constituted a breakthrough into the 'stream of consciousness' modernist form, it was also synergetic with key aspects of visual culture and technology, giving birth to cinematicity on screen.

The 1914–15 *Portrait* (that Joyce began writing in Triestine exile in 1907 and was still drafting while famously opening one of Dublin's first cinemas in December 1909),[3] has long been regarded as a stage towards the filmic styles of *Ulysses* (as Eisenstein recognized), particularly in relation to the first-person interior monologue.[4] It certainly extends *Dubliners'* effect of a highly mobile, intra-diegetic 'gaze' to a virtually claustrophobic degree, because Joyce's free indirect discourse filters every sight (and for that matter all other sensory experience) through Stephen's developing consciousness as sole 'focalizer'. Indeed, *Portrait's* themes and method are specifically regarded as elaborating the first three stories of *Dubliners* (published 1914, but mostly composed in about 1904) with their anonymous boy protagonists, although without their matching first-person retrospective. Both the emergent 'cinematicity' of late nineteenth-century optical culture and Joyce's fiction were predicated on what Anne Friedberg calls a *'mobilized "virtual" gaze'*, a characteristic feature of modernity: 'The *virtual gaze* is not a direct perception but a *received* perception mediated through representation [. . .] that travels in an imaginary *flânerie* through an imaginary elsewhere and an imaginary elsewhen.'[5] Alan Spiegel points out that the increasingly radical nature of Joyce's focalization technique makes his protagonists like observing consciousnesses or intra-diegetic 'camera eyes', rather than characters in the more traditional sense who are physically described from an external viewpoint. We generally *see with them*, rather than *see them* (except for rare moments of explicitly extra-diegetic third-person narrative interjection for 'tracking' their position objectively in the present, or when presenting them from another observer's equally subjective point of view).[6] Paradoxically, although this narrative strategy can appear strikingly cinematic, film itself has problems sustaining presentation of characters solely as 'observing consciousnesses', rather than externally visualized *dramatis personæ*, because mainstream audiences find this effect challenging. Using the 'subjective camera'[7] in a thoroughgoing way turns screen protagonists, *de facto*, into invisible men (or women), usually leaving film-goers with only an intra-diegetic, first-person 'voice-over' to identify with after the coming of sound.[8] In *Portrait*, Stephen is almost never described in physical detail, except through the act of remembering his own experiences or fantasizing about future situations. Paradoxically, he becomes corporeally 'visible' in textual descriptions only when *he visualizes* past selves or when he imagines future ones, even though our reading experience locates us intimately within his senses and mind. In a typical example, the adolescent Stephen's review of his days of preparatory school innocence ends with a sudden materialization of his lost childhood self beside him, as virtual, oblivious and detached as a projected photographic image, but also now visible for the first time: 'It was strange *to see his small body appear again for a moment*: a little boy in a grey belted suit' (78; italics mine). The same effect of self-externalization, as if watching a virtual duplicate from another time, occurs under emotional pressure to join the Jesuits. Imagined scenes of Spartan living in the novitiate are figured through the repeated phrase, 'He saw himself' (135, and discussion below).

A *Portrait* and Photographic Analysis

The development of Joyce's novel references visual technologies pre-dating cinema. In particular, it epitomizes literary emulation of visual analysis of movement over time. This was one of the primary scientific and technological drives leading to the creation of the medium in the first place. Modernist writing and scientific research using cameras shared a preoccupation with fixing 'decisive' but transient moments for inspection. Hence Virginia Woolf recognized in 1918 that *Ulysses* (then being serialized) was '[p]ossibly like a cinema that shows you very slowly, how a horse does jump'. Crucially, she added, 'all the pictures were a little made up before. Here is thought made phonetic – taken to bits.'[9] Woolf was obviously comparing the ultra-mimetic precision of Joyce's textual descriptions to how technologically enhanced vision in slow-motion scientific films made it possible to replicate and anatomize natural phenomena in ways impossible for the naked eye. But her second comment also noted astutely how Joyce represents both phenomenon observed *and* the subject perceiving and reflecting on it. She implied, in effect, that Joyce carried out simultaneous 'vivisection' (to echo *Stephen Hero*'s term[10]) of the consciousness behind the perception: 'Here is thought made phonetic – taken to bits.' Indeed, as Stephen emphasizes in *Ulysses*' 'Proteus' chapter, the phenomenal world is both seen and 'thought through my eyes', as he tries to understand its visible signatures.[11] This underscores Joyce's own project to represent consciousness itself through what and how his protagonist sees.

In 1872, Anglo-American Eadweard Muybridge's innovative rapid photographic 'animal locomotion studies' proved that all four of a horse's hooves momentarily leave the ground in the so-called 'flying gallop'. Woolf's notes on *Ulysses* indicate that she was working out how his fiction's cinematic presentation of visual reality is traceable back to this 'Eureka' moment, but also how that is connected with Joyce's *equally* cinematic presentation of consciousness. In the preceding section of her notebook, Woolf refers to the simultaneity of '[t]he inner thought and then the little scattering of life on top to keep you in touch with reality'; then to 'Queer *jerking* variety of thought', suggesting both the stuttering effect of early projected images and the associative, elliptical movements of Joyce's characters' 'streams of consciousness'.[12]

Joyce's artist friend Frank Budgen recollected him saying of *Ulysses* that '[i]n my book the body lives and moves through space and is the home of a full human personality'. Moreover, Budgen recollected him saying that his protagonists' minds were inseparable from their simultaneous sensations and perceptions.[13] Similarly, Budgen thought that 'Proteus' contained the best 'word picture' of a dog ever written. In the same way that no-one had seen how a horse really gallops before Muybridge, for Budgen Joyce provided a more precise image of how a dog actually behaves.[14] However, Alan Spiegel regards the running dog passage as more than just coldly and photographically precise, because Joyce's metaphors also make us simultaneously aware of the manoeuvrings of the mind behind its enhanced vision.[15] In 'Proteus', Stephen certainly meditates on the processes and effects of vision, particularly in relation to depth and perspective (as well as referencing the stereoscope, another common optical toy available from the 1850s).[16] Stephen takes a hypothetical mental snapshot (albeit possibly referring as much to the sound of the photographic mechanism as to patent stereoscopes, as their double images 'click' into the right focal position for the individual viewer to appreciate their three-dimensional effect): 'Flat I see, then think distance, near, far, flat I see, east, back. Ah, see now. Falls back suddenly, frozen in stereoscope. Click does the trick' (*Ulysses*, 48).[17] However, Joyce's 'anatomizing' tendency, simultaneously visual and psychological, can be traced to far earlier. *Portrait*'s distinctive form of cinematicity is rooted in speculations about a method for representing the processes of a mind developing over time in Joyce's first version. The 1904 'A Portrait's' cryptic metaphors grope towards a new form of representation arguably derived from the context of visual analysis and especially the '*chronophotographie*' (literally 'time photography'), practised by Étienne-Jules Marey, whose work complemented Muybridge's. Moreover, Joyce's metaphors point towards an experimental psychological purpose and 'moving' form lost amid the inert and sprawling naturalism of Joyce's discarded and much longer second version, *Stephen Hero*,[18] but eventually borne out in the published fiction of 1914–15. As 1904's opening paragraph states:

> The *features of infancy are not commonly reproduced in the adolescent portrait*, for, so capricious are we, that we cannot or will not conceive the past in any other than its iron memorial aspect. *Yet the past surely implies a fluid succession of presents, the development of an entity of which our present is a phase only.* Our world, again, recognises its acquaintance chiefly by the characters of beard and inches and

is, for the most part, estranged from those of its members who seek through some art, by some process of the mind as yet untabulated, *to liberate from the personalised lumps of matter that which is their individuating rhythm*, the first or formal relation of their parts. But for such as these a portrait is not an identificative paper but rather *the curve of an emotion*.[19]

The unconventional idea of the 'features of infancy' still showing forth through 'the adolescent portrait' suggests overlapping images from different places, times or states like the magic lantern's chronological shuffling, dissolves and superimpositions as referenced in *Dubliners*.[20] However, new leading concepts and dynamically visual phrasing here – 'the past [. . .] implies a fluid succession of presents, the development of an entity [. . .] to liberate from the personalised lumps of matter that which is their individuating rhythm [. . .] the curve of an emotion' – recall other key moments in cinema's cultural and technological prehistory. From the 1860s and 1870s onwards, electric shutter mechanisms and instantaneous plates made it possible to defamiliarize reality temporally – to see the ordinarily invisible. Fixing images at fractions of a second enabled scientists 'to fix attitudes too transitory for the ordinary eye', as H. G. Wells put it.[21] Muybridge and Marey inspected phenomena in a kind of action replay, but also anticipated the filmstrip. Muybridge had first broken what Ian Christie calls the 'monumental stillness'[22] necessitated by early long exposures through an impression of continuous movement using consecutively arranged batteries of cameras with tripwires. But he and Marey, by their respective methods, in effect, materialized time by mechanical means. Such rapid photographic techniques sliced up and recomposed continuous action into a series of related moments, in order to apprehend its physical reality more accurately than merely organic vision can.

Joyce's epigraph – '*Et ignotas animum dimittit in artes . . .*' – invokes the mythical inventor, Daedalus, who became an artificial 'bird man' in order to escape from the Cretan Labyrinth and furnishes the *Leitmotif* for *Portrait*. The Latin from Ovid's *Metamorphoses* translates as, 'So then to unimagined arts he set his mind'; it continues, 'and altered nature's laws'.[23] Thus Joyce was staking his claim as literary experimenter on the crest of a modernity looking out on wonders such as moving images and artificial flight. By auspicious coincidence that would have pleased Joyce with his triangulated interests in vision, wordplay and modern/mythological parallelisms, the 'Zoëtrope' or 'Wheel of Life', an optical toy key to the development of cinematicity, was originally christened the 'Daedalum' in 1834. Although its principal form dates to second-century China, its modern form was invented by British mathematician William George Horner. This ingenious device animated sequences of images by taking advantage of the eye-conning 'persistence of vision' effect (as it was then known).[24] Rechristened the zoëtrope by an

American, William F. Lincoln, who patented a mass-manufactured version, it became enormously popular from the 1860s onwards. The zoëtrope consists of a horizontally spinning drum, pierced by viewing slots, inside which is a strip of figures in various stages of movement that spring into jerky but vivid action. Typical subjects included acrobats jumping through hoops, jugglers, arcing dolphins and (most Joyceanly suggestive) gulls skimming the sea.[25] The phrase 'Wheel of Life' was applied to other patent innovations, such as the 'Wheel of Life Lantern', a miniature 'Phenakistoscope' marketed from the 1870s. By means of a revolving glass disc, it animated drawings on its rim, but also projected them.[26] (Dublin supplier of lanterns and other entertainments, Robinson's, promoted this version of the Wheel of Life as a 'new optic wonder'.)[27] Similarly, Muybridge's 1879 patent 'Zoopraxiscope', combining phenakistoscopic rotation with magic lantern projector, eventually animated his stills into the appearance of a genuinely 'fluid succession of presents', to borrow Joyce's evocative phrase.[28] Thence Victorian experiments in cinematicity moved inexorably towards the point where a mechanical device 'could convincingly represent empirical reality in motion', as David A. Cook puts it.[29]

Whereas Muybridge's work segmented continuous action into a series of visual moments, Marey overlapped moments to create a distinctively complementary effect. In 1882 he developed a special 'chronophotographic gun', and then a high-speed camera on rails. By 1888 and 1890, paper roll film succeeded by celluloid enabled making extended strips of images of black-suited gymnasts against ebony backgrounds (lines of muscular thrust picked out in white highlights).[30] Marey's subjects were thus ambiguously 'dematerialized' and fetishistic, but with presence as physical force. In terms of Joyce's 1904 tropes, Marey effectively 'liberate[d]' the 'individuating rhythm' of a body in action from shots of separate moments, making its action visible as an abstract curve rising and falling in space. Muybridge's work mutually influenced Marey's own studies of 'Animal Mechanism' and, in turn, Thomas Alva Edison and his researcher W. K. L. Dickson, whose Kinetoscope loop subjects resemble their work closely and whose machine finally inspired the Lumière brothers' *cinématographe*.[31]

Muybridge's principal publications – *Locomotion* (1887), *Animals in Motion* (1891) and *The Human Figure in Motion* (1901) – aroused interest globally,[32] as did Marey's vast chronophotographic survey, *Le Mouvement*, published in 1894 and translated into English the following year. Moreover, visual analysis fascinated Dublin's intelligentsia as much as mainland Britain's when Joyce was growing up. As early as 1876, Michael Angelo Hayes (founder member of Dublin's Photographic Society and Royal Hibernian Academy fellow) published *The Delineation of Animals in Rapid Motion*, quite independently of

Muybridge's research. Hayes's detailed illustrations similarly show the exact positions of a galloping horse's legs and were also animated by phenakisto-scope.[33] If Hayes had not drowned in 1877, it is perfectly conceivable that his research would have continued to develop. Muybridge himself was invited to lecture to the Photographic Society in Dublin's Antient Concert Rooms on 17 February 1890, demonstrating his studies by Zoopraxiscope.[34] Captivated by chronophotography, Joyce's Dublin contemporary Lucien Bull (born 1876 to a French mother) attained a post at the 'Institut Marey' in 1902 (the same year that Joyce first stayed in Paris), becoming Marey's personal assistant. After Marey's death in 1904, Bull became his scientific heir. With Pierre Nogues, Bull extended his mission through X-ray, microscope and high-speed analysis films.[35]

Chronophotography dissolved individual identity into curves of poetic dynamism. Anticipating Cubist painting but also Futurism's fascination with cinematically multiplied after-images, it demonstrated how innovations in science and cultural representation were interconnected. Archie K. Loss detects echoes of such developments in the representation of movement in *Ulysses*.[36] Moreover, William Rubin argues that such dynamism was in fact 'a *narrative*, not a *plastic* innovation' and probably had more importance for subsequent development of modernist writing than art.[37] Either way, in his 1904 attempt at 'A Portrait', Joyce hypothesized a means for figuring both physical *and* psychological motion to present the rhythm of a consciousness developing over time equivalent to the way rapid photography (feeding into cinema) dissected and recomposed living motion, using such experiments as both technical precedent and guiding metaphor for the project he would eventually realize in the 1914–15 novel.

Significantly, Joyce's famous definition of 'epiphany' (Greek for 'showing forth'), referring to 'the gropings of a spiritual eye which seeks to adjust its vision to an exact focus', hints at photography's enhancement of organic vision and its defamiliarizations of mundane phenomena and experience through close-ups.[38] Just as epiphany is central to Joyce's own work, the photographic interventions of Muybridge and Marey resulted in a cultural epiphany of incalculable significance and led directly to the development of projected moving images. The 1914–15 *Portrait* eventually realized the *ekphrastic* method of 'picturing time' (to borrow the title of Marta Braun's 1992 study of Marey) only speculated about in Joyce's 1904 version: to present the rhythmic development of Stephen's consciousness, through present perception, reflection and memory.[39] Although epiphany is not explicitly named in *Portrait*, Joyce weaves the concept into its structure, opting for a more satisfyingly 'dynamic' deployment of its principle in action.

A MOBILIZED VIRTUAL GAZE

Few Anglophone texts predating *Portrait* rival the sustained intra-diegetic focalization that Joyce gives to Stephen's point of view. This presents an effect of seeing phenomena with virtually photographic precision, expanding the impression of a 'mobilized virtual gaze' beyond the limits of *Dubliners*.[40] Joyce highlights mediated vision from the opening page (symbolized by Simon Dedalus's monocle), foregrounding Stephen's viewpoint with its developing fascinations and susceptibilities. He vicariously immerses us in Stephen's infant sensorium like a moving camera-eye: '[H]is father looked at him through a glass: he had a hairy face.'[41] Episodically structured like rapid slide substitution or montage come swift exchanges between locations and times, although always implicitly sutured by Joyce's stylization of the unconscious logic of Stephen's mind. In the preparatory school sports passage, displaced from the nursery centre of parental regard, Stephen's intra-diegetic viewpoint is now literally marginalized, although we continue to share its slant. Joyce mimics the young boy's eyesight like a kind of fuzzy camera tracking the *mêlée* across the field:

> The evening air was pale and chilly and after every charge and thud of the footballers the greasy leather orb flew like a bird through the grey light. *He kept on the fringe of his line*, out of sight of the prefect, out of reach of the rude feet, feigning to run now and then. He felt his body was small and weak, amid the throng of players and *his eyes were weak and watery*. (6; italics mine)[42]

Sporting dynamics were frequent subjects of photographic analysis and early films. Similarly, Joyce mimics Stephen's viewpoint on the action, literally dissecting his visual field and what it frames. As Stephen peers downwards through the thicket of flailing legs after the ball, Joyce presents a dynamic moving synecdoche, suggestive of multiple, after-image-like effects: 'Then Jack Lawton's yellow boots dodged out the ball and all the other boots and legs ran after' (6). This characterizes how Joyce's simultaneous anatomization of movement and cognition frames and defamiliarizes significant details only, cropping scenes into moving parts, detaching legs from bodies, and then boots from legs, by verbal close-up – giving them a visually expressive life of their own.

Paradoxically, precise mimesis of vision is intensified after Stephen breaks his glasses in a cycling accident, adding the virtual impressionism of sharing his 'hyperopic' condition[43] through relativistic effects of distance and distorted focus, thus anticipating the 'subjective camera' of Expressionist films, notably F. W. Murnau's *Der letzte Mann* (*The Last Laugh*, 1925). The term was coined to recognize cinema's potentials for presenting a mobilized intra-diegetic gaze convergent with literary experiments such as Joyce's:

The fellows were talking in little groups here and there on the playground. The fellows *seemed to him to have grown smaller*: that was because a sprinter had knocked him down the day before [. . .] and his spectacles had been broken in three pieces [. . .]

   That was why the fellows seemed to him smaller and farther away and the goalposts so thin and far and the soft grey sky so high up. (34; italics mine)

During lessons, Joyce's meticulous simulation is maintained in virtually microscopic close-up, the typography of Stephen's text blurring in and out of focus as he cranes over it: '[T]he lines of the letters were *like fine invisible threads* and it was only by closing his right eye tight and staring out of the left eye that he could *make out the full curves* of the capital' (38; italics mine). As Joyce's focalizer reads, we simultaneously 'see' the text as he does. Similarly, in *Der letzte Mann*, the text of the letter demoting Murnau's proud, but ageing, doorman to toilet attendant is only directly visualized after he dons reading glasses. Shock causes magnified letters of the fatal phrase – 'der Grund dieser Massnahme ist Ihre Alterschwäche' ('the reason for these measures is the weakness of your old age') – to fill the screen and oscillate in and out of focus.

Stephen's optical occlusion increases when victimized by Father Dolan, 'stumbl[ing] into the middle of the class, *blinded by fear and haste*' (41; italics mine). A blurry, monochromatic outline of the prefect of studies features (also framed by lenses, now conferring authoritarian menace) looms above to summarily convict him of slacking (42). Thus, the narrative simulates Stephen's gaze as if presenting every detail through a moving, intra-diegetic camera. Symptomatically, Luigi Pirandello's *Si, gira!* (translated as *Shoot!*), one of the first novels about the Italian film industry, which also appeared in 1915, is narrated from the impassively 'camera-eyed' viewpoint of its cinematographer-protagonist.[44] Joyce had absorbed Frenchman Edouard Dujardin's pioneering 'interior monologue', *Les Lauriers sont coupés* (*The Bays are Sere*, 1888) (that he discovered in Paris in 1903), by the time of starting to write *Portrait*.[45] However, he had also been living in an increasingly movie-minded, Italian-speaking Trieste for a decade by the time that *Portrait* was finished. Hence if *Portrait* was not yet cast in the thoroughgoing 'Dujardinesque' grammar of *Ulysses*' first-person interior monologues, where deictic 'telling' is removed almost altogether for direct 'showing' of perception and thought, Joyce's continuous mimesis of what Stephen sees and feels nonetheless approaches them, as, for example, when Stephen braves the rector's office to protest:

– Come in.

   He turned the handle and opened the door and fumbled for the handle of the green baize door inside. He found it and pushed it open and went in.

> He saw the rector sitting at a desk writing. There was a skull on the desk and a strange solemn smell in the room like the leather of old chairs.
>
> His heart was beating fast on account of the solemn place he was in and the silence of the room; and he looked at the skull and at the rector's kindlooking face. (47)

In this passage of *Portrait*, Joyce simulates Stephen's eye movements alighting on 'objects of attention' on a virtually moment-by-moment basis, contracting and expanding his text's *ekphrastic* 'visual field' as Stephen moves through its spaces. Entering the narrow vestibule, we focus vicariously with Stephen on his own hand fumbling the inner door handle. We then share his vision opening out into the room beyond, with the rector at its centre, followed by its nervous downward flicker towards the *momento mori*, before resting reassuringly on the 'kindlooking face'.

Indeed, *Portrait* goes beyond such peripatetic observing into effects of mechanized virtual locomotion, in which Stephen's viewpoint itself becomes mobilized relative to different forms of transport. His trips are presented kinaesthetically as a kind of 'phantom ride', the vicarious and immersive experience of travel afforded spectators by moving panoramas or photographic lantern 'tours' to exotic destinations and extended through the virtual motion of early films shot from speeding vehicles.[46] Joyce contrives a strikingly mobilized viewpoint through accelerated and rhythmically repeated details in Stephen's train journeys. Geographical landmarks and recurrent infrastructural fixtures rush past Stephen's framed gaze with a flowing permutation characteristic of rail films: 'And the train raced on *over the flat lands and past the hill of Allen. The telegraph poles were passing, passing*' (16; italics mine). In Stephen's 'night mail' ride to Cork, this visual rhythm intensifies.[47] As he gazes backwards through his 'still' compartment window (a key motif in proto-cinematization of Victorian culture, according to historians),[48] the landscape is suggestively conjured into converse, accelerated movement by mechanization and artificial light. This modern visual relativity is neatly caught by Joyce's verb 'flung', repeated as though the train were unreeling the visible world alongside it: 'He saw the *darkening lands slipping past him*, the silent *telegraph-poles passing his window swiftly every four seconds*, the *little glimmering stations*, manned by a few sentries, *flung by the mail behind her* and *twinkling for a moment* in the darkness *like fiery grains flung backwards* by a runner.' In another visual match suggestive of railway film clichés, a memory of the telegraph-wires continuously sliding past his eye evokes musical notations (73).

Seeing with the Eyes of Memory

As Woolf would note about *Ulysses*, *Portrait* also focuses simultaneously on processes of reflection and recollection. Hence Joyce mimics what Stephen's present perceptions of phenomena evoke in his inner vision, to (in her terms) 'mak[e] thought phonetic – taken to bits'.[49] Thus Stephen continually sees with 'remembering eyes' (190), both in the sense of impressions becoming imprinted, but also new ones being perceived through those already stored up. The 'individuating rhythm' of Stephen's developing consciousness is simultaneously *Portrait*'s underlying subject and form, in a reflexively structural sense. It is narrated not just as a cinematically 'fluid succession of presents' as the 1904 sketch puts it, but an associative shuttling back and forth along the chronological axis to fulfil its methodological propositions. Interjections by Joyce's (otherwise famously 'invisible') third-person narrator foreground the continuous dynamism of this process: 'And he tasted in the language of memory [. . .] and saw with the eyes of memory' (196).

The protagonist's body and mind in the modernist fiction that *Portrait* exemplifies tend to simultaneously inhabit 'then and there' as much as the 'here and now' of their ongoing narrative present. Representation of interiority is based on imagistic association that continuously 'overlaps' perceptions and accumulating memories, tracing a timeline from the past that nonetheless drives dynamically onwards to assert Stephen's vocational future. Hence the rising and falling 'curve' of his emotional progress inscribes a pattern of both recurrent challenges and adaptive responses. *Portrait* added a new kind of cinematicity to the *Bildungsroman*, revolutionizing how the genre 'pictures time', both in terms of photographic visualization of individual moments and also how they become dynamically choreographed. This explains Joyce's final exasperation with *Stephen Hero*: Its conventional chronology and inert naturalism, largely un-animated by such qualities, obscured Joyce's integral psychological and aesthetic purpose. One of the principal challenges thrown up by radical economization between the two versions is that the reader must actively interconnect its 'montage' of imagistic fragments – events, motifs and themes – to actively follow this underlying perceptio-cognitive rhythm: so much so that *Portrait* appeared formally chaotic to some early reviewers.[50]

Joyce employed many methods of creating chains of associative imagery that lace the narrative and suggest its individuating rhythm to the reader. Just as Marey picked out his athletes' lines of muscular thrust in white, highlighting the integral rhythm of pure movement over individual shots of bodies, Joyce highlights particular motifs to foreground the distinctive rhythm of Stephen's developing consciousness through what he notices and recollects. Each new experience is filtered through cumulative memories by association of ideas, leading to some *'epiphanic'* correspondence. The process is often triggered by some sight or other sensation in the present. Such Bergsonian *'memoire involontaire'* also occurred occasionally in *Stephen Hero*,[51] but did not constellate into a larger pattern. In *Portrait*, memories, reveries and speculations stir, as if spontaneously, at crucial moments, to continually foreground the 'individuating rhythm' of Stephen's thought processes. Joyce's imagistic stylization of this complex interaction constitutes the modernist breakthrough of the final version, as well as a progression of techniques tried out in *Dubliners*.

Space–time shifts associated with memory often exhibit the instant materialization associated with projected images. Sometimes they seem conjured up like lantern pictures: 'A sudden memory had carried him to another scene, *called up as if by magic*' (65; italics mine). Joyce's deliberately ambiguous phrasing seems to treat memories almost palpably, as if they were manifested outside of Stephen's subjective consciousness or will. Significantly, Stephen's undergraduate theorizing connects artistic creativity with processing and externalizing images: 'The esthetic image in the dramatic form is life purified in and reprojected from the human imagination' (181). Hence *Portrait* builds on *Dubliners'* imagistic techniques, not least (lantern-like) dissolutions of one time or space into another and projection of detached pictures into other contexts, but pushes them much further. It continuously mixes the outer space of present perception with the internalized space of recollection and fantasy, blurring boundaries between objective and subjective reality with images so vividly and concretely visualized for Stephen that they seem to hover between the two.

The most sustained interruption of *Portrait's* forward narrative drive by 'flashback' typically dilates from an involuntary perceptual 'cue' in the present – the micro-close-up on a mouth. It shares the projective materialization of other visual shifts, but instantly transports Stephen into the sensory environment of elsewhen like a psycho-physiological time machine:

> The confession came only from Stephen's lips and, while they spoke the words, *a sudden memory had carried him to another scene called up, as if by magic*, at the moment when he had noted the faint cruel dimples at the corners of Heron's smiling lips. (65; italics mine)

Heron teasingly cajoles Stephen to 'admit' an adolescent crush, simultaneously tapping a cane across his calf. This propels Stephen back four years earlier to an accusation of writing 'heresy' and a brutal schoolboy inquisition. The dilation returns to the present as Stephen realizes that his ability to rise above past traumas is a mark of growing maturity, while its ongoing action is still 'replaying' in his consciousness – another instance of rhythmic space–time overlapping and projective imaging: 'While he was still repeating the *Confiteor* amid the indulgent laughter of his hearers and *while the scenes of that malignant episode were still passing sharply and swiftly before his mind* he wondered why he bore no malice now to those who had tormented him' (italics mine). The phrase 'scenes [. . .] passing sharply and swiftly before his mind' is practically formulaic by this point in deliberate suggestion of a mechanized procession of images like slides or film-frames. The flashback's sustained nature clearly anticipates the frequency and elaboration of similar effects in the interior monologues of *Ulysses*.

Since the text is marked by dynamic 'overlapping' of successive moments, 'past layers' of Stephen's experience continuously show through the present. Therefore, just as in Marey's sequences of athletes, the rhythm of movement can be traced both forward and backward in time, simultaneously marking recurrence and change. Joyce's increasingly complex sensory contrasts and matches trace the rhythm of Stephen's consciousness and his rising and falling Daedalian 'flightpath' towards artistic transcendence. In another pivotal example, torn by the rector's invitation to join the Jesuits, it is precisely involuntary memory that visualizes Stephen's emotional resistance and prefigures his conscious rejection of the 'tempting' offer. Multi-sensory associations dredged from memory induce a feeling of suffocation as Stephen exits to the street. Joyce effectively overlaps three separate layers of time like lantern images or film scenes shimmering in and out of one another – interweaving narrative present, past and possible future. Note *Portrait*'s habitual use of cinematically suggestive terms: 'shadow' implying both foreboding and recorded or projected pictures, and the transverse effect of a moving slide or filmstrip in 'passed [. . .] over' as Stephen imagines the fate awaiting him if he chooses wrongly:

> The *shadow*, then, of the life of the college *passed gravely over* his consciousness. It was a grave and ordered and passionless life that awaited him, a life without material cares. *He wondered how he would pass* the first night in the novitiate and with what dismay he would wake the first morning in the dormitory. *The troubling odour of the corridors of Clongowes came back to him and he heard the discreet murmur of the gasflames.* At once from every part of his being unrest began to irradiate. A feverish quickening of his pulses followed and a din of meaningless words drove his reasoned thought hither and thither confusedly. His lungs dilated and sank as if he were inhaling a warm moist unsustaining air which *hung in the bath at Clongowes above the sluggish turf-coloured water.* (135; italics mine)

Disquiet about the order's repressive discipline awakens traumas nesting into one another. Hallucinatory nightmares from Clongowes bleed back into the mind and body of the Belvedere youth: The 'square ditch' into which the prep-schoolboy was bullied, picking up a fever, and fetid communal bath conflate into an 'immersive' and powerfully somatic warning from Stephen's own unconscious against regressing into institutional and creative stagnation through moral vanity. This is at once mimesis of present perceptions, imaginative processes and a perfect example of *Portrait*'s cinematic organization as narrative. An entry in Stephen's undergraduate diary comments on Joyce's presentation of time as structural rhythm in this way: 'The past is consumed in the present and the present is living only because it brings forth the future' (211). Note the ambiguity of 'consumed': that is, not erased by the-here-and-now, but re-experienced afresh by continually 'showing through' it in existentially significant ways. Thus Joyce creates *Portrait*'s effect of a virtual gaze, moving not just through *physical*, but also *mental* space and time, simultaneously picturing Stephen's perceiving *and* remembering consciousness and revolutionizing the *Bildungsroman*.

The individuating rhythm of Stephen's own consciousness always shows through like the abstract curves tracing the distinctive muscular thrust through Marey's athletes' bodies. In this way, it is possible to view *Portrait*'s advances in *ekphrastic* cinematicity – especially Joyce's method of 'picturing time' – as in direct line of development from his earlier work. *Portrait* builds on subjective focalization and re-visualization through memory in many stories from *Dubliners* and lays the basis for refining such techniques in the interior monologues of *Ulysses*, confirming the last's position as *the* superlatively intermedial modernist text in a world saturated with cinema by its publication in 1922.

Notes

1. Eisenstein received a copy of *Ulysses* as early as 1928, but he had also read *Portrait* a few years previously. For a recent round-up of research on Eisenstein and Joyce, see Keith Williams, 'Odysseys of Sound and Image: "Cinematicity" and the *Ulysses* Adaptations', in John McCourt, ed., *Roll Away the Reel World: James Joyce and Cinema* (Cork: Cork University Press, 2010), pp. 158–73.

2. For the history of *ekphrasis* see *Pictures Into Words: Theoretical and Descriptive Approaches to Ekphrasis*, eds Valerie Robillard and Els Jongeneel (Amsterdam: VU University Press, 1998), especially 'Introduction', pp. ix–x.

3. For the background to the Volta Cinematograph, see Denis Condon, 'The Volta Myth', *Film Ireland* 116 (May/June 2007), 43, and Luke McKernan, 'James Joyce and the Volta Programme', in McCourt, ed., *Reel World*, pp. 15–27.

4. See Sergei Eisenstein, 'Sur Joyce', *Change* (May 1972), 51. Robert A. Gessner argued that the influence of Joyce's Italian movie-going came out in flashback, cross-cutting and 'editing of time and space with the intensity and concentration of the camera'; see *The Moving Image: A Guide to Cinematic Literacy* (London: Cassell,

1968), p. 266. To Alan Spiegel, *Portrait*'s 'temporalized space' comes alive cine-matically, 'as *process*, developing, changing, infinitely flexible, quick with advances and recessions, expansions and contractions, openings and closings, accumula-tions and dissolutions'; see *Fiction and the Camera Eye: Visual Consciousness in Film and the Modern Novel* (Charlottesville, VA: University Press of Virginia, 1976), pp. 164–5. Neil Sinyard considers the four sections of Chapter 1 to constitute 'one of the finest examples of montage in fiction'; see *Filming Literature: The Art of Screen Adaptation* (London: Croom Helm, 1986), p. viii. Robert A. Armour drew attention to the novel's distinctive audio-visual strategies to argue that it is more 'cinematic' than Joseph Strick's 1977 film adaptation; see 'The "Whatness" of Joseph Strick's *Portrait*', in Michael Klein and Gillian Parker, eds, *The English Novel and the Movies* (New York, NY: Frederick Ungar, 1981), pp. 279–90. More recently, Luke Gibbons suggests that Joyce counterpointed sound and image to signify unconscious processes. Gibbons also argues that Strick's adaptation is less cinematic, comparing their respective Christmas dinner scenes and the interplay between dialogue and emblematic colours – red and green, to dramatize conflict between the progressive nationalism and Catholic morality conditioning Stephen's outlook from childhood onwards; see 'Visualizing the Voice: Joyce, Cinema, and the Politics of Vision', in Robert Stam and Alessandra Raengo, eds, *A Companion to Literature and Film* (Oxford: Blackwell, 2004), pp. 171–88.

5. Anne Friedberg, *Window Shopping: Cinema and the Postmodern* (Berkeley, CA: University of California Press, 1993), pp. 2–3; italics in original.

6. Spiegel, *Fiction and the Camera Eye*, p. 142.

7. The term 'subjective camera' was coined to describe intra-diegetic viewpoints in Expressionist silent cinema. See David A. Cook, *A History of Narrative Film* (New York, NY and London: Norton 2004, 4th edn), pp. 103–5.

8. Hollywood's most extended experiment with intra-diegetic visual narrative was *Lady in the Lake* (dir. Robert Montgomery, 1946), where the entire film is shot as if seen directly through gumshoe Philip Marlowe's eyes. Materialized on the soundtrack as recollecting voice-over, or in dialogue with other characters, the effect of Marlowe's absent presence is uncannily like the viewpoint of an Invisible Man (except for brief moments when his image is reflected in mirrors or casts shadows).

9. See Virginia Woolf, 'Reading Notes for "Modern Novels" (Joyce)', 1 volume (April 1918), '*Ulysses* VII, Dark Blue', in New York Public Library Berg Collection (also available in microform, Reel 11, M91). I am indebted to Dr James Stewart (an editor for the Cambridge University Press Edition of the Writings of Virginia Woolf) for ascertaining that the key noun is 'horse'. The section on 'Joyce, Woolf and "The Moment"', in Bonnie Kime Scott, ed., *The Gender of Modernism* (Bloomington, IN: Indiana University Press, 1990), p. 643, mis-transcribes it as 'hare'.

10. *Stephen Hero* (written *c.* 1904–6, albeit surviving chapters were not published until 1944) opposes the magic lantern's 'transformative and disfiguring' light to the steady and uncompromising critical illumination of 'the modern spirit':

The modern spirit is vivisective. Vivisection is the most modern process one can conceive. The ancient spirit accepted phenomena with a bad grace. The ancient method investigated law with the lantern of justice, morality with the lantern of revelation, art with the lantern of tradition. *But all these lanterns have magical properties: they transform and disfigure.* The modern method examines its territory by the light of day. [. . .] It examines the entire community in action and reconstructs the spectacle of redemption [. . .] here you have the spectacle of the esthetic instinct in action.

This quote is from *Stephen Hero* (Frogmore: Granada, 1977 [1944], revised edn), p. 167; italics mine. Subsequent page references in text. It should also be noted that 'vivisection' implies anatomizing 'living' things – in this case social practices and institutions – with scientific objectivity and lack of preconceptions like the camera's analysis of living movement. Stephen's metaphors imply a radical break with 'phantasmagoric' illusions of the past through a defamiliarizing aesthetic based on new modes of vision.

11. James Joyce, *Ulysses* (1922), ed. with an intro. and notes by Jeri Johnson (Oxford: Oxford University Press, 1998), p. 37. Subsequent page references in text.
12. Woolf, 'Reading Notes for "Modern Novels"', '*Ulysses* VI, Green'; italics mine.
13. Frank Budgen, *James Joyce and the Making of* Ulysses (1934), repr. in *James Joyce and the Making of* Ulysses *and Other Writings* (Oxford: Oxford University Press, 1972), p. 21.
14. Budgen, *James Joyce and the Making of* Ulysses, p. 54; also *Ulysses*, p. 46.
15. Spiegel, *Fiction and the Camera Eye*, pp. 113–14.
16. The stereoscope was created by Sir Charles Wheatstone in 1838 to investigate the physiology of binocular vision, but it was produced for the mass-market by inventors such as Oliver Wendell Holmes. See Laura Bird Schiavo, 'From Phantom Image to Perfect Vision: Physiological Optics, Commercial Photography, and the Popularization of the Stereoscope', in Lisa Gitelman and Geoffrey Pingree, eds, *New Media, 1740–1915* (Cambridge, MA: The MIT Press), pp. 113–38. Ray Zone discusses its key role as a precedent for effects of virtual tangibility and immersion in film space in his *Stereoscopic Cinema and the Origins of 3-D Film, 1838–1952* (Lexington, KY: University of Kentucky Press, 2007), especially pp. 76–7.
17. For an alternative view on Joyce, Muybridge and *Ulysses*, see Louise E. J. Hornby, 'Visual Clockwork: Photography, Time and the Instant in "Proteus"', *JJQ* 42–3.1–4 (Fall, 2004/ Summer, 2006), 49–68.
18. Joyce reduced *Stephen Hero*'s epically conceived sixty-three chapters to just five in *Portrait*. The surviving manuscript (that only covers Stephen's student days) is two hundred pages in itself, subsequently condensed into a mere section of *Portrait*'s Chapter V. The novel's length is estimated to be only a third of that of *Stephen Hero* as a whole; see 'Composition and Publication History', in James Joyce, *A Portrait of the Artist as a Young Man* (1914–15), ed. with an intro. and notes by Jeri Johnson (Oxford: Oxford University Press, 2000), pp. xl–xliii.

19. 'A Portrait of the Artist' (1904), in Robert Scholes and Richard M. Kain, eds, *In the Workshop of Daedalus: James Joyce and the Raw Materials for* A Portrait of the Artist as a Young Man (Evanston, IL: Northwestern University Press, 1965), pp. 60–8 (p. 60); italics mine.

20. For *Dubliners'* emulation and critique of lanternism, see Keith Williams, '"I Bar the Magic Lantern Business"? *Dubliners* and Pre-Cinema', in John Nash, ed., *James Joyce in the Nineteenth Century* (Cambridge: Cambridge University Press, 2013).

21. See *The King Who Was a King: The Book of a Film* (London: Ernest Benn, 1929), p. 9.

22. *The Last Machine: Early Cinema and the Birth of the Modern World* (London: BFI/BBC, 1994), pp. 69–70.

23. Ovid *Metamorphoses*, Book viii., trans. A. D. Melville (Oxford: Oxford University Press, 1986), p. 177.

24. See Horner, 'On the Properties of the Daedalum, a New Instrument of Optical Illusion', *London and Edinburgh Philosophical Magazine* (January 1834); repr. in vol. I of *A History of Pre-Cinema*, ed. Stephen Herbert (London and New York, NY: Routledge, 2000), pp. 271–6.

25. See Olive Cook, *Movement in Two Dimensions: A Study of the Animated and Projected Pictures which Preceded the Invention of Cinematography* (London: Hutchinson, 1963); repr. as vol. III of *A History of Pre-Cinema*, ed. Stephen Herbert (London and New York, NY: Routledge, 2000), pp. 127–8. Claire Wallace also discusses the zoëtrope in '"Ghosts in the Mirror": Perception and the Visual in *Giacomo Joyce*', in Louis Armand and Claire Wallace, eds, *Giacomo Joyce: Envoys of the Other* (Prague: Litteraria Pragensia Books, 2006, 2nd enlarged edn), pp. 207–27, see especially pp. 213–15, 222.

26. The phenakistocope was invented by the Belgian Joseph Plateau in 1841. For the 'Wheel of Life' lantern, see *Encyclopaedia of the Magic Lantern*, eds David Robertson, Stephen Herbert and Richard Crangle (London: The Magic Lantern Society, 2001), pp. 321–22.

27. See Kevin and Emer Rockett, *Magic Lantern, Panorama and Moving Picture Shows in Ireland, 1786–1909* (Dublin: Four Courts Press, 2011), p. 52.

28. For a development of the Zoopraxiscope, see Amy Lawrence, 'Counterfeit Motion: The Animated Films of Eadweard Muybridge', *Film Quarterly* 57.2 (2004), 15–25.

29. Cook, *History of Narrative Film*, p. 1.

30. By coincidence, I presented this research at the 2010 James Joyce Symposium in Prague, famous for its 'black theatre', in which human movement is 'dematerialized' so that objects can be manipulated invisibly. (I am grateful for a British Academy travel grant to do this.)

31. Tate Britain staged a major exhibition of Muybridge's work, including a demonstration of the Zoopraxiscope (September 2010–January 2011), with accompanying catalogue: Philip Brookman, *Eadweard Muybridge* (London: Tate, 2010). Links between series photography and cinema have also been extensively his-

toricized in (among others): Gordon Hendricks, *Eadweard Muybridge: The Father of the Motion Picture* (London: Secker and Warburg, 1977); Rebecca Solnit, *Motion Studies: Time, Space and Eadweard Muybridge* (London: Bloomsbury, 2003); Marta Braun, *Picturing Time: The Work of Étienne-Jules Marey* (Chicago, IL and London: University of Chicago Press, 1992). Volume I of Herbert's *History of Pre-Cinema* reproduces key images and facsimiles of documents in pp. 39–217.

32. For example, Poet Laureate, Alfred Lord Tennyson attended one of Muybridge's most prestigious lectures in 1882, along with T. H. Huxley, William Gladstone and the Royal family. See Hendricks, *Eadweard Muybridge*, p. 141.

33. See illustration and discussion in Edward Chandler, *Photography in Ireland: The Nineteenth Century* (Dublin: Edmund Burke, 2001), p. 66. See also Rockett, *Magic Lantern,* pp. 150–1. Joyce certainly knew about Hayes, enrolling him among 'Irish heroes and heroines of antiquity' in *Ulysses*, see 'Cyclops', pp. 284–5.

34. Chandler, *Photography in Ireland*, p. 89.

35. For the significance of Bull's work, see (among others): Chandler, *Photography in Ireland*, p. 89; Stephen Herbert and Luke MacKernan, *Who's Who of Victorian Cinema: A Worldwide Survey* (London: BFI, 1996), pp. 29–30; *The Encyclopedia of Early Cinema*, ed. Richard Abel (London: Routledge, 2010), p. 86.

36. See Umberto Boccioni *et al.*, 'Futurist Painting: Technical Manifesto' (1910), in *Futurist Manifestos*, ed. Umbro Apollonio (London: Thames and Hudson, 1973), pp. 27–8; also Archie K. Loss, *Joyce's Visible Art: The Work of Joyce and the Visual Arts, 1904–1922* (Ann Arbor, MI: UMI Research Press, 1984), pp. 62–3.

37. Quoted in Loss, *Joyce's Visible Art*, p. 63; italics in original.

38. Joyce, *Stephen Hero*, chapter XXV, p. 189. See also Scarlett Baron, 'Flaubert, Joyce: Vision, Photography, Cinema', *Modern Fiction Studies* 54.4 (2008), 689–714.

39. According to the online concordance to *Portrait*, the noun 'time' (in just about every sense) occurs on no less than one hundred and nineteen occasions and 'times' occurs at least twenty-one times. 'Memory' occurs thirty-seven times and the word 'memories' occurs six times. These also collocate with forty-one occurrences of the verb 'remember', plus forms thereof: 'remembered' (twenty-two), 'remembering' (four) and 'remembers' (five). The concordance is viewable at: <www.doc.ic.ac.uk/~rac101/concord/texts/paym/> (accessed 1 January 2013).

40. According to the online concordance to *Portrait*, 'sight' occurs seventeen times and the verb 'see' occurs eighty-three times, plus the variants – 'saw' (seventy times), 'seeing' (sixteen times) and 'seen' (twenty-eight times).

41. Joyce, *A Portrait of the Artist as a Young Man*, p. 5. Subsequent page references in text.

42. Accounts differ as to whether this is rugby or Gaelic football. If it is rugby, then the oval ball's description as a spinning 'orb' is mimetic of Stephen's eyesight and, hence, it is another example of dynamic distortion.

43. For the case that Joyce depicts his own condition of long-sightedness rather than short-sightedness (as often assumed), see Francisco J. Ascaso and Jan L. van Velze, 'Was James Joyce Myopic or Hyperopic?', *BMJ* (2011); 343: d7464;

doi: 10.136/bmj.d7464 (published 15 December 2011), pp. 1–3, at: <www.bmj.com> (accessed 1 January 2013). See also Jan Leendert van Velze, 'James Joyce on his Blindness', at: <http://deficienciavisual14.com.sapo.pt/r-James_Joyce-On_his_blindness.htm> (accessed 21 June 2012).

44. See *The Notebooks of Serafino Gubbio (Shoot!)*, trans. C. K. Scott Moncrieff (Sawtry, Cambridgeshire: Dedalus, 1990).

45. For Dujardin as Joyce's model for interior monologue form, see Richard Ellmann, *James Joyce* (Oxford: Oxford University Press, 1982, new and revised edn), pp. 126, 665; also the introduction to the edition *The Bays Are Sere*, trans. Anthony Suter (London: Libris, 1991), pp. xi–lxvii.

46. For phantom rides see Raymond Fielding, 'Hale's Tours: Ultrarealism in the Pre-1910 Motion Picture', in John R. Fell, ed., *Film Before Griffith* (Cambridge, MA: Harvard University Press, 1983), pp. 116–30; Tom Gunning, 'Landscape and Fantasy of Moving Pictures; Early Cinema's Phantom Rides', in Graeme Harper and Jonathan Rayner, eds, *Cinema and Landscape* (Bristol: Intellect, 2010), pp. 31–69.

47. Interestingly, the route overlaps with scenic lantern tours such as 'The Lakes of Killarney and Glengariff, via Cork and Bantry' (1894), slides and text published by Dublin firm William Lawrence that specialized in them; also with Mitchell and Kenyon's film *Ride from Blarney to Cork on Cork & Muskerry Light Railway* (1902). For Mitchell and Kenyon's other Irish phantom rides and Dublin panoramas, see Robert Monks, 'The Irish Films in the Mitchell and Kenyon Collection', in Vanessa Toulmin, Simon Popple and Patrick Russell, eds, *The Lost Worlds of Mitchell and Kenyon: Edwardian Britain on Film* (London: BFI, 2006), pp. 75–97, and the *Mitchell and Kenyon in Ireland* DVD (London: BFI National Film and Television Archive, 2006).

48. 'Panoramic perception, in contrast to traditional perception, no longer belonged to the same space as the perceived objects: the traveller saw the objects, landscapes, etc. *through* the apparatus which moved him through the world. That machine and the motion it created became integrated into his visual perception; thus he could only see things in motion.' Wolfgang Schivelbusch, *The Railway Journey: The Industrialization of Time and Space in the 19th Century* (Berkeley, CA: University of California Press, 1986 [1976], new edn), p. 64; emphasis in original. Many films shown at the Volta featured mechanical transport (planes, cars, ships and so forth) or simulated 'tours' through the natural or architectural spectacles of foreign countries.

49. Woolf, 'Reading Notes for "Modern Novels" (Joyce)', '*Ulysses* VI, Green'.

50. Edward Garnett, for example, who turned it down for Duckworth, rejected it as 'formless' (quoted in Ellmann, *James Joyce*, p. 404).

51. See, for example, Stephen's queasy flashback to communal feeding at Clongowes, when feeling alienated from fellow students at University College (*Stephen Hero*, p. 165).

CHAPTER 6

Nature Caught in the Act: On the Transformation of an Idea of Art in Early Cinema

NICO BAUMBACH

In a well-known anecdote, Georges Méliès, an audience member at the first screening of projected film in the Grand Café in Paris, 1895, is said to have encountered the potential of cinema and his own destiny as a filmmaker in the detail of moving leaves in the background of the Lumières' film *Le Repas de Bébé* (*Baby's Meal*).[1] In 1944, in what was to be his final interview, delivered from a hospital bed, D. W. Griffith claimed, 'What the modern movie lacks is beauty – the beauty of the moving wind in the trees.'[2]

What do Méliès, the figure most associated with the introduction of illusion, special effects and fantasy into cinema, and Griffith, the figure most associated with the development of film as a story-telling medium and enhancement of its narrative codes and conventions, both see in this detail whose attraction may seem to derive from precisely its resistance to manipulation or codification?

To begin to answer this question, let us first note the gap between Méliès and Griffith. For Méliès, the wind in the trees was an image of the future of cinema, a sign that the new medium offered something that needed to be harnessed and explored. For Griffith, nearly fifty years later, this same image has come to stand for what the cinema has lost. What happened to this image within this half-century?

In the first volume of his *Histoire générale du cinéma* (1946), Georges Sadoul comments on the fact that in the surviving reports from the 1895 screening at the Grand Café, seemingly minor details tended to be of greater interest to the audience than the supposed main attractions of the ten films on the Lumière programme. Sadoul is struck by the fact that newspaper reports of the time made repeated reference to incidental details like smoke, waves and, especially, 'the trembling of the leaves through the action of the wind' ('le frémissement des feuilles sous l'action du vent') when, as he claims, these are images that would no longer make an impression.[3]

The lure of the incidental detail in the margins of the frame complicates Tom Gunning's description of the aesthetic of early cinema as delivering 'a brief dose of scopic pleasure'.[4] The train arriving in the station remains the archetypal image of early cinema as the primal scene and an image of the shock effect of the early attractions. Smoke, waves and the wind in the trees seem to provide a rather different sense of the viewing habits of early spectators, albeit a sense just as unavailable to us today. The phrase Sadoul highlights from an 1896 write-up singling out the leaves is, 'It's nature caught in the act' ('c'est la nature prise sur le fait').[5] Unlike Griffith, Sadoul does not lament the loss of this experience but explains it by proposing that it derived from sheer amazement at the novelty of cinema. But this does not take us very far. Why would the novelty of cinema be made visible in images of smoke, waves or leaves moving in the wind and not in the images of people moving or, for that matter, anything else? And why, on the other hand, would cinema be needed to catch nature in the act?

On the surface, Griffith's claim looks just as mysterious. Whatever his opinion of the value of location shooting over sets, surely he did not mean in any literal sense that nature was not and could not be filmed any more, that one could not find wind in the trees (even if sometimes in the form of rear projection) in the background of films being shown on screens across America in 1944. Let us take a look at precisely what he says: 'What the modern movie lacks is beauty – the beauty of the moving wind in the trees.' He continues, 'That they have forgotten entirely – the moving picture is beautiful; the moving of wind on beautiful trees is more beautiful than a painting.'[6] What Griffith claims that movies have lost is *beauty*, a specific form of cinematic beauty, exemplified in the wind in the trees, which exceeds the beauty of painting, presumably even the painting of the same image.

Griffith makes no distinction between 'the moving picture' and 'the moving of wind on beautiful trees'. The beauty of the moving picture is equivalent to the beauty of nature. In *Critique of Judgement*, Immanuel Kant makes a categorical distinction between the beauty of art and the beauty of nature. It is often remarked how Kant reserved the sublime for nature and denied it to art, and how modern art can be demarcated by the introduction of the sublime as an effect of art. The train entering the station in the Lumière film *L'Arrivée d'un train à La Ciotat* or Edison's *Black Diamond Express* can be used to link early cinema to this development of aesthetic modernity. But this narrative ignores the fact that Kant's definition of the sublime was based on a more fundamental distinction between art and nature that was equally significant for the question of the beautiful. For Kant, an interest in the beauty of nature directs the individual to the ultimate purpose of humanity: the morally good. This is decidedly not the case for the beauty of art, which commands only a judgement of taste but has no bearing on morality. The nature/art distinction highlights the fact that aesthetic experience for Kant is not a matter of mere appearance but is dictated by the origins and ends of the aesthetic object. It is in this sense that beauty is 'purposeful' despite Kant's famous claim that, at the same time, it is 'without purpose'. Indeed, Kant goes so far as to claim that if the man of good soul who has been taking a direct interest in the nature around him were to discover that the wild flowers he contemplated were actually fake flowers artfully crafted to deceive him, his direct interest and the accompanying moral feeling would 'promptly vanish', leaving him either without interest and just a judgement of taste or with a vain interest that comes from society.

Kant explains the distinction: 'Art is distinguished from nature as doing (*facere*) is from acting or operating in general (*agere*); and the product or result of art is distinguished from that of nature, the first being a work (*opus*), the second an effect (*effectus*).'[7] This distinction has its roots in Aristotle, who claimed in *Nicomachean Ethics*: 'Action [*praxis*] and production [*poiesis*] are generically different. For production aims at an end other than itself; but this is impossible in the case of action, because the end is merely to do what is right.'[8]

Art is a matter of doing or making and it takes the form of a work. Nature is an effect of acting or operating in general. Art has an end other than itself unlike nature. Art, grasped as developing out of mimesis or play, from Aristotle to Schiller, implies an intention. As Hans-Georg Gadamer proposes, even the avant-garde's attempt to make the 'effect' a 'work' implies intention because 'something is *intended as something*, even if it is not something conceptual, useful, or purposive, but only the pure autonomous regulation of movement'.[9] Duchamp's ready-made is a 'work' because there is a minimal difference between the object as effect and the 'something' it is intended as that makes it a work, even if this 'something' is not specifiable. This idea of art in terms of mimesis does not imply resemblance, as is often claimed, so much as a gap between *agere* and *facere*.

'La nature prise sur le fait' has been translated as 'nature caught in the act', but this does not reverse the distinction we find in Kant between *agere* and *facere*, in that 'act' in the phrase 'caught in the act' implies that the act was intended by a doer, as in a crime. The statement 'la nature prise sur le fait' literally means 'nature grasped as fact or deed' – as that which was done or made, nature apprehended as crime or artwork. This is then another way of stating André Bazin's cryptic claim in 'The Ontology of the Photographic Image' that 'nature at last does more than imitate art: she imitates the artist'. In the cinematic image, it is as if making and operating, work and effect, can no longer be distinguished. Bazin went on to claim: 'All the arts are based on the presence of man. Only photography derives an advantage from his absence. Photography affects us like a phenomenon in nature, like a flower or a snowflake whose vegetable or earthly origins are an inseparable part of their beauty'.[10] Photography takes on the beauty of nature not just because it shows nature as it is, but because it takes on the qualities of nature itself. Photography, he claims, 'contributes [. . .] to natural creation'. Bazin continues by saying, 'photography can even surpass art in its creative power', suggesting that photography is not an art, not because it is not creative, but because the creativity is out of man's hands.[11]

In the image of the moving leaves, nature was confronted as doing or making itself, participating in its own self-presentation. Art, at the same time, became an effect rather than (just) a work. The spectators of the first films were not like Kant's fictitious spectator thrust out of their moral contemplation of nature by the recognition that what they were watching was only a movie. Instead, they were encountering a simultaneous transformation of both nature and art. Recall Jean Epstein and Louis Delluc's claims in the 1920s that the art of cinema was encountered in something called *photogénie*, defined as the enhancement of the 'moral aspect' of things through their 'filmic reproduction'.[12] The moral aspect that the French Impressionists recognized in film evokes Kant's definition of natural beauty. In a sense, faces and objects were revealed as nature.

Walter Benjamin would grasp in film this mutual transformation of the Kantian categories of nature and art, but derive a different conclusion. For Benjamin it was not that art had acquired a moral aspect by becoming nature, but that nature had lost its moral aspect by becoming art. Art, in turn, became a question of politics because what Epstein identified as *photogénie* was in fact 'the optical unconscious', which was not a revealing of the mysteries of nature through art, but a neutralization of the mysteries of art through an elimination of art's distance from nature.[13] This is how I grasp Benjamin's famous claim that film was the most significant sign of the decay of the 'aura' of the work of art. Recall that the 'aura' of the work of art, defined as a 'unique existence in time and space', has its origins for Benjamin in man's experience of nature. In a fragment, Benjamin writes: 'Derivation of the aura as the projection of a human social experience onto nature: the gaze is returned.'[14] For Benjamin, film did not bring art closer to natural beauty, but rather the opposite: It severed the relation between the two.

How do we reconcile these apparently opposing conclusions? It is worth returning to Griffith's claim that the moving image of the wind in the trees was more beautiful than any painting. This desire to preserve transient nature unadorned was already part of late nineteenth-century painting before the invention of the *cinématographe*. In 1878, Theodore Duret in his study 'The Impressionist Painters' wrote that Monet has succeeded in setting down the fleeting impressions which his predecessors had neglected or considered impossible to render with a brush. The thousand nuances that the water of the sea and rivers take on, the play of light in the clouds, the vibrant coloring in the flowers and the checkered reflections of the foliage in the rays of the burning sun that have been seized by him in all their truth.[15]

For the Impressionists, fidelity to nature meant a turn away from the sublime landscapes of mid-nineteenth-century French painting and towards nature in its diurnal or ordinary manifestation. To use the terms adopted by Deleuze in his *Cinema* books, nature was to be conceived as 'any-instant-whatever' rather than a transcendent pose and was subject to the same interest as human-made spectacle and fashion.[16] As Meyer Schapiro and T. J. Clark have emphasized, the subject of Impressionist painting was often the bourgeoisie in nature – not only the play of light on the leaves of trees but picnics, promenades and boat trips, but these images of bourgeois leisure were to be rendered *as nature* insofar as nature was understood as the transient world of appearance.[17]

Monet made no distinction between completely surrendering to nature and painting what was on his retinas. The Impressionists adopted an anti-representationalism in the name of optical truth. For Monet, line was to be dispensed with in favour of vibrations of colour in order to, as Jules Laforgue put it at the time, 'render nature as it is', not in its permanence, 'but in the fleeting appearances which accidents [. . .] present to him'.[18]

But how pure was the seizing of sensation in such a way that it preceded cognitive processing or, as Henri Bergson might say, 'cinematographical perception'?[19] As T. J. Clark has proposed, it came at no small effort in which the 'normal habits of representation [. . .] must somehow or other be outlawed'.[20] In other words, the Impressionist painter was not merely the neutral vehicle for seizing the immediacy of external appearance. As Laforgue put it:

> [O]ne's work will never be the real equivalent of the fugitive reality but rather the record of the response of a certain unique sensibility to a moment which can never be reproduced exactly for the individual, under the excitement of a landscape at a certain moment of its luminous life which can never be duplicated. [. . .] In the flashes of identity between subject and object lies the nature of genius.[21]

Indeed, the legibility of Impressionism as art derived from the very impossibility of the stated project. It was the impossibility of a surrendering to *opsis* and evacuating representation that was both mobilized by its detractors to suggest that the paintings looked unfinished and was seen by its defenders as making possible the expressive mark of the artist and revealing his genius. According to the latter, what was recorded ultimately was not nature in some generic sense but rather the unique sensibility of the artist. In Laforgue's comments we can see two reasons for this impossibility that makes Impressionism an art: time and movement. The artist is always limited by the fact that nature and sensation are always in flux, and the attempt to seize hold of the transient in a static painting is never pure. No matter how many paintings Monet makes of haystacks or the Rouen Cathedral, he will never have a movement-image. But this becomes a strength of Impressionism as an art. Ultimately, objective nature and subjective genius are seen as inextricable, but if these contraries could be synthesized, this synthesis was justified by a tension thought to be captured in the paintings themselves. In other words, if a Monet painting was said to seize the beauty of ephemeral nature without interpretation or adornment, it nonetheless remained clear that it was Monet and not nature that was the artist.

What happens with the advent of cinematography is that film actualizes an Impressionist axiom to render the artist passive in the face of nature. But if this is true, and if, as Bazin claimed, nature truly becomes the artist in film, and if nature here is what the Impressionists mean by nature, which is nothing other than transient optical appearance, then why isn't this equally true of all films? What is special about a cinematic image of wind blowing through leaves, and how is it that whatever is special about this image is visible in the 1890s in a way that is no longer visible in the 1940s?

The image of wind in trees has a history in Romantic poetry and literature as a generic image of familiar romantic tropes: interiority, melancholic longing and temporal dislocation. In Hegel's *Encyclopedia*, he uses the word '*Rauschen*', or rustling, as an example of the kind of word in the German language mistakenly thought to have profound implications because it evokes what is 'sensuous and insignificant'.[22] Thomas Pfau in *Romantic Moods* suggests that the recourse to rustling trees had become so overtly clichéd in the German Romantic lyric that repetition of that image in Joseph von Eichendorff's poetry of the 1820s and 1830s functions as a thematization of the lyric form – that is, as a kind of proto-modernism that draws our attention to the rustling not of leaves, but, in Roland Barthes's phrase, of language itself. Pfau emphasizes that in Eichendorff it is an acoustic-image and suggests that 'the poetic sign here assumes the character of a simulacrum, a copy (or pseudo-memory) for which no original can ever be produced'.[23]

If Eichendorff and Monet may seem to have little else in common, in both examples rustling or moving leaves and other images of transient nature were indices for the returned gaze or mute speech of the material or physical world that found their truth in aesthetic abstraction. Whatever their vast differences, both German Romantic poetry and French Impressionist painting share a nineteenth-century idea of art that believes in an interiority and subjective perception that was only grasped by the murmur or gaze of an indifferent external world. Both Eichendorff and Monet attempt to neutralize this belief without escaping from it by returning us to the materiality of their respective mediums. In the German lyric, the rustling of leaves was to be reduced to an acoustic image indexing the materiality of language, and in French Impressionist painting transient nature was to be reduced to pure varying intensities of colour.

If this image of nature found its truth in sound and colour, these were both absent from the earliest Lumière films. Maxim Gorky's famous response to the Lumière programme emphasizes precisely this fact: 'Last night I was in the Kingdom of Shadows. If you only knew how strange it is to be there. It is a world without sound, without colour. Everything there – the earth, the trees, the people, the water and the air – is dipped in monotonous grey. [. . .] Noiselessly, the ashen grey foliage of the trees sways in the wind.'[24] Colourless and noiseless, for Gorky, cinema drained nature of its beauty. For this very reason, it was an artless medium. Yet for Benjamin this loss of 'beautiful semblance' was the key to what cinema could reveal about the transformation of aesthetic experience.[25] Following Benjamin, we might see that Gorky's image of cinema suggests its potential to go further than Eichendorff or Monet to neutralize a proto-Fascist Romantic idea of art that sought in the link between art and nature a mysterious beauty that harboured the secret to authentic interiority. If so, it did this not through what it added to the image of transitory nature but what it subtracted from it: not only sound and colour, but the expressive hand of the artist.

But is this truly what Méliès or Griffith grasped in this image? We should remind ourselves that during the early years of cinema, the era dominated by what Tom Gunning refers to as 'the cinema of attractions', no film was ever made in which wind moving through leaves was the express attraction. As noted at the start of this essay, the film Méliès saw and remarked on was called *Le Repas de Bébé*. Far from being a film centred on nature, *Le Repas de Bébé* – a film of Auguste Lumière and his wife and child dining outside on their estate – distinguishes itself from the other nine films on the first Lumière programme by being the only film in medium shot as opposed to long shot and the only film to feature human figures facing the camera for its duration. Although the theatrical staging evokes the family snapshot more than any genre or tradition of painting, its subject matter bears some relation to those images of bourgeois idylls so common to Impressionist painting.

Many recent studies of early cinema have emphasized the importance of the indexical sign to an idea of cinema that was especially relevant to the genre of actualities that dominated the industry's first ten years, and of which the Lumière films are the prototype. The claim is that cinema, by bearing the trace of the pro-filmic, a past event that precedes the viewing of the film and exceeds the control of the filmmaker, harboured an anarchic potential through what Mary Ann Doane calls 'contingency' or Dai Vaughan calls 'spontaneity'.[26] The index, as formulated by C. S. Peirce, signifies through an existential bond between the sign and the object. It is directly caused by its object but cannot be mistaken for it. According to Doane, the index is 'evacuated of content; it is a hollowed-out sign'.[27] It testifies to an object's existence, but offers only its effect. Not only is a film an index for a pro-filmic event, but moving leaves are an index of the wind. According to Peirce, 'an index is a sign which would, at once, lose the character that makes it a sign if its object were removed, but would not lose that character if there were no interpretant'.[28] In other words, the index harbours a potential meaningless-ness by being a mark of only the mere fact of existence. Nature leaves its mark whether or not a subject perceives it. To modify a familiar riddle, wind blows the leaves of trees even if no camera is there to film it. To catch nature in the act is thus thoroughly ambiguous. It is a proof or evidence of mere brute fact, but says nothing about meaning.

The wind arrested by the film is an index of an index, and as such drew attention to the potential of this new medium. The inscription of the moving leaves visible in the projection of the filmstrip provides an image of cinema's ability to make visible an absent cause, but no recipe for what to do with it. Art acquired the qualities of nature at the same time that nature lost the capacity to testify to an experience outside of the life of people. The fascina-tion of this image that is now lost to us was tied to the potential of cinema and, as such, its meaning could not be explicitly stated because it remained to be determined. If the image is now an image of loss, it can be resuscitated to still harbour a certain potential as long as we do not return to Griffith's Victorian sensibility and link that potential to a nostalgic desire to restore natural beauty to art, but rather see it for the opposite effect – the linking of art to politics by freeing art from both moral and occult projections. The importance of this image is its transformation over time: its role in the history of film and the meaning derived from film in the history of aesthetic experi-ence. We can revive its potential only by deflating its mystery. Louis Lumière famously claimed that cinema is 'an invention without a future', and so it is no accident that the moving leaves can be found in a film depicting the domestic comfort of one of cinema's inventors, lodged in the margins of the frame outside of his field of vision.

Notes

1. See, for example, Mary Ann Doane, *The Emergence of Cinematic Time* (Cambridge, MA: Harvard University Press, 2002), p. 177. The film is alternately known as *Le Déjeuner de Bébé*, 'Baby's First Meal', 'Baby's Breakfast' and 'Baby's Lunch', among other variants.
2. Ezra Goodman, *The Fifty-Year Decline and Fall of Hollywood* (New York, NY: Simon and Schuster, 1961), p. 19.
3. See Georges Sadoul, *Histoire générale du cinéma*, vol. 1: *L'Invention du cinéma 1832–1897* (Paris: Denoël, 1948), pp. 291, 294. The reference is found in Siegfried Kracauer's *Theory of Film: The Redemption of Physical Reality* (Princeton, NJ: Princeton University Press, 1997), p. 31. Kracauer cites Sadoul, who in turn was citing journalist Henri de Parville.
4. Tom Gunning, 'An Aesthetic of Astonishment: Early Cinema and the (In)Credulous Spectator', in Linda Williams, ed., *Viewing Positions: Ways of Seeing Film* (New Brunswick, NJ: Rutgers University Press, 1995), p. 121.
5. Sadoul, *Histoire*, p. 291. My translations throughout unless otherwise stated.
6. Goodman, *The Fifty-Year Decline*, p. 19.
7. Immanuel Kant, *Critique of Judgment*, trans. Werner Pluhar (Indianapolis, IN: Hackett, 1987), p. 170.
8. See Giorgio Agamben, *Infancy and History: The Destruction of Experience*, trans. Liz Heron (London: Verso, 2007), p. 154. The original source is *Nicomachean Ethics*, Book 6, 1140b.
9. Hans-Georg Gadamer, *The Relevance of the Beautiful and Other Essays*, ed. Robert Bernasconi, and trans. Nicholas Walker (Cambridge: Cambridge University Press, 1986), p. 24; italics in original.
10. André Bazin, *What Is Cinema?*, vol. 1, trans. Hugh Gray (Berkeley, CA: University of California Press, 1967), p. 13.
11. *Ibid.*, p. 15.
12. Jean Epstein, 'On Certain Characteristics of Photogénie', trans. Tom Milne, *Afterimage* 10 (Autumn, 1981), p. 20.
13. Walter Benjamin, 'The Work of Art in the Age of Its Technological Reproducibility: Second Version', in *Selected Writings: 1935–1938*, trans. Edmund Jephcott and Harry Zohn (Cambridge, MA: Harvard University Press, 2002), p. 117.
14. Walter Benjamin, *Selected Writings: 1927–1934*, trans. Rodney Livingston (Cambridge, MA: Harvard University Press, 1999), p. 173. For Benjamin, arguably, the distinction between film and photography is quantitative rather than qualitative. The decay of the aura is defined as something that is happening in 'present day perception' (p. 104). The first example given of the masses' desire to overcome the uniqueness and distance of objects is 'the reproduction [of an object], as offered by illustrated magazines and newsreels'. This example seems to include both photography and film. See *Selected Writings*, vol. 3, pp. 104–6.

15. *Impressionism and Post-Impressionism 1874–1904: Sources and Documents,* ed. and trans. Linda Nochlin (Englewood Cliffs, NJ: Prentice-Hall, 1966), p. 30.

16. Gilles Deleuze, *Cinema 1: The Movement-Image,* trans. Hugh Tomlinson and Barbara Habberjam (Minneapolis, MN: University of Minnesota Press, 1991), p. 6.

17. See Meyer Schapiro, 'The Nature of Abstract Art', *Marxist Quarterly* (January–March 1937), 77–98 (p. 83); and T. J. Clark's comments on Schapiro's essay in *The Painting of Modern Life: Paris in the Art of Manet and his Followers* (Princeton, NJ: Princeton University Press, 1984): 'The few lines [of Schapiro's essay] devoted to Impressionist painting still seem to me the best thing on the subject, simply because they suggest so tellingly that form of the new art is inseparable from its content – those "objective forms of bourgeois recreation in the 1860s and 1870s"' (p. 5).

18. In Nochlin, *Impressionism,* p. 17.

19. Henri Bergson, *Creative Evolution,* trans. Arthur Mitchell (Mineola, NY: Dover, 1998), p. 306.

20. Clark, *Painting,* p. 20.

21. In Nochlin, *Impressionism,* p. 18.

22. See Hegel's *Philosophy of Subjective Spirit,* Part 3 of *Enzyklopädie der philosophischen Wissenschaften im Grundrisse,* ed. and trans. M. J. Petry (Dordrecht: D. Reidel, 1978), p. 181.

23. Thomas Pfau, *Romantic Moods: Paranoia, Trauma and Melancholy 1790–1840* (Baltimore, MD: Johns Hopkins University Press, 2005), pp. 255–6.

24. Maxim Gorky, review of the Lumière programme at the Nizhni-Novgorod Fair (4 July 1896), in *In the Kingdom of Shadows: A Companion to Early Cinema,* eds Colin Harding and Simon Popple (London: Cygnus Arts, 1996), p. 5.

25. See Benjamin, *Selected Writings,* vol. 3, p. 127.

26. See Doane, *The Emergence of Cinematic Time*; Dai Vaughan, *For Documentary: Twelve Essays* (Berkeley, CA: University of California Press, 1999), p. 7.

27. Doane, *Emergence,* p. 94.

28. Quoted in Doane, *Emergence,* p. 94.

Part 3

Cinematicity in the 'Classic' Cinema Age

Cinematicity of Speech and Visibility of Literature: The Poetics of Soviet Film Scripts of the Early Sound Film Era

ANKE HENNIG

This chapter focuses on the relationship between literature and film in the Soviet film culture of the 1930s.[1] What directors like Sergei Eisenstein, Vsevolod Pudovkin and Grigori Aleksandrov[2] feared most in this new era of sound film was that the spoken word, once admitted, would change cinema forever. Film would never again be a 'pure' medium. Soviet cinematic dramaturgy and its attendant discourses brought these debates into sharp focus. Well-known scriptwriters such as Mikhail Bleiman proclaimed the film script as an artwork in its own right, and claimed for it the status of a new genre, fourth in line with epic, drama and poetry. Repeatedly, however, Bleiman's scripts were criticized for not being cinematic enough on the grounds that they told the story but did not show it. This obvious difference between literature and film – one tells; the other shows – hides another much more complex distinction: that between story and plot. Not telling the story in effect entails the creation of a story without plot, or the importation of the cinematic plot into the script. As we shall see, this meant that the borderline between literature and film came to be relocated into the written text itself. The same was also true for film. Once the spoken word had become part of film, its borderline with literature was relocated into cinema. In consequence, the inclusion of literary forms (sound, the spoken word and story) into the world of film pushes a narrowly conceived notion of cinematicity beyond the 'purely' visual.

Film-theoretical discussions in the Soviet Union of the 1920s, which took the form of radical manifestoes and heated debates about the nature of film, are remembered today for their antagonism between defenders of narration and partisans of showing. It was Viktor Shklovsky's *Literature and Cinematography* (1923)[3] that made this polemic juxtaposition, at least in part, so influential. Even the title of the book is indicative of where he thought the battle lines should be drawn. By conceiving of literature and film as two modes of presentation, the separation between narrating and showing is made all the more acute. The poetics of cinematic dramaturgy – that is, the writing of film scripts – was profoundly shaped by this opposition from the very beginning. The scriptwriter Natan Zarkhi's claim that 'cinematic film does not narrate, it shows'[4] not only echoes this position, but also implies that there is such a thing as 'pure cinematics' that must be safeguarded from contamination by the other arts, especially literature.

The demand then that 'cinematic' scripts have to show rather than narrate is made as early as the 1920s; it is also a demand to which cinematic drama-turgy continued to respond throughout the 1930s.[5] This said, the poetics of cinematic dramaturgy by no means always conformed to these demands, giving rise to widespread complaints about the 'non-cinematic' nature of film scripts. In the 1930s, these complaints increased extensively. On the one hand this had to do with language gaining new powers over cinema in the era of sound film, and, on the other, it had to do with an altered conception of film more generally: 'Pure cinematics' began to be relegated to the past. Pudovkin, for example, lamented: 'An abundance of conversational scenes, purely theatrical monologues, in which the story replaces the showing typical of cinema, creates a slowness and heaviness so alien to the most dynamic of the arts – cinema.'[6]

In addition, the demands for showing and for the exclusion of narrating entered into new contexts: While film script-related criticism was part of film-theoretical discourses in the 1920s, such criticism was assimilated into the history of literature during the course of the 1930s. The view that the film script is a fourth genre of literature – a view affirmed by the 1934 Soviet Writers' Congress – inscribes the questions of narrating and showing within a context of literariness. This raises two attendant questions: What could a literary text without narration be? How does showing stand in relation to the literariness of the film script?

It is worth recalling here that the exclusion of narrating touches on one of the foundational questions concerning the constitution of literary texts as 'literary'. Twentieth-century theories of prose offer a number of ideas: the narratological concept of the *plot*, the formalist concept of the *sujet*, Roland Barthes's *narrativity*, Tzvetan Todorov's *discourse*, Karlheinz Stierle's *Text der Geschichte* (text of the story/history) or Gérard Genette's *narrative*.[7] All of these terms seek to capture the communicative level of narrative, that is, the level at which the message is truly poetically stylized. It is precisely and only at this level that an originary self-referentiality of the literary emerges; and it is finally only when this level is reached that literariness has access to its own medium, that is, language. When it came to the genre of the film script in the Soviet view, however, none of this was to be relevant: 'It is not written the way a fiction writer writes his works, who conducts his narrative in his own name or in the name of one of his characters, who subordinates the depiction of behaviour and the conversation of his characters to his narrative style, who crafts language and who uses purely verbal means of figuration'.[8] This statement by Valentin Turkin, like 1930s writings on cinematic dramaturgy more generally, shows itself unaware of the fact that in trying to exclude narration, one in effect also eliminates an entire level of literary textuality. This has far-reaching consequences for the system of genres as a whole, but also for particular genres and their conventions. If narration is to be excluded in order to attain immediate transparency of meaning (that the Stalinist symbolic order was of course obsessed with), the potentials for meaning-construction are radically reduced. In consequence, all those genres that are constituted primarily on the level of narration disappear from the formal canon of Stalinism; this includes autobiographies, diaries, memoirs and genres of prose structured by rhythms and leitmotifs. Even the novel is reduced to the narrative dimension of action (*rasskaz*).[9]

Furthermore, those genres, the narratives of which contain the level at which the message is organized (*plot*, *sujet*, *discourse* and *narrativity*), are also affected. Exemplary in this regard are those genres in which the level of communication is tied negatively to the story (*fabula*) – namely, mystery novellas, intrigues of defamation and various crime fictions, which presuppose a level of the plot that can be organized independently, and in which information can be hidden from the reader, falsified or postponed. These particular genres are unthinkable within the formal canon determined by Stalinism, although none of them was in fact ideologically suspect or explicitly prohibited. Ultimately, this results in the deliberate de-differentiation of the formalist distinction between *fabula* and *sujet*, undertaken by the scriptwriter Aleksandr Chirkov in 1939.[10] Meanwhile, those genres that focus on a dialectics of hero and action increasingly make do without a narrative plot.

THE CINEMATICITY OF SPEECH: MIKHAIL BLEIMAN'S POETICS

It could be argued that Mikhail Bleiman's search for an alternative to narration manifests itself in the poetics of speech of his scripts.[11] As Bleiman and his co-author Manuel' Bol'shintsov put it with reference to *The Great Citizen* (1938):

> It was difficult and complicated to create the script. And when we had written it, it became clear that it could either not be filmed at all or that it had to be filmed as it had been written. We were horrified by the abundance of text, the absence of external effects, the script's paucity in outwardly expressed action. We tried to get back to the 'cinematograph'. It didn't work. Almost against our will, the scenario turned out to be an incursion into the domain of speech cinema, where the text does not compensate for the action but *is* the action.[12]

Bleiman and Bol'shintsov also elaborate on how their poetics of speech construction raises problems for shooting and montage:

> It was clear that the usual methods of shooting and editing would only spoil the script. In the analysis of each scene, it became obvious that the jerking caused by montage in the transition from frame to frame destroys the continuity of the text and of the action. [. . .] The task determined the structure of frames, camera angles, and the *mise en scène*.[13]

Of all the films made in the 1930s, *The Great Citizen* has the longest lasting shots and the greatest spatial depth in its *mise-en-scène*.[14] It is the poetics of speech that gives this film its particularity; although we should keep in mind here that it was not until the 1950s that Soviet film practice developed the kind of off-screen sound in which speech could reverberate without a visible source on screen, such as is the case here. It was only after the Second World War that scriptwriters such as Evgeny Gabrilovich first suggested the use of voice-over narration, for instance. Before then, such a practice was widely regarded as an intrusion of literariness into the domain of film.

In this context it is not surprising why Bleiman should have faced considerable criticism. His entire *oeuvre* is comprised of scripts based on a strong poetics of speech sound.[15] The intensive use of speech was criticized as early as 1933 with reference to his libretto *Capital Overhaul* (*Kapital'nyi remont*): 'Thought is revealed in the libretto mainly through conversations, whereas it should flow from the major conflicts of the work.'[16] The rejection of his 1934 script *The March* also lists the poetics of speech as a reason. The report states: 'In addition to the script being unacceptable for political reasons, there are several artistic shortcomings. (a) In the script, there is no dynamic development of the action. Most / a large part of the action is overburdened with long conversations.'[17] It is possible, therefore, to understand the use of speech in Bleiman's scripts as a material instantiation of the *sujet* in the formalist sense of the term. This includes, on the one hand, the attempt at a thoroughgoing structuration of the work and, on the other, the attempt to establish a material communicative basis with the reader, both of which determine the *sujet*. What is striking about the *March* script is not just the intensity of speech but also its experimentation with the structure of the *sujet*. Instead of the usual format of sequencing the scenes by tying them to a particular plot (*sujet*), this script uses fifteen episodes to visualize its theme. Each of these episodes simultaneously concretizes a whole series of *sujet*-like structures. The introduction, for example, is comprised of three *sujet*-like structures: the opening credits,[18] the paratext of the fiction[19] and a musical overture:

> The intertitles appear on the screen. Softly drawn, the figure of Lenin emerges from the card.

Leaning, as if rushing forward, over the wooden barrier, he speaks / the words in the intertitle /
WE HAVE ABSOLUTELY NO INTENTIONS AGAINST THE INDEPENDENCE OF POLAND ...
There is a young man in the crowd, with big eyes, smiling /. This is Petrov – the hero of our film. He's excited. He sees Lenin. He hears his voice /.
REMEMBER, COMRADES, YOU GO TO THE FRONT NOT AS OPPRESSORS BUT AS LIBERATORS.
The words on the background of the card.
And now we see the movement of our troops – the rapid counter-attack of the Red Army. Breakthrough near Zhitomir.
Rising and developing into a sound of enormous power, the overture evolves into battle march – a marching song.
/ This musical theme resounds later in the film, organically fused with the structure of the *sujet*. It is a part of the film /. [20]

Several modes of expression are synthetically superimposed here, among which speech (highlighted in capital letters) is privileged. Lenin's speech is presented in alternation with intertitles, script-image (*Schriftbild*), and sound. The symptosis of different media forms – of sound and writing, or image and space – is illustrative of the way in which the entire script retains its consistency, linking the episodes with one another and with the overall subject matter. This is to say, Lenin's speech has inspired the March: the military action as well as the film about it. Emblematic of this procedure is the fact that Bleiman, in the introduction just quoted, assigns the 'multipoint' (*mnogotochie*) to Lenin's speech.[21]

What is remarkable above all in this early script of Bleiman's is the transition of speech from the level of the *sujet* to the level of the *fabula*. This can be seen, for example, in the translation of the narrating authority 'our': 'Our film' becomes 'our troops'. Similarly, the transition from the actor's name to the image of his body marks the translation from *sujet* to character: The 'hero of our film' is still bracketed by the narrative commentary, but the *fabula* speaks of the 'movement of our troops'. This shows that the de-differentiation of *fabula* and *sujet* is not just a theoretical position in the Soviet film culture of the late 1930s; rather, it also determines the poetics of the script and, as can be seen from the diminishing stock of genres available to filmmakers, it directly influences filmmaking.

In Bleiman, speech seeks to participate in the structuring power of the *fabula* by transforming characters into authors and their speech into narratives. His *The Journey to Arzrum at the Time of the 1829 Campaign* (1937) syncretically superimposes *fabula* and *sujet* as well as author and character. It is a travel script in which the main character is none other than the Russian poet

Aleksandr Pushkin. Like most of Bleiman's scripts, it follows the chronotope of a path or route, with a central figure following that path. The journey as minimal model of an adventure *fabula* attempts to take up and manifest the entire cycle of the literary word, that is, of the *sujet*.[22] The speech of the author Pushkin unfolds along the path, and he describes the locales on the wayside, and has encounters that develop into conversations. The conversations take place not only on the occasion of such encounters, but the occasions that give rise to conversations in turn are central topics of the conversations themselves.

Bleiman's script adapts an episode from one of Pushkin's own travel descriptions where Pushkin is enjoying a Kalmuck woman's hospitality at a roadside inn. The poem that describes this encounter with the Kalmuck woman comes up again later in the course of the journey when Pushkin presents the poem, written on a piece of paper, to an illiterate guard as a transit pass. Just as in the film *The Great Citizen*, the writing here too is 'curiously illegible'.[23] The poem is shown and made public but stripped of the legibility that characterizes the specific visibility of written literature.[24] There is a difference in the treatment of this episode as it occurs in Pushkin's narrative (*Erzählung*) and in the Bleiman script. On the level of the narrated (*Erzählten*), it is introduced in the same manner as it is by Pushkin, by being presented as a pass written on paper to someone who does not know how to read Russian. On the level of the narrative, however, Bleiman incorporates a poem, now entitled 'To the Kalmuck Woman', which Pushkin had written during the journey but had not included in his narrative. The poem is therefore inserted on the level of the *sujet*, and only on this level is it legible.

The character of this script is the author; his words are inserted into the dialogue of the *fabula*, but being the author's Word, it is not *fabula*-like. Bleiman adds a postscript to the Pushkin script in which he explains that he has used historical and verified biographical material.[25] The oddness of Bleiman's description of the way he used the material is particularly striking against the background of the dramaturgical rules for cutting down material in screen adaptations of literary texts:[26] 'Individual episodes of Pushkin's text and the text of the memoirs have been completely transferred to the narrative.'[27] Bleiman obviously translates the 'text of history'[28] instead of the 'history'. He does not reduce the episodes to their motifs but transfers the texts in their entirety. Recalling Boris Tomashevsky's definition of the *sujet*, this complete text is nothing other than the order of the *sujet*: 'the same motifs in that order and connection in which they are given in the work'.[29] Bleiman attempts to let Pushkin's authority speak: He gives a voice to words that are not concretizations of the *fabula* but of the *sujet* in order to attain a pure literary communication without object. The translation of Pushkin's journey sketch also turns this material into an argument in favour of memoirs – those forms of expression that, as narrations without *fabula*, are excluded from the Stalinist system of genres: 'Besides the *Journey to Arzrum* and Pushkin's correspondence, we used the memoirs of Yuzefovich, Savastayanov, Pushchin, Lorer, Gaigeblor, Potosky, Tornau, Filipson, Belyaev, Rozen, Bestuzhev.'[30] In referring to the authority of Pushkin's authorial Word, Bleiman thus brings together the entire repertoire of just the kind of narrative literariness discussed above: sketches of journeys, diaries, factographic biographies, exchanges of letters and memoirs.

In this script, with its intensified literariness, Bleiman seeks to promote a cinematicity of speech. In a later scene, the travellers cross the river Archapay (or Akhuryan). It originates in Armenia and flows south, forming a natural border between Russia and Turkey, until it flows into the Aras, which originates in Turkey and passes the biblical Mount Ararat. Pushkin describes his impression in a poetic metaphor, that is, he compares the sublime beauty of Archapay on the Russian side of the border to the biblical Mount Ararat on the Turkish side. In Pushkin we read:

> Before us shone a small river, which we had to cross. – 'Here is the Archapay river', the Cossack said to me. Archapay! Our border! It was worth Mount Ararat. I rode down to the river with an inexplicable feeling. I had never seen a foreign land. The border was something mysterious to me; from childhood on, adventures were my favourite dream.[31]

Bleiman, by contrast, renders this passage as:

> Before them shone a small river, which they had to cross. The Cossack halted his horse and held out his hand holding his whip: Here is the Archapay river. Our border – he explained. Pushkin spurred his horse. The Cossack looked at him with a blank look. Archapay! It was worth Mount Ararat. He rode down to the river with an inexplicable feeling. He had never seen a foreign land. The border was something mysterious to him; from childhood on, adventures were his favourite dream.[32]

Parts of the text are given to the Cossack who is also ascribed the function of visually commenting on Pushkin's overtly poetic impression of the Archapay river by way of a pointing gesture and the cut to his blank face. The use of personal pronouns (I/he, we, our) in combination with direct, indirect (him), and narrating speech runs through various degrees of visual concreteness and refines these degrees around the centrepiece phrase 'Archapay! It was worth Mount Ararat'. Ultimately, however, Pushkin's comparison of the Archapay river to the biblical Mount Ararat itself remains purely verbal.

Bleiman assigns his adaptation of Pushkin's narrative to the genre '*povest*'. How then is a 'plot for the cinema' (*povest' dlya kino*) different from a 'cinematic

story' (*kinorasskaz*)? The 'cinematic story' is an instrument for turning literature into film; in the Soviet Union of the 1930s, it was a preliminary stage
to the film script. We may approximate it to the stage called, in English, the
film 'treatment'. The importance of the cinematic story becomes apparent
in articles written for the review *Gazeta Kino* around the big film script competition of 1938. Time and again, the claim is made that the cinematic story
is a preliminary form of the film script.[33] The article 'What is a Cinematic
Story?' ('*Chto takoe kinorasskaz?*') explains: 'The conditions of the competition announced by the Committee for Cinema Affairs permit not only scripts
that are completely prepared but also narratives for the cinema or cinematic
stories.'[34] Yet, instead of showing the *fabula*, which is the goal of the cinematic
story (*kinorasskaz*), Bleiman's 'plot for the cinema' attempts a 'narrating'
(*povestvovanie*) for the cinema. Thus, he undertakes not just a visualization of
narrative structures, but he describes the emergence of narrative speech from
non-verbal visuality.

THE VISIBILITY OF LITERATURE

In the years from 1933 to 1940, Bleiman attracts attention with a series of
critical articles, such as, 'What is a Script?' ('Chto takoe scenary?'),[35] 'On
the Most Miscellaneous Things' ('O samykh raznoobraznykh veshchakh')[36]
and 'Appearance in a Debate' ('Vystuplenie v preniyakh').[37] They clarify
the paradoxical function of speech for the cinematic nature of the script. In
Bleiman's case, speech as the guarantor of literary expression does not refer
to the sound of film but to its visuality. Here, the tension between language
and visibility is no longer a tension *between* 'purified' literariness and 'purified'
cinematicity, evoked at the beginning of this chapter; rather, the tension is
modelled as a dynamics *within* literariness and *within* cinematicity. Here, a
reversal of perspective becomes palpable: what is necessary for survival from
the perspective of cinematic dramaturgy, namely to emphasize the verbal
character of cinema in its conflict with the *mise-en-scène*, precisely does not
serve the interests of literature. For literature, the interest of the script lies
in its being a text meant to be visualized. In this context, the script does not
act as a substitute for literature in film but, for a number of scriptwriters, it
marks the search for the point at which cinematicity is already inherent in
literariness. Volkov, for example, writes: 'I have already pointed out how
much the study of literature can give script writers as far as the visual and
audible quality of the image [*obraz*] is concerned.'[38] Within literature, it is the
script, the 'fourth major genre' of literature, which names the engagement of
literature with its visibility. Time and again, scriptwriters' engagements with
the cinematicity of literature go beyond contemporary forms of the filmic

medium and appeal to a more comprehensive concept of cinematicity.

This cinematicity of literature manifests itself as the exact negative image of the then-current filmic practice of showing (*pokaz*) the *fabula* or the narrative: the cinematic story (*kinorasskaz*). The 'showability' of meaning-making derives from the relation between literature and theatre, a relation that is conspicuous in the third major genre: drama. Drama mediates words in the gestures of the one who acts. In *showing*, visuality is incarnation. The more cinematic dramaturgy is oriented towards drama, the more visuality tends to be reduced to showing.

For Bleiman, the image as something shown is related to expression, but as something seen, it is related to representation (*izobrazhenie*). Speech must become material and visible in order no longer to appear as simply the expression of meaning. Thus speech exceeds the limits of literature in that something that cannot be expressed in the latter here finds form. Oksana Bulgakova writes about *The Great Citizen*: 'The text represented in the film functions only as a marker of and a reference to the unspeakable and the non-spoken.'[39] What is crucial here is that this unspeakable does not denote silence but refers to seeing. The source of subjective, individual speech is a seeing that lies beyond speaking. This thematizes a difference that is in many ways central to cinematic dramaturgy: The confluence of speaking and seeing reveals that seeing has undergone a reduction in its visual dimension. 'Seeing, as a special act of individualization, is present here only negatively, as a threat. Seeing that speaks is not visual.'[40] The Russian avant-garde filmmakers had already favoured a non-objective seeing[41] and, accordingly, they did not reflect on the visual substance of shooting films. Further, the above mentioned 'showing' practices a mode of presentation in cinema that makes meaning perceptible without attaining a concrete visuality. This is made particularly clear by a juxtaposition suggested in the 1950s by the inventor of montage, Lev Kuleshov. Kuleshov distinguishes between meaningful seeing (*videnie*) and staring (*glazet'*) and rejects the latter as a blank registering of the visible. The philosopher Mikhail Ryklin summarizes the problem of mere seeing: 'Banal visibility is equivalent to its desacralization.'[42]

In his essay 'What is a Script?' (1933), Bleiman is concerned with the visibility of literature. When he claims that the arts generally are synthetic and criticizes the separation of literature and film in particular, a separation that turns the script into a mere stage or step in the process of filmic creation without any artistic expression of its own, he argues for a sensual figuration of literary expression. For Bleiman, the script can attain its own expression only if film practice eliminates the separation of literature and film. In his view, the idea that the script acquires its full literary value, as proven by Sergei Eisenstein or Vsevolod Pudovkin, inverts the problem: It addresses the literariness of film instead of raising the question of the visuality of literature. The script's 'achieved' literariness is insufficient because it cannot account for the value of orienting the script towards the film. In Bleiman, the script is (film-)'oriented' literature. Bleiman refuses to see in this 'orientation' towards film an insufficient literariness or to reject the interest taken by literature in film as a self-estrangement of literature. A conception of literature that appeals to the view that 'Goethe was able to do without cinema'[43] is too narrow for him.

The film script, to conclude, incarnates the orientation of literature towards its 'visibility' and 'audibility'. It testifies to the interest literature takes in its elaboration, materialization and sensual reception. Accordingly, Bleiman in 1935 polemicizes against Béla Balázs's 'The Spirit of Film',[44] which, in his view, touches neither on the sensuality of the filmic nor on the sensuality of the literary. By insisting on the sensual figuration of literary expression, Bleiman thus appeals to a more comprehensive concept of cinematicity that is equally capable of capturing the cinematicity of speech and the visibility of literature.

Translated by Nils F. Schott

Notes

1   This chapter is based on my book, *Sowjetische Kinodramaturgie: Konfliktlinien zwischen Literatur und Film in der Sowjetunion der dreißiger Jahre* [*Soviet Cinematic Dramaturgy: Lines of Conflict between Literature and Film in the Soviet Union of the 1930s*] (Berlin: Verlag Vorwerk 8, 2010). Unless otherwise noted, all translations from the Russian are my own and have been checked against the original.

2. See their jointly drafted 'Notes on Sound', in Ian Christie and Richard Taylor, eds, *The Film Factory: Russian and Soviet Cinema in Documents 1896–1939* (Abingdon: Routledge, 2002), pp. 234–5. Here, they warn that 'an incorrect understanding of the potential of the new technical invention might not only hinder the development and improvement of cinema as an art form but might also threaten to destroy all its present formal achievements to date' (p. 234).

3. Viktor Shklovsky, *Literatura i kinematograf* (1923)/*Literature and Cinematography*, trans. Irina Masinovsky, intro. Richard R. Sheldon (Champaign: Dalkey Archive Press, 2008).

4. «[. . .] кинофильма показывает, а не рассказывает.» N. Zarkhi, Kniga Kinematurgiya'. [nezakonchennyi avtograf]. mashinopisnaya kopiya. – RGALI (Russian State Archives). 2003; op. 1; ed. chr. 93, 214. According to Tokareva, one of the typical flaws of most film scripts is that they do not show actions but merely narrate the result of actions. M. Tokareva, 'Itogi stsenarnogo konkursa', *Iskusstvo kino* 3 (1939), 53–5 (p. 55).

5. See, for example, Valentin Turkin, 'O kinosyuzhete i kinostsenary', *Iskusstvo kino*

8 (1938), 28–31 (p. 28); Nikolai Kolin, 'V pomoshch' nachinayushchemu stsena-ristu', *Konkurs na kinostsenary* (Moscow: Goskinoizdat, 1938), p. 11.

6. «Изобилие разговорных сцен, чисто сценических монологов, в которых рассказ заменяет типичный для кино непосредственный показ, создают медлительность, тяжеловесность действия, столь несвойственные самому динамическому из искусств – кино.» Vsevolod Pudovkin, *Osnovnye zadachi kinoiskusstva*, 1934, Sobranie sochineny v trekh tomakh (Moscow: Iskusstvo, 1975), p. 160. The survival of this *topos* among directors is due, in particular, to montage cinema's resistance to sound film and an insistence on the media ontology of silent film.

7. See Roland Barthes, *Selected Writings*, ed. Susan Sontag (London: Fontana, 1983), p. 285; Tzvetan Todorov, 'The Categories of Literary Narrative', *Papers on Language and Literature* 16.1 (1980), 3–37; Karlheinz Stierle, *Text als Handlung* (Munich: Fink, 1975), p. 53; Gerard Genette, *Narrative Discourse: An Essay in Method*, trans. Jane E. Lewin (Ithaca, NY: Cornell University Press, 1983), p. 25.

8. «Он не пишется так, как пишет свои произведения писатель-беллетрист, который ведет повествование от своего имени или от имени того или другого своего персонажа, подчиняет стилю повествования изображение поведения, разговоры своих героев, обрабатывает язык и использует средства чисто словесной образности.» Valentin Turkin, 'O kinosyuzhete i kinostsenary', *Iskusstvo kino* 8 (1938), 28–31 (p. 30). Here, Turkin emphasizes once again that a script is not supposed to narrate but to show.

9. Compare Vladimir Nemirovich-Danchenko's observation that the novel is too powerful for theatre and cinema ('Ob instsenirovkach v teatre i kino', *Iskusstvo kino* 3 (1936), 20–1 [p. 20]). E. Zil'ver articulates a critique of the dominance of drama-oriented scripts and a demand for an orientation towards the *sujet* of the novel ('K probleme syuzheta', *Iskusstvo kino* 3 (1936), 12–15 (p. 15).

10. Aleksandr Chirkov, *Ocherki dramaturgii filma* (Moscow: Goskinoizdat, 1939), pp. 44–5.

11. There is an incomplete list of his scripts in *Stsenaristy sovetskogo kino, 1917–67* (Moscow: Iskusstvo, 1972), pp. 46–7. It lists thirty-three scripts in the years 1924 to 1970; *The March*, which was written in 1934 and will be discussed in what follows, is not listed.

12. «Сценарий создавать было сложно и трудно. И когда он был написан, нам стало ясно, что либо его нельзя снять совсем, либо его нужно снимать так, как он был написан. Нас ужасало изобилие текста, отсутствие внешних эффектов, бедность сценария внешне выраженным действием. Мы пытались вернуть дело к 'кинематографу'. Не выходило. Сценарий оказался почти невольно для нас, выпадкой в область кино речевого, где текст не компенсирует действие, а является основным действием.» *Gazeta Kino*, 11 February 1938. Two months later, the authors are already convinced that with 'pure speech cinema' they have successfully opened up a new path and that speech is not a flaw but the script's 'main dramatic element'. Mikhail Bleiman,

Manuel' Bol'shintsov and Fridrikh Ermler, 'Rabota nad stsenariem', *Iskusstvo kino* 4–5 (1938), 30–1 (p. 30).

13. «Было ясно, что обычные методы съемки и монтажа только испортят сценарий. При анализе каждой сцены становилось очевидным, что монтажные рывки при переходе с плана на план уничтожают игровую и текстовую непрерывность. ... Это задание определило построение кадра, точки съемки, мизансцены.» *Gazeta Kino*, 11 February 1938.

14. Maya Turovskaya, 'Kino totalitarnoi epochi', *Kino: Politika i lyudi, 30e gody* (Moscow: Materik, 1995), p. 49.

15. For his work on *My Motherland* (*Moya rodina*) one would have to consult the film, because the only excerpt of the script ever to be published appeared under the title 'The Bridge' ('Most') in *Gazeta Kino*, 30 June 1932. In the film, the appearance of language is staged as emerging from childish-expressive mumbled speech and from refugees' speech, which mixes languages to the point of indiscernibility, and as an initiation into Russian (Evgeni Margolit, 'Problema mnogoyazychiya v rannem sovetskom zvukovom kino (1930–1935)', *Sovetskaya vlast' i media*, eds Sabine Hänsgen and Hans Günther (St. Petersburg: Akademichesky proekt, 2006), p. 384.

16. «Мысль выявляется в либретто преимущественно в разговорах, тогда как она должна вытекать из основных конфликтов произведения.» Mikhail Bleiman, Gosfil'mofond; national fond; personal files; fond 241/1; Kapital'nyi remont. sentence GUK 27 November 1933, 9.

17. «Помимо неприемлемости сценария по политическим соображениям, в сценарии наличествуют недостатки творческого порядка. а) В сценарии нет динамического развития действия. Больше всего/большая часть/ действия загружена длинными разговорами.» Mikhail Bleiman, Gosfil'mofond; national fond; personal files; fond 241/1; Pochod. sentence GUK 11 October 1934, No. 15–17.

18. The missing reference to the director corresponds to the naming of authors and actors.

19. See Gerard Genette, *Paratexts: Thresholds of Interpretation*, trans. Jane E. Lewin (Cambridge: Cambridge University Press, 1997). Of the paratexts listed by Genette, the opening of Bleiman's script superimposes several at once: the editorial information page, the cardboard of the book cover and the title page vignette.

20. «Надписи проходят. Мягким контуром через карту проступает фигура Ленина. Наклоняясь стремительным движением вперед, через деревянный барьер трибуны – он говорит/ слова и надписью/:
НИ МАЛЕЙШИХ ЗАМЫСЛОВ ПРОТИВ НЕЗАВИСИМОСТИ ПОЛЬШИ МЫ НЕ ИМЕЕМ ...
[...]
Вот в толпе молодой парень с большими глазами с улыбкой/. Это Петров – герой нашей фильмы. Он взволнован. Он видит Ильича. Он слышит его голос/.

ПОМНИТЕ, ТОВАРИЩИ, ВЫ ИДЕТЕ НА ФРОНТ НЕ КАК УГНЕТАТЕЛИ, А КАК ОСВОБОДИТЕЛИ.

Слова на фоне карты. И вот мы видим движение наших частей – стремительный контрудар Красной Армии. Прорыв под Житомиром.

Порастая и развиваясь в звучание огромной мощности, увертюра переходит в боевой марш-походную песню.

/Эта музыкальная тема прозвучит потом в фильме, органически спаянная в сюжетную композицию. Она составная часть картины/

[. . .].»

Mikhail Bleiman and Yuri Tarich, *Pokhod: Zvukovoi stsenary* (Leningrad, 1934). Gosfil'mofond; national fond, personal files. Mikhail Bleiman, Yuri Tarich, item 241/1, 1–3.

21. On the function of the dash in silent film intertitles as a sign of a cut, compare Yuri Tsivyan, 'K semiotike nadpisei v nemom kino: Nadpis' y ustnaya rech', *Zerkalo: Semiotika zerkal'nosti*, Trudy po znakovym sistemam XXII (Tartu: 1988), 152; on the 'multipoint' ('mnogotochie') in scripts as an index of a continual alternation between media, see my article, '"I otkrylos' tret"e dobavochnoe ucho": K pafosu medial'nogo perevorota v kinodramaturgii 30-ych godov', in K. Aymermakher, G. Bordyugov and I. Grabovsky, eds, *Kul'tura i vlast' v usloviyakh kommunikatsionnoi revolyucii XX. Veka* (Moscow: Airo, 2002), pp. 168–75.

22. Evgeni Margolit, in a conversation with the author, claims that there is a second script of this kind from 1939: *Balzac in Russia* (*Bal'zak v Rossii*).

23. Oksana Bulgakova, 'Ton und Bild: Das Kino als Synkretismus-Utopie', *Musen der Macht*, eds Juri Murashov and Georg Witte (Munich: Fink, 2003), pp. 173–86 (p. 184).

24. See Maurice Blanchot, *The Gaze of Orpheus, and Other Literary Essays*, trans. P. Sitney (Barrytown, NY: Station Hill Press, 1981), p. 116.

25. Also in Mikhail Bleiman, 'Puteshestvie v Arzrum', *Iskusstvo kino* 2 (1937), 25–6 (p. 25). Compare Slonimsky and Shklovsky's articles on their Pushkin scripts: Aleksandr Slonimsky, 'Pushkin v licee', *Iskusstvo kino* 2 (1937), p. 24, and Viktor Shklovsky, 'Stsenary "Kapitanskaya dochka"', *ibid.*, p. 47.

26. See, in particular, the rules for cutting established by Turkin – that Bleiman's procedure clearly violates – in Turkin's adaptation of Serafimovich's *The Iron Flood*, «отбрасывались описания (пейзажи, литературные характеристики) повествовательные экскурсы в прошлое [. . .], рассуждения и лирические отступления, недейственные жанровые картинки». Valentin Turkin, 'O kinoinstsenirovke literaturnykh proizvedenii', in I. Popov, ed., *Kak my rabotaem nad kinostsenariem* (Moscow: Kinofotoizdat, 1936), pp. 107–47 (p. 134).

27. «Отдельные эпизоды из пушкинского текста и текста мемуаров целиком перенесены в повесть.» Mikhail Bleiman and I. Zil'bershtein, 'Puteshestvie v Arzrum vo vremya pokhoda 1829 g.: povest dlya kino', *Zvezda* 1 (1937), 67–101 (p. 100).

28. Karlheinz Stierle, *Text als Handlung* (Munich: Fink, 1975), p. 53.

29. «совокупность тех же мотивов, той последовательности и связи, в

которой они даны в произведении.» Boris Tomashevsky, *Teoriya literatury. Poetika* (Moscow, Leningrad: Gosizdat, 1925), p. 138.

30. «Кроме ‚Путешествия в Арзрум' и переписки Пшкина мы использовали воспоминания Юзефовича, Савастьянова, Пущина, Лорера, Гаигеблора, Потоского, Торнау, Филипсона, Беляева, Розена, Бестужева.» Mikhail Bleiman and I. Zil'bershtein, 'Puteshestvie v Arzrum', p. 101.

31. «Перед нами блистала речка, через которую мы должны переправиться. 'Вот и Арчапай', сказал мне казак. Арчапай! Наша граница! Это стоило Арарата. Я поскакал к реке с чувством неизъяснимым. Никогда еще не видал чужой земли. Граница имела для меня что-то таинственное; с детских лет путешествия были моею любимою мечтой.» Aleksandr Pushkin, *Puteshestvie v Arzrum*, ed. Boris Tomashevsky (Leningrad: Goslitizdat, 1936 [1836]), p. 646.

32. «Перед ними блестела река, через которую они должны были переправиться. Казак остановил коня и протянул руку нагайкой: – Вот и Арчапай! Наша граница, – пояснил он. Пушкин пришпорил коня. Казак смотрел на него с недоумением. Арчапай! Это стоило Арарата. Он скакал к реке с неизъяснимым чувством. Никогда не видел он чужой земли. Граница имела для него что-то таинственное; с детских лет путешествия были его любимой мечтой.» Mikhail Bleiman and I. Zil'bershtein, 'Puteshestvie v Arzrum', p. 79.

33. «Не старайтесь сразу написать профессиональный сценарий. Пишите рассказ для кино.» Viktor Shklovsky, 'Pervye shagi', *Gazeta Kino*, 5 September 1938.

34. *Gazeta Kino*, 17 August 1938.

35. *Gazeta Kino*, 10 June 1933.

36. 'O samykh raznoobraznykh veshchakh' (1940), in Mikhail Bleiman, *O kino: Svidetel'skie pokazaniya. 1924–1971* (Moscow: Iskusstvo, 1973), pp. 209–14.

37. 'Vystuplenie v preniyakh ', in Bleiman,*O kino*, pp. 214–20.

38. «[…Я] уже указывал, как много может дать сценаристу изучение художественной литературы с точки зрения звукозрительности образа.» Nikolay Volkov, *Sovetskoe kino* 11 (1933), p. 61.

39. Oksana Bulgakova, 'Ton und Bild: Das Kino als Synkretismus-Utopie', *Musen der Macht*, eds Yuri Murashov and Georg Witte (Munich: Fink, 2003), pp. 173–86, (pp. 184–5).

40. «[. . .] зрение как особый акт индивидуализации присутствует здесь только негативно, как угроза. Речевое зрение не визуально.» Mikhail Ryklin, *Terrorologiki* (Tartu: Eidos, 1992), p. 29.

41. Thomáš Glanc, *Zrenie russkikh avangardov* (Prague: Nakl. Karolinum Press, 1999).

42. «Банальная зримость равносильна их десакрализации.» Mikhail Ryklin, *Terrorologiki*, p. 17.

43. Mikhail Bleiman, 'Gimnazichesky urok', *Sovetskoe kino* 6 (1934), 38–45 (p. 39).

44. Mikhail Bleiman, 'Grezy dukhovidtsa', *Sovetskoe kino* 8 (1935), 56–9. Béla Balázs's 'The Spirit of Film' was written in 1930 and translated into Russian in 1935.

CHAPTER 8

Making America Global:
Cinematicity and the Aerial View

JEFFREY GEIGER

In 1936, in the pages of *National Geographic*, readers could witness a view over Earth like none other seen before. A pull-out supplement revealed a 'global panorama' of the Black Hills of North Dakota, shot from the manned balloon Explorer I at an elevation of 72,395 feet, near 'the division between the troposphere and the stratosphere'. The image revealed 'the actual curvature of the earth – photographed from the highest point ever reached by man'.[1]

Even as such spectacular documentary images were challenging how people related to the world, motion pictures were altering modern perception itself. As outlined in this book's Introduction, the early decades of the twentieth century saw cinema being remediated into literature, the arts – into the very fabric of the thought process. By the 1920s, cinema-going was an established 'universal pastime' and by the early 1930s, two-thirds of the population of the United States was going to the cinema weekly.[2] Operating alongside related media such as radio and photojournalism, movies were a key means for the public to garner facts and information about the world: 'Not inconsequentially,' Maren Stange writes, 'the camera, with its image both realistic and mass reproducible, rose to become [as James Agee wrote] the "central instrument of its age".'[3] At the same time, new amateur and home-viewing technologies were being marketed widely, and these in turn enhanced and intensified cinematic means of perceiving and consuming space, time and movement. Film had entered into the lifeblood of popular entertainment, self-expression and individual and collective memory: It was an intimate counterpart to – rather than just an abstract reflection of – direct experience of the world.

This chapter explores connections between aerial perspectives and the moving image at a time when technological advances were producing a myriad of new ways of coming to terms with an increasingly globalized world. Aerial life, in particular, was transforming social perceptions of space and terrain, and influencing how those spaces were managed and controlled.

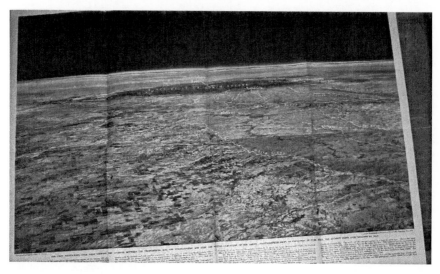

Figure 8.1 '*Global panorama'*, National Geographic *(May 1936), supplement.*

According to M. Christine Boyer:

> The rapid growth of aviation during the interwar period was mercurial, dramatically reshaping perception of the world and of space. There were daring flights of aviators challenging the breadth of oceans and deserts, the heights of Everest, the length of Africa, the uncharted terrain of the North and South Poles. The airplane not only internationalized cartography; it was a tool for exploring and controlling the colonies.[4]

The years between the wars also saw new pressures being placed on motion pictures – at one time associated chiefly with mass entertainment – to guide the public's political and moral sensibilities: to instil knowledge and understanding of citizenship, national belonging, and one's place in the world at large.[5] The Production Code of 1930 summed up mounting social concerns about the movies and the essential function they were playing in modern life:

> The motion pictures which are the most popular of modern arts for the masses, have their moral quality from the minds which produce them and from their effects on the moral lives and reactions of their audiences. [. . .] In the case of the motion pictures, this effect may be particularly emphasized because no art has so quick and so widespread an appeal to the masses. It has become in an incredibly short period, *the art of the multitudes*.[6]

Widespread demands regarding the moral outlook and quality of this 'art of the multitudes', mixed with the rise of photojournalism and public faith in the photographic document, meant that conditions were ripe for promoting the moving image as both educational and enlightening. Documentary film – an emerging form in its own right – was beginning to be seen by many as a key solution to what John Grierson called the 'great dilemma of mass education'. The answer to questions of national cohesion and social responsibility lay 'in the realm of the imaginative training for modern citizenship and not anywhere else'.[7] Grierson's influential approach foregrounded documentaries as principal vehicles for defining and shaping the role of modern citizen-subjects.

In the United States, the Griersonian approach was met with some scepticism among filmmakers and policy makers alike, but by the mid-1930s documentaries were becoming more widely used for persuasive, educational and public information purposes. Indeed, the 'films of merit' made by Pare Lorentz and funded by the Roosevelt administration resonate with Grierson's views about documentary's role in modern citizenship. As a result, what remains striking about these government films is the comprehensive outlook they strive to capture: The rhythmic coordination of image and sound works to embody a sense of national cohesion and unified civic responsibility. Without wishing to downplay the key role of voice and sound in these films,[8] my focus here will be on the strategic uses of panoramic and elevated views and, especially with the coming of the Second World War, aerial photography. During the war, the moving image and flight became aligned to a distinctly American version of global awareness – as in *Northwest USA* (aka *Pacific Northwest*, 1944), where American citizen-subjects are figured as gazing up towards, and down from, open skies. Perhaps this is due in part, as Denis Cosgrove argues, to the sense that the American scene, with its vast scale and varied topography, is most clearly revealed through 'the synoptic, aerial perspective'.[9] At the same time, with the United States on the verge of superpower status, the emotional and psychic power of aerial cinematography provided a profound illustration of – and an essential counterpart to – the nation's emerging global dominance.

THE WORLD AS PICTURE

Some of cinema's earliest innovations emerged side by side with developing modes of flight. At the Paris Universal Exposition of 1900 a key attraction was the Cineorama, where fairgoers could participate in a simulation of a hot-air balloon flight over Paris, with ten synchronized 70 mm projectors creating a 360-degree panorama of the city. Spectators gazed across intricate patterns of parks and elegant boulevards that offered an aesthetic experience far removed from the gritty streets and everyday life of the world beyond the Exposition grounds.[10] But it was only after the First World War that the development of what Paul Virilio has called 'global vision' was realized through innovations both in photography and flight,[11] breaching what formerly seemed impossible aeronautical and topographical boundaries.

The 1930s, despite the privations of the Great Depression, saw the extensive growth of global mobility (particularly for the moneyed elite): In addition to cinema's virtual tours, improved modes of transportation facilitated vast increases in tourists travelling to the far-flung corners of Earth. The 'round-the-world' cruise was becoming a fixture in the popular imagination, with unprecedented numbers circumnavigating the globe on luxury passenger ships such as the RMS *Empress of Britain* and the M/Y *Stella Polaris*, bringing the sights back home on amateur black and white and Kodachrome colour film stock. At the same time, commercial air travel became a feature of modern life: In 1935 Pan American Airlines initiated scheduled services between San Francisco and Manila, with the *China Clipper* 'an object of widespread publicity and American pride'.[12] But not all forms of globetrotting were quite so expensive: For twenty-five cents (the average price of a ticket in the early 1930s) cinemagoers could encounter wild Africa in *Trader Horn* (1931) or exotic Pacific islands in *The Pagan* (1929) while supplementing the experience with a travelogue through Argentina, Fiji, Japan or Ceylon, thanks to popular series such as James A. FitzPatrick's *Traveltalks* newsreels, distributed by MGM, Paramount and Warner Bros., and screened in thousands of theatres.

Taken together, these diverse yet interlinked phenomena indicate the emergence of what Martin Heidegger called, in 1938, the 'Age of the World Picture [*Weltbild*]', assisted by technologies that complemented and at times competed with direct experience. Heidegger surmised that 'world picture, when understood essentially, does not mean a picture of the world but the world conceived and grasped as a picture. What is, in its entirety, is now taken in such a way that it first is in being and only is in being to the extent that it is set up by man, who represents and sets forth.'[13] Consuming the world in images becomes a matter of mastering the world through making and viewing it as a (man-made) picture. At least one aspect of this phenomenon is familiar to most of us: the anticipation of framing and taking the photograph or moving image that threatens to usurp the immediacy of direct experience: The idea of the image precedes being in the world.

Along with the panorama, elevated and aerial views would become central instruments in 'conceiving and grasping' the world picture. Captured in moving images, these views could not only reveal the distant corners of Earth to the observer/cinemagoer, but fuel a sense of global engagement while situating national citizens – not unproblematically or in any ideologically neutral sense – as seeing and feeling global subjects. With the United States entrance into the Second World War, the widespread use of aerial photography came to reflect not only the military and public obsession with war being fought in and from the skies, but also latent tensions around a militarized mindset, national identity and an increasingly palpable global subjectivity. Like *Northwest USA*, information and propaganda films ranging from *The World at War* (1942), *The Valley of the Tennessee* (1944) and *The Bridge* (1944), to William Wyler's colour films *The Memphis Belle* (1944) and *Thunderbolt!* (1944/1947), all employ the skyborne viewpoint to dramatically visualize rapidly changing interfaces between the individual, national and global.

While opening on to seemingly limitless horizons, aerial views also could convey highly subjective and ideologically restricted impressions of world citizenship and global stewardship. One of the earliest aviation movies, for example, Elvira Notari's *The Heroism of an Aviator in Tripoli* (1912), constructs air pilots as heroes fighting for the colonial conquest of Libya. In the US context we find the *Pathé Review* (aka *American Travelogue*) release *Zooming over Luzon* (1930), a travelogue featuring soaring views over the Philippines, the intertitles proclaiming it, 'the first aerial motion picture log of our chief island possessions to be presented on any screen'. Here, serene views taken from high above Manila and the bays of Luzon help to convey a sense of order and control over a possession occupied by the United States, and not long past the throes of a far more disordered and fervent period of war and 'insurgency'. Indeed by 1930, numerous Philippine independence missions to Washington had been demanding self-rule (finally granted in 1946), a fact that the film's sublime airborne aesthetic helps to suppress. Hence aerial views, as Paul Virilio has convincingly argued, indicate a critical period in modernity when 'the image was starting to gain sway over the object'.[14]

I would, nonetheless, contest the 'normative' account of aerial views as emblematic 'of an acquisitive imperious and transcendent modern subjectivity'.[15] As this essay suggests, rather than the technologized aerial eye serving merely as 'a lens, hard, distanced, with no emotion or sentimentality',[16] the aerial view can engage with embodied perception, 'creating birds-eye views that are both graphic and haptic'.[17] Certain aerial views (Google Maps™, for example), as Amir Soltani argues, may invoke a sense of detachment, yet aerial views can also be intimately linked to bodily sentience. As Maurice Merleau-Ponty has suggested, embodied vision should be seen 'not as a chunk of space or a bundle of functions but that body which is an intertwining of vision and movement'.[18] Ultimately, I would call for a more dialectical reading of the role of the cinematic aerial view in modern perception, one that emphasizes how the 'aerial subject'[19] simultaneously can encompass seemingly opposed experiences of abstract distancing and emotional connection, 'objective' overseeing and embodied feeling. In this sense, the development of global perception through cinematic aerial views does not always necessarily anticipate a dehumanized modern perception – the 'desert of the real' that characterized highly restricted point-of-view aerial combat footage of the first Gulf War (1991)[20] – but can indicate the virtual *and* embodied nature of, for example, virtual reality (VR), gaming technologies, and the 'highly subjective and chaotically intense' moving images of recent conflicts such as the war in Iraq.[21]

CINEMATIC PERCEPTION

Image production and consumption can help make and remake subjective relations to the world. Significantly, the period leading up to the Second World War, during which the United States was establishing itself as a global power, corresponded with the 'feverish production of views of the world, an obsessive labor to process the world as a series of images', as Tom Gunning points out.[22] The consuming passions of travel and picture-making intensified over the course of the early twentieth century through a range of interlinked phenomena including travel by rail, balloon, aeroplane, ship and automobile, and through virtual travels such as the simulated rail or aeroplane ride and the international and ethnographic displays at World's Fairs. Complementing these experiences was a dizzying array of increasingly sophisticated still photographic and motion picture views – snapshots, post-cards, slide show projections, panoramas and aerial photography – ranging from the railway and automobile subgenres of the early 1900s to the airborne travelogues of the 1930s.

As Gunning elaborates, the technologizing of the tourist gaze, argu-ably, formed part of a widespread technologizing of perception itself. Yet this technologized perception did not in any simple or straightforward way produce the 'mechanical eye' (and 'mechanical ear') – the complex 'I, a machine' prosthesis – envisioned by Dziga Vertov.[23] Cinema, as Vivian Sobchack has contended, is a medium that is also felt as much as it is seen (and heard). Indeed for Merleau-Ponty, any one-dimensional conception of the relationship between vision and the instruments of vision would need to be contested: He argues, 'our organs are not instruments; on the contrary, our instruments are added-on organs. [. . .] I do not see according to an exterior envelope; I live it from the inside; I am immersed in it.'[24] Extrapolating from Merleau-Ponty, Sobchack further stresses the need to recognize key struc-tural and perceptual links between cinematic and direct experience. Cinema transposes modes

> of being alive and consciously embodied in the world that count for each of
> us as *direct* experience: as experience 'centered' in that particular, situated, and

solely occupied existence sensed first as 'Here, where the world touches' and then as 'Here, where the world is sensible; here, where I am'.[25]

This is not to say that cinematic and direct experience are identical, but it does suggest that cinema, through its employment of 'modes of embodied existence', may be seen not as a medium that just reflects human experience, but as a co-extension of our experience, engaging with human subjectivity 'through common structures of embodied existence, through similar modes of being-in-the-world' (5). Moreover, Sobchack argues, cinema can open up the singular and uniquely embodied world of the subject's vision and senses to a collective audience, thus making individual experience 'accessible and visible to more than a single consciousness who lives it' (9). Similarly Annette Kuhn, in her study of cinemagoing in the 1930s, stresses cinema's relationship to the sentient experience of the modern body and the collective production of 'cultural memory': Film experience 'can combine the kinetics of the moving image with the kinesis of the moving body in an all-encompassing, embodied cinema memory'.[26] These insights into cinema's address to collective experience become especially valuable when considering the uses and impact of aerial views, which I would argue are often less about individual and isolated experiences of overlooking the world picture than about using aerial cinema as a means to negotiate common and collective perceptions of national and global identities.

The links between modern and cinematic perception have been explored quite extensively, notably in the works of (among others) Giuliana Bruno, Lynn Kirby, Thomas Elsaesser, Wolfgang Schivelbusch and Anton Kaes.[27] Describing the connections between modern and cinematic perception in Walter Ruttmann's 'city symphony', *Berlin: Symphony of a Metropolis* (1927), for example, Kaes succinctly sums up the parallels between 'fast moving and transitory' modern perception, and cinematic perception:

> Nature, things, people – condensed into abstract forms (dots, lines, stripes and streaks) – disappeared the very moment they were perceived. As velocity increased, an ever-larger number of visual impressions had to be processed, producing a stimulus overload in the train traveler's perception, and we might add, in the moviegoer's perception as well. Indeed, the train traveler, sitting in an immobile state, peering out of a window, has a structural affinity with the moviegoer looking out at the screen. Neither controls the distance from the objects flying by, neither influences the sequence of what appears before one's eyes. By showing the landscape through a window – fast-moving and transitory – Ruttmann's film reflects on the conditions and practices of cinematic perception itself.[28]

Yet along with these altered states of speed and movement, perhaps nothing encapsulated the giddy intensifications of modern spatial relations more than the aerial view. From the canted and destabilizing shots taken from skyscrapers in Paul Strand's and Charles Sheeler's *Manhatta* (1921) to the gargantuan scale of photogrammetric topographical surveys that were finally being realized in the 1930s, viewing the world from the air was a 'new perception and experience of landscape hitherto unknown'.[29] Indeed the aeroplane, as Cosgrove asserts, 'is the most visible of a great range of modern technologies that [. . .] progressively annihilated space and time' over the course of the twentieth century.[30]

GIDDY HEIGHTS

Like the map and the aerial photograph, the cinematic aerial view is a graphic representation and its comprehension depends upon the instruments of vision. Such sights offer 'an Apollonian perspective of the wide earth', encouraging 'visions of rational spatial order to be written across the land', the kinds of visions that animated not only modernist planners and architects, but imperialist and military tacticians.[31] As early as 1920 the president of the Royal Geographic Society, addressing a meeting in London, offered a critique of aerial photography that underlined opposing perspectives from earth and sky: 'They soar up aloft and glide gracefully over the most terrible obstacles, insurmountable to us geographers. We dislike them especially for a very nasty habit they have contracted of taking photographs of us from that superior position in which men appear like ants, mountains like mole-hills'.[32] Sixty years later Michel de Certeau, viewing New York City from the 110th floor of the World Trade Center, described the aerial gaze as totalizing and omniscient, tied to the regime of the 'cancerous growth of vision' and signalling the divisions between mapped space and 'intimate' embodied place[33] (although even here, arguably, the instruments of vision are not separable from the sentient body suspended above the city).

Recently Teresa Castro has contributed to outlining the embedded compulsions towards the aerial viewpoint; citing a debt to Svetlana Alpers, Castro charts a history of a 'mapping impulse' and of 'cartographic reasoning' that underlies connections between photography, aerial views and the actual and psychic acquisition and conquest of topographic space. In animating and bringing motion to the map and the still image, however, the cinematic aerial view delivers not just a totalizing gaze, but a 'double kineticism': an 'intense sensorial stimulation' via the immediate and physical experience of simultaneous height and motion.[34] Expanding on the model of the motion picture phantom ride to invoke kinesthetic responses, films such as the Smithsonian National Air and Space Museum's *To Fly* (1976) are so immersive that they even come with exhibitor warnings about dizziness and motion sickness.

As a result, aerial cinematicity engages both with a mapping impulse – that, as Castro argues, strives to 'create an image of the totality of the world . . . *a means to organize visual knowledge*' – while also providing a stimulating '*cinematographic sensation*' of the world.[35]

Cinema's moving worlds, as Bruno has shown, can 'embody a haptic sense of space'. She suggests that 'in the hub of filmic traveling and dwelling, we are absorbed in the stream of emotions and experience an embracing affective transport'.[36] Aerial cinematography transports us to the skies, soaring far above the intimate streams of everyday street-level life, yet does not necessarily always construct the spectator as a disengaged or disembodied subject. In fact in the films discussed below flight is consistently shown as a process initiated and mediated by human agency, while the aerial view is almost always inserted into a narrative frame and motivated by a look attached to an identifiable human figure. The filmgoer as aerial subject is always doubled by a physical presence in the films: a body gazing at the skies or moving through the air.

Forms of mobile embodiment in aerial cinema may be seen already in early aerial motion picture surveys. One such film, *En dirigeable sur les champs de bataille* (*In an Airship above the Battlefields*), has had wide circulation as part of the BBC documentary *The First World War From Above* (2010). Made in the summer of 1919, the film links together a number of disparate shots – taken from a camera strapped to an airship as it flies over the destroyed fields and towns bordering northern France – to create the appearance of a continuous survey over the remnants of intense combat. As it moves across ruined towns such as Ypres, above fields pock-marked with thousands of shell holes and over jagged trenches angling away into the distance, the film vividly demonstrates Virilio's argument relating to the symbiotic aerial and cinematic turn of the First World War. The war, Virilio contends, saw a new and more complete alignment of violent combat, surveying and aerial photography: Indeed during the conflict, aerial views taken from as high as 15,000 feet could be blown up to detect footprints in the mud. During the course of the twentieth century, war and aerial cinematography would become increasingly imbricated: There is for Virilio a 'deadly harmony' that 'always establishes itself between the functions of eye and weapon'.[37]

Yet rather than see *En dirigeable sur les champs de bataille* as indicative primarily of the growing alliance of aerial technology and industrialized warfare (where 'the concept of man had changed, time and space had been emptied of experience'),[38] Castro reads the film not only as revealing the geographic and quantitative *scale* of the devastation but also as delivering an 'unquestionable source of emotion: emotion linked to the visual pleasure of discovering the earth's surface from a new and exciting angle of vision, emotion attached to the sudden revelation of the territory as yet another injured body'.[39] Such associations between aerial movement and emotion, landscape and body, are crucial for considering further strategic uses of aerial photography discussed below. Indeed, what is interesting about *En dirigeable sur les champs de bataille* is that it offers not just an overview of destruction, but a face and figure that shares in the overseeing: the airman/cameraman himself, Jacques Trolley de Prévaux. The mobile and tactile effect created by the travelling shot is enhanced: We travel with the camera across the destroyed cities and fields from a position just behind Prévaux's head as the airship moves forward. Occasionally he turns towards the camera/spectator, creating a palpable sense of frisson between the vision of ruins below and the vertiginous yet pleasurable experience of airship flight. Aerial cinematicity can thus link spatial overseeing to a motion picture immediacy that engages with structures of affective connection and identification.[40]

AERIAL NATION

The aerial view remains deeply paradoxical: providing an emotionally charged opening onto a potentially globalizing perspective and an abundance of detail that can at the same time result in highly restricted and obscurantist views of the world. For Cosgrove, aerial images give rise to a troubling duality: They can instil 'a new sensitivity to the bonds that bind humanity to the natural world' even while, sometimes simultaneously, encouraging visions of control and spatial and territorial conquest.[41] Peter Adey further indicates the contradictions at the heart of aerial life, asking 'just what kind of life our aerial world has produced': a life that is both 'supported, shunted, and made good by the aeroplane, and simultaneously dropped, punished, and treated as less than human.'[42]

Indeed, even as a newfound Apollonian perspective was appearing to unveil a world without borders, the space of the air was itself becoming territorialized. The control and nationalization of airspace was well underway by the 1920s, as Liz Millward has shown:

> [A]fter four years of war and another demoralizing year of demobilization, the Versailles victors sat down to carve up the world's sky, just as they had carved up the world map, and produced the Convention Relating to the Regulation of Aerial Navigation. This Convention formed the basis of international air regulations during the interwar period, including the recognition that 'every Power has complete and exclusive sovereignty over the air space above its territory' (Canada 1920, Article I).[43]

Mirroring the territorializing of land and sea, airspace was progressively harnessed between the wars towards political ends. The aerial viewpoint thus provided forms not just of spatial orientation but of ideological positioning. Adey's shorthand list of landmark events in aviation history readily confirms the 'political spectacle of flight as an object of visual capital':

> Alan Cobham's arrival in England on the Thames. Lindbergh's landing at Paris. [. . .] Hitler's stage-managed mobility across Germany by aircraft [. . .] Propaganda is high on the list of the aeroplane's functions.[44]

These emerging 'choreographies of the [aerial] body' become paralleled by and intimately engaged with other demonstrations of nationalized mobility: the intricately choreographed 'performance of national space' of the military air show;[45] the elaborate routines of air travel, with identities validated via passports and carefully designed airport zones; the jingoistic and nationalist identifications encouraged by films such as *Top Gun* (1986) and by computer games such as *Aces High: F-15 Strike* and *Skies of War*. These activities, spaces and participatory spectacles conjoin flight, aerial subjectivity and national allegiance.

Even the professed educational value of the Smithsonian's *To Fly* (which, the Smithsonian claims, 'has been seen by more Americans' than any other film)[46] lies precisely in political spectacle and its contribution to a sense of national belonging. In the Smithsonian's educational guide detailing 'how *To Fly* and its associated classroom extensions meet specific national standards of learning', teachers are encouraged to stress that 'using a balloon, airplane, or satellite as an observation platform provides enormous advantages in: military reconnaissance, resource exploration, land-use planning, navigation, and in other uses'. Finally, the guide states: 'Flight, in all its forms, is part of the Human condition, part of our Destiny.' Here the 'we', as *To Fly*'s narrative arc emphasizes, is distinctly American: Flight is aligned in the film to a mythic national narrative ('Destiny') of 'westward expansion over the last 200 years, climaxing with [America's] venture into space'.[47]

As Adey argues, 'as a key component of contemporary mobile life, aero-moblities have shaped and defined the scope of our movements: the sorts of places we may go; the kinds of violence we may inflict; the scale, extent, and manner of our surveillance'.[48] In this sense, the panoramic and aerial views of the 1930s and 1940s encapsulate the paradoxes of an increasingly global sense of the world: at once testing, challenging and potentially breaking down established perceptions of spatial limits and boundaries even while the world was to be engulfed in that most radical experience of restricted and divided experience – global warfare.

ENVISIONING THE MODERNIST STATE

By the second half of the 1930s, a significant re-vision of national priorities and the duties of citizens was emerging under Franklin D. Roosevelt's administration, with the liberal-left coalitions of the Popular Front – with the discourse of the collective need of 'the people' and the idea of a unified 'public interest' – helping to settle the intense political rifts of the early Depression years. As Jonathan Kahana notes, the ambitious state-sponsored projects carried out in the 1930s with regards to land management, social welfare and industrial and economic regulation can be described as 'an all-powerful vision that mapped both space and social relations'.[49] Taylorized and Fordist mass production systems were promoted as key to 'scientifically managing' diverse and often unpredictable social, economic and natural forces through orderly design. At the same time, 'documentary photography and cinematography were perfectly suited to the optic of social, scientific, and economic rationality [. . .] of the high modernist state'.[50] Hence the rise of documentary as both an explicit and implicit apparatus of the US state shared with its counterparts in countries such as Germany and the Soviet Union certain elements of construing an 'all-powerful' national vision.

The effort to shore up American identity and purpose is clearly visible in the marriage of the aesthetics and ideology found in the New Deal documentaries directed and produced by Pare Lorentz and made with President Roosevelt's support. Not coincidentally, in films such as *The Plow that Broke the Plains* (1936) and *The River* (1938), panoramic and elevated shots feature prominently. Panoramas respond, for Castro, to a desire both 'to embrace and to circumscribe space'.[51] Here they reproduce the viewer's attempt to take in the vastness of the land: visually surveying and claiming space in the name of the people and the nation at a time when documentary was itself undergoing a process of 'maturation' as a nation-building apparatus.[52] Panoramic views in *The Plow*, for instance, envision the open space of the prairie as the potential of a new nation, asserting longstanding and powerful psychic links between landscape and national identity. A similarly-employed panoramic shot, although more insidious in its uses, would a few years later conclude the notorious propaganda film *Japanese Relocation* (1943). The film was made by the recently formed Office of War Information to persuade average Americans of the pressing need to 'relocate' (that is, imprison in remote camps) more than one hundred thousand people of Japanese descent, including American citizens. Here the film's concluding shot traces a wide arc across a valley, the gaze of the camera mimicking the slow movement of the eye across the land, embracing mountains and desert, with patterns of prisoner huts stretching across the landscape, the voice-over assuring the

Figure 8.2   The Land *(Flaherty, 1941), courtesy of The British Film Institute.*

nation that 'we are protecting ourselves without violating the principles of Christian decency'.

Although not always so explicit, the marrying of aesthetics and ideology to visualize the aims of the modernist state can be seen in the overhead image of the highway cloverleaf and the orderly patterns of the urban grid that feature in films such as *The City*, a documentary collaboration by Willard Van Dyke, Ralph Steiner and Aaron Copland made for the 1939 New York World's Fair. It is visible too in the aerial images of land management employed by Robert Flaherty in *The Land* (1941), made for the US Film Service. As Kahana sees it, these documentary visions offered images both 'strange and beautiful', mixing landscape and ideology to reveal spaces as socially constructed, ordered and rational: visible evidence of a highly – and 'scientifically' – managed environment.[53]

Used strategically, the meeting of airborne imagery and documentary's social currency could do more than supply awe and wonder to visions of national order and unity; it could serve as potent propaganda. Leni Riefenstahl's widely admired – and feared – *Triumph of the Will* (1935) revealed the extreme ideological uses of aerial footage: In its artful opening sequence, panoramic shots taken from the windows of the Führer's plane sweep the skies. As the plane gradually descends towards Nuremberg airport, the camera floats above the city, gazing across elegant spires and streets. Complementing its emotional impact, the scene's allegorical message is clear: The point of view is at once that of the viewer and the Führer, a union fused with the landscape below, caressed by the camera – a vision of a nation united with its iconic leader through love of land and country. The synoptic vision from the air is mirrored on the ground, where Riefenstahl intercuts images of Hitler being greeted by the integrated choreographies of the adoring masses.

Precisely because of the profound impact of films such as *Triumph of the Will*, intellectuals and government officials in the United States debated the uses of motion picture propaganda, voicing concerns about government intervention in film production and mass distribution to the public. Hence even with the production of films such as *The Plow, The River* and Joris Ivens's *Power and the Land* (1940, screened in more than five thousand theatres), government filmmaking remained modest in scale. Yet with the US entrance into the Second World War, when ideas of global responsibility were lensed through strict patriotic alliances, documentary's adoption by the state as a means to define public and national interests expanded enormously. At the same time, the skyborne image would offer up the war's definitive point of view.

AERIAL WAR

The attack on Pearl Harbor on 7 December 1941 not only shifted the US government agenda on state-sponsored propaganda, it dramatically confirmed the power of war from the air, setting in motion, Cosgrove notes, 'sustained discussions among American intellectuals and strategists about the "airman's war" and, more broadly, the "airman's vision".' As Archibald MacLeish conjectured: 'The airman's earth, if free men make it, will be truly round: a globe in practice, not in theory.'[54] In the meantime, the coalescing image of the world as a finite 'single sphere' (MacLeish's term) came up against, and was redefined by, an acutely restricted and hyper-nationalized worldview, as clearly expressed in the Manichean imagery of Frank Capra's *Prelude to War* (1942), where the future of the world is represented by two globes: one light and one dark, one free and one enslaved.

With anti-fascist passions running high, many of the experienced documentarists who had come of age amidst the leftist collective movements of the 1930s began working on propaganda films for the US government and related organizations. These included Van Dyke, who before the war contributed to *The City*, was a cinematographer on *The Plow that Broke the Plains* and later made *Valley Town, A Study of Machines and Men* (1940), a bleak portrait

Figure 8.3 Northwest USA *(Van Dyke, 1944), PublicResource.org (screen capture).*

of mass unemployment of factory workers that strives to create a unifying vision of America's economic plight through a focus on a single industrial town. In *The Bridge* (1942, with Ben Maddow), planned before the United States entered the war but completed after Pearl Harbor, the totalizing viewpoint emerges less through narrative and themes than through explicit visual imagery: Maps and graphics evoke an aerial perspective, indicating the potential of air transport links ('the bridge') between dispersed Latin American and North American countries.[55] *Northwest USA* marks a shift towards an even more comprehensive global image, representing the Northwest as the 'crossroads of the air': a gateway and means to manage international trade routes with Russia, Latin America and East Asia. Reflecting the wartime preoccupation with the skies, the film's opening shots imagine Earth from high above its surface, where an aeroplane (representing a historic flight of June, 1937, from Moscow to the Pacific Northwest over the Arctic Circle) draws together widely dispersed nations, suggesting the paradox of a globalized and intimately connected world in crisis, and in need of unification (here, through US trade and aerial mobility).

The Russians are introduced as 'neighbours who dropped in from the sky', having flown across the top of the world. Ensuing shots are carefully sequenced, starting with an animated god's eye view over Earth that concretizes the collapse of temporal, physical and spatial boundaries, a perspective just beyond the limits of representation – although no longer inconceivable. These shots shift seamlessly into aerial photography, gradually moving from the skies to the world at street level. The sequence articulates concrete and palpable relations between a global perspective, aerial embodiment and the realms of the earth-bound and everyday. Moreover, the visual juxtapositions remind us that, even if invisible to the naked eye, day-to-day fluxes and transformations of average American lives may be conceived in orderly,

Figure 8.4   Northwest USA, *PublicResource.org (screen capture).*

comprehensible patterns if seen from a different, elevated perspective. The film's final images move back to the skies, focusing on a child looking towards the camera as an aeroplane flies over; the close-up – what Gilles Deleuze would call the 'affection image' of the face[56] – providing an intimate and emotive double to the overseeing eye of the airborne camera. In many government films, close-ups of children looking upwards, and then directly towards the camera, feature as tropes for the projected future. The child's face may move and inspire the viewer as he or she gazes towards a new and newly globalized world – the 'geography of the air' as the film calls it – guided by commonly held, and dearly protected, American values.

Similarly didactic and uplifting in turns, Alexander Hammid's *Valley of the Tennessee* (1944) dramatizes the theme of waterway and flood management explored in *The River*. As in Lorentz's film, Hammid surveys the problems of flooding, and the solutions brought about by the New Deal and the Tennessee Valley Authority. *Valley of the Tennessee* opens with the camera perched on a seaplane taking off from San Francisco Bay, an aerial perspective surveying the American scene, before returning to earth and images of everyday life: here, impoverished children in a run-down schoolhouse. Government initiatives, the voice-over insists, are designed to address these wants and are performed for and by the people: 'The development of people is the first concern of democracy.' The film later moves decisively back from earth to sky: cutting from models of dams being examined by children in a schoolroom to an animated sequence that gives a god's-eye view of dams built along the Tennessee Valley – visioning a scientifically engineered and industrially efficient nation. Seen from high above (and, by extension, from the child's eye), the American landscape is revealed as a body that mirrors our own: The land is at once vibrant and vulnerable, yet made stronger by management and the solutions of science. Rivers and tributaries branch out like veins and capillaries, with their waters now 'dispatched, as trains are

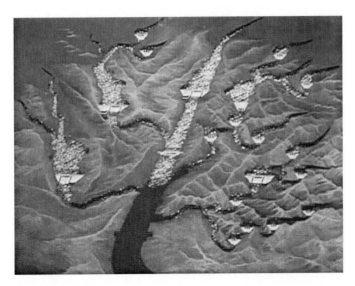

Figure 8.5 Valley of the Tennessee *(Hammid, 1944), PublicResource.org (screen capture).*

dispatched on a railroad system'. This is a social body managed by ingenuity, discipline and efficiency, 'by and for the people' as the voice-over asserts.

As in *Northwest USA*, the overlapping of different representational strategies (animation and aerial photography, panoramas and close-ups) conspires with the integration of moving image, voice and music, culminating in a documentary experience that feels both immersive and comprehensive, that feels as if it adds to the growth of the viewer's knowledge and perception. Hammid's final, sweeping shots of water resources managed by sophisticated dam-building technologies are juxtaposed with a zoom towards the face – again – of a child, her expression shifting from awe to determination. The meeting of a totalizing perspective and the 'affection-image' brings the film full circle, recalling the imagery that opened the film while at the same time positing a new, revitalized America well-prepared to lead the global future. While the domestic focus of such films may seem far from the bombing raids, air battles, and aerial surveillance and reconnaissance that were conspicuous features of the 'total war' in Europe and the Pacific,[57] such synoptic and airborne perspectives over a changing American landscape evoke the new world being created by modern aerial life.

Aerial views were thus central to imagining the warring nation's relationship to emerging domestic and global realities. The aerial perspective, as mentioned above, constructed a point of view at once masterful, overseeing and highly restricted, hence its usefulness as propaganda. The crucial value of harnessing virtual airspace as a tool for winning the 'real' war was clear from early on: The US Army Air Forces (USAAF) film *Winning Your Wings* (1942)

Figure 8.6 Target for Today *(Army Air Forces, 1944), PublicResource.org (screen capture).*

starred a folksy yet decidedly manly Lieutenant James Stewart, and reputedly helped attract more than one hundred thousand recruits through its masculine appeal to young men and its sexy aerial footage. Once recruited, fighters were trained for aerial combat through virtual warfare; motion pictures also documented and promoted their efforts to the public (the First Motion Picture Unit of the USAAF produced more than four hundred films during the war). In the training picture *Target for Today* (1944), for instance, the forensic build-up to a bombing raid culminates in an extensive sequence where, as in video gaming, the viewer directly occupies the position of a bomber, and sees through the lens that sights (and films) targets being destroyed.

The *Fight For the Sky* (1945) similarly embodies an aerial viewpoint through virtual engagement, but adds psychological and emotional force by showing the faces of pilots emerging from dynamic shots taken from cameras mounted on the noses of planes as targets are being destroyed. Again, the close-up of the face is juxtaposed with – here also superimposed on – the flyer's point of view, enhancing the film's 'e-motion' and haptic sensations of aerial cinematicity. Similarly, the colour film *Fortress of the Sky* (1944) (essentially an extended advertisement for Boeing, which was building B-17 bombers) aims to further glamourize the air war, opening with a flyer's sketch of a glamour girl, after which we see him affectionately patting and going into his B-17, called 'Glamor Gal'. *Fortress* draws on an established visual and acoustic grammar of the virtual air war to knit the spectator both optically and physically into the frame: juxtaposing a participatory voice-over, engine noise and close-ups of flyers' faces with point-of-view shots of bombing raids from the air.

Perhaps the most celebrated of the aerial combat films are William Wyler's *The Memphis Belle* (1944) and *Thunderbolt!* (released in 1947 from footage shot in 1944). Like the films mentioned above, *The Memphis Belle* draws on the seductions of aerial perception and the seeming mastery of its view. But it does more as well, complexly combining narrative suspense with the heightened sensations of flight and the intense excitement of aerial combat. Soon after the mission takes off, the camera pans around the cramped interior of the plane, gazing through windows and through gun sights at planes in formation alongside, and at the land slipping away below. Ideology and aesthetics are united in aerial warfare: The sunlight glistening off planes and the clear blue sky create an undeniable impact. The voice-over intones over the distant hum of engines:

> Higher and higher, climbing [. . .] so high you can't be seen from the ground with the naked eye. So high that after one minute without oxygen, you lose consciousness. After twenty minutes, you're dead. [. . .] Higher and colder, temperature forty degrees, below zero. Take off your glove and you lose some fingers. You look out at the strange world beyond, reflections in plexiglass, like nothing you ever saw before outside of a dream. Higher and higher, into the lifeless stratosphere.

Through the interrelation of aerial photography, poetic voice-over and minimal ambient sound, the film evokes the sensation of the vulnerable body confined within the B-17 bomber and suspended in air. Inside the B-17 with its crew, the spectator is drawn into the drama, the film stimulating the senses by invoking flight, weightlessness, extreme cold, excitement and agitation. Soaring high above Earth with a seemingly limitless view, the film nonetheless strategically stresses the limitations and restricted viewpoint from the B-17, mirrored by the war's straightened ideologies and closely watched patriotic allegiances. Here the paradox at the heart of aerial life manifests itself: the 'life on the move', which the aeroplane has produced, and yet also 'threatens to undo'.[58]

Thunderbolt!, released just after the war, mirrors aspects of *The Memphis Belle*'s combat narrative but expands – without ever negating – its ideological and perspectival restrictions. It even opens by self-reflexively revealing the cameras sited around the plane, panopticon-like, underlining the film's participatory effect: Cameras are (the voice-over states) 'behind the pilot, shooting forward and back, under the wing, in the wing, timed with the guns, in the wheel well, in the instrument panel, photographing the pilot himself'. The film also explicitly shows the 'collateral damage' of war on the ground – with images of children filing past ruined buildings and hiding their faces from mangled corpses – long before it engages in the first-person perspective of the P-47 attack missions. Near its end, we see the scorched corpse of an airman being pulled from a burning crash. In this sense, unlike *The Memphis Belle*, the film works to situate aerial combat within a sense of 'total war'. The film suggests an awareness of both the seductions and deceptive elisions of the airborne perspective: 'From the air,' the voice-over states, 'Italy is more

Figure 8.7   Thunderbolt! *(Wyler, 1947), Romano-Archives (screen capture).*

remote. The airman never sees the face of the people, only the face of the country. [. . .] For the airman, the ground war is remote. The only war you ever really understand is the air war. You can see a pattern to it'. The 'pattern' revealed four minutes into the film is of ruined towns and cities reminiscent of the destruction of the previous world war, captured in *En dirigeable sur les champs de bataille*. Hence the film begins with war's human impact and the aftermath, before moving on to the grim and thrilling scenes of aerial battle.

Thunderbolt! is, however, very far from an anti-war picture, and includes lengthy sequences of strafing and bombing that mirror (and draw from) combat training films (and prefigure video war games). Its extensive use of documentary combat footage, constructed to key up and draw in the viewer through first-person voice-over and dynamic cinematography, touches on ethically precarious territory. The voice-over admits that strafing can allow flyers to choose their own targets, with 'every man his own general'; with its adrenaline-fuelled point-of-view shots that involve the viewer in strafing trains and random houses, even gunning down a bystander in a field and a man on a motorcycle, it is difficult to suppress its momentary resemblance to a 'snuff' film. Whether the spectator-body here becomes machinelike or the flying/filming machine becomes 'added-on organ', both phenomena engage with the brain and body conditioned for war. But the film's message and impact is more multifaceted and potentially darker than the wartime propaganda of *The Memphis Belle*. We do see contexts behind 'combat mode' and states of heightened sensation where the enemy body is reduced to a dehumanized target. The film's final image, 'The End' with a red question mark superimposed over it, reverses and unsettles any overriding postwar optimism. As Hiroshima and Nagasaki had already proven by 1947, the new global order faced threats from the air far more terrible than even imagined during the more 'innocent' battles for Italy in 1944.

AERIAL DEATH

As revealed in the extraordinary and baffling nuclear test films made for military training purposes, such as the declassified US Air Force film *Operation Ivy* (1952),[59] aerial cinematicity would come to reveal both the sublime open vistas, and heightened terrors, of global awareness. With the overhead image of the mushroom cloud, aerial life truly does seem to annihilate space, time and matter itself. In *Operation Ivy*, as planes fly right through the nuclear cloud to collect radiation samples, the voice-over notes that 'manned jet fighters are being used exclusively on this operation; experience has proven that manned aircraft are just as efficient and much less costly to put in the air than are drones for sample collecting'. These images of aerial death in the name of scientific and military advancement nonetheless still manage to foreground, as in military recruitment advertisements, the aesthetic and physical allure of flight – here at 45,000 feet and at jet speeds.

With the coming of the space age, the world was captivated by photographs taken from the moon during the Apollo 11 mission, the sphere of Earth appearing fragile and alone amid the black void of space. Earth, the world picture, was a powerful icon and an emotional site for meditating on holistic and ecological issues, for exploring fears about total warfare and nuclear obliteration threatened by the Cold War. At the same time, it was difficult to ignore the American flag prominently placed in the foreground of the lunar landing images. Aerial life and the aerial view, then, continue to enable and restrict, expanding imagined national affiliations and reaching towards global potentialities even while inciting impulses towards mastery, ownership and territorialization – as the events, spectacular images and ensuing global turmoil of the 9/11 attacks so profoundly affirmed.

Notes

1. Albert W. Stevens, 'Man's Farthest Aloft', *National Geographic Magazine* 69.1 (January 1936), p. 90. The balloon was manned by Captains Albert Stevens and Orvil Anderson; the flight was sponsored by the National Geographic Society. The early 1930s saw many flight records being broken, with the exploits of

aviators and scientists such as Ruth Nichols and the Piccards (Auguste, his brother Jean, and Jean's wife Jeannette) widely reported.

2. Ian Christie, 'Cinematography and the Body', in Colin Blakemore and Sheila Jennett, eds, *The Oxford Companion to the Body* (Oxford: Oxford University Press, 2001), p. 158.

3. Maren Stange, *Symbols of Ideal Life: Social Documentary Photography in America, 1890–1950* (Cambridge: Cambridge University Press, 1989), p. 107.

4. M. Christine Boyer, 'Aviation and the Aerial View: Le Corbusier's Spatial Transformations in the 1930s and 1940s', *Diacritics* 33.3–4 (2003), 93–116 (p. 94).

5. See, for example, Barbara Low, 'Mind Growth or Mind Mechanization?' (1927), in James Donald, Anne Friedberg, and Laura Marcus, eds, *Close Up, 1927–1933: Cinema and Modernism* (London: Cassell, 1998), pp. 247–9.

6. 'The Production Code of 1930', at: <http://www.und.edu/instruct/cjacobs/ ProductionCode.htm> (accessed 15 December 2012); italics in original.

7. Quoted in Bill Nichols, 'Documentary Film and the Modernist Avant-Garde', *Critical Inquiry* 27.4 (Summer, 2001), 580–610 (p. 602).

8. For an analysis of voice and sound in Depression-era documentaries, see Jonathan Kahana, *Intelligence Work: The Politics of American Documentary* (New York, NY: Columbia University Press, 2008), pp. 89–140.

9. Denis Cosgrove, *Geography and Vision: Seeing, Imagining and Representing the World* (London: I. B. Tauris, 2008), p. 87. The strategy is not far from the use of shots of people looking skywards towards a 'Communist future' that Lev Manovich identifies in 1920s Soviet films in Chapter 12 of this collection.

10. For a more detailed description, see David Sweetman, 'A Tale of Two Cities', *The Observer* (London), 2 January 2000, at: <http://www.guardian.co.uk/theobserver/2000/jan/02/featuresreview.review1>.

11. Paul Virilio, *War and Cinema: The Logistics of Perception*, trans. Patrick Camiller (London: Verso, 1989), p. 1.

12. Cosgrove, *Geography and Vision*, p. 195.

13. Martin Heidegger, *The Question Concerning Technology*, trans. William Lovitt (New York, NY: Colophon, 1977), p. 129. Tom Gunning cites the notion of the world picture as an 'aggressive appropriation of space'; see 'The Whole World Within Reach: Travel Images without Borders', in Jeffrey Ruoff, ed., *Virtual Voyages: Cinema and Travel* (Durham, NC: Duke University Press, 2006), pp. 25–41 (p. 32).

14. Virilio, *War and Cinema*, p. 1.

15. Mark Dorrian, 'The Aerial View: Notes for a Cultural History', *Strates* 13 (2007), at: <http://strates. revues. org/5573> (accessed 3 August 2012). Dorrian also contests this 'normative' view.

16. Bernd Hüppauf, 'Modernism and the Photographic Representation of War and Destruction', in Leslie Deveraux and Roger Hillman, eds, *Fields of Vision: Essays in Film Studies, Visual Anthropology, and Photography* (Berkeley, CA: University of California Press, 1995), p. 105.

17. Amir Soltani, 'Embodied Airborne Imagery: Low-Altitude Urban Filmic

Topography', in Stuart Dunn, ed., *Proceedings of the 2011 International Conference on Electronic Visualisation and the Arts* (Swinton: British Computer Society, 2011), pp. 108–15 (p. 108).

18. Maurice Merleau-Ponty, 'Eye and Mind', in Ted Toadvine and Leonard Lawlor, eds, *The Merleau-Ponty Reader* (Evanston, IL: Northwest University Press, 2007), pp. 351–78 (p. 353).

19. Peter Adey, *Aerial Life: Spaces, Mobilities, Affects* (Oxford: Wiley-Blackwell, 2010), p. 21.

20. Jean Baudrillard, 'The Precession of Simulacra', in *Simulations*, trans. Paul Foss and Paul Patton (New York, NY: Semiotext(e), 1983), p. 2.

21. Patricia Pisters, 'Logistics of Perception 2.0: Multiple Screen Aesthetics in Iraq War Films', *Film-Philosophy* 14.1 (2010), 232–52 (p. 243).

22. Gunning, 'Whole World', p. 32.

23. Dziga Vertov, *Kino-Eye: The Writings of Dziga Vertov*, ed. Annette Michelson, trans. Kevin O'Brien (Berkeley, CA: University of California Press, 1985), p. 17.

24. Merleau-Ponty, 'Eye and Mind', p. 367.

25. Vivian Sobchack, *The Address of the Eye: The Phenomenology of Film Experience* (Princeton, NJ: Princeton University Press, 1992), p. 4; italics in original. Subsequent page references in text.

26. Annette Kuhn, *An Everyday Magic: Cinema and Cultural Memory* (London: I. B. Tauris, 2002), p. 193.

27. Rereading Lacan from a cinematic standpoint, Jonathan L. Beller has situated cinema at the heart of the unconscious itself. See 'Kino-I, Kino-World: Notes on the Cinematic Mode of Production', in Nicholas Mirzoeff, ed., *The Visual Culture Reader* (New York, NY: Routledge, 2002), pp. 60–85.

28. Anton Kaes, 'Leaving Home: Film, Migration, and the Urban Experience', *New German Critique* 74 (Spring–Summer, 1998), 179–92 (p. 182).

29. Hüppauf, 'Modernism and the Photographic Representation', p. 105. On photogrammetric surveys see Peter Collier, 'The Impact on Topographic Mapping of Developments in Land and Air Survey: 1900–1939', *Cartography and Geographic Information Science* 29.3 (2002), 155–74.

30. Cosgrove, *Geography and Vision*, p. 88.

31. *Ibid.*, p. 89.

32. Quoted in Adey, *Aerial Life*, p. 1.

33. See Michel de Certeau, *The Practice of Everyday Life*, trans. Steven Rendall (Berkeley, CA: University of California Press, 1984), p. xxi.

34. Teresa Castro, 'Cinema's Mapping Impulse: Questioning Visual Culture', *The Cartographic Journal* 46.1 (February 2009), 9–15 (p. 14).

35. *Ibid.*, pp. 13–14; italics in original.

36. Giuliana Bruno; talk based on *Atlas of Emotion: Journeys in Art, Architecture, and Film* (London: Verso, 2002), presented at the Institut pour la ville en movement, Paris, March 2004, at: <http://www.ville-en-mouvement.com/chaire_universitaire/conferences> (accessed 15 December 2012).

37. Virilio, *War and Cinema*, p. 69.

38. Hüppauf, 'Modernism and the Photographic Representation', p. 100.

39. Castro, p. 14.

40. Prévaux's daughter, watching the footage as part of the BBC documentary, is moved to tears by the combined images of post-war destruction and the seemingly direct experience of her (long deceased) father glancing at the camera.

41. Cosgrove, *Geography and Vision*, p. 89.

42. Adey, *Aerial Life*, p. 9.

43. Liz Millward, 'The "Aerial Eye": Gender and the Colonization of Airspace', *Michigan Feminist Studies* 13 (1998–9), at: <http://quod.lib.umich.edu>.

44. Adey, *Aerial Life*, p. 9.

45. Adey, *Aerial Life*, p. 53. See also Michael Paris, *From the Wright Brothers to Top Gun: Aviation, Nationalism, and Popular Cinema* (Manchester: Manchester University Press, 1995).

46. Jeffrey Ruoff, 'The Filmic Fourth Dimension: Cinema as Audiovisual Vehicle', in Ruoff, ed., *Virtual Voyages: Cinema and Travel* (Durham, NC: Duke University Press, 2006), pp. 1–24 (p. 14).

47. See the Smithsonian website, '*To Fly!*', at: <http://www.si.edu/imax/movie/1>, and '*To Fly!*', IMAX film (Smithsonian educational guide), <https://si.edu/Content/SE/Educator%20Guides/To_Fly_Standards.pdf>. Synopsis by Robert C. Cowdery, Kansas Geological Foundation, at: <http://www.kgfoundation.org>.

48. Adey, *Aerial Life*, p. 8.

49. Kahana, *Intelligence Work*, p. 89.

50. *Ibid.*

51. Castro, p. 11.

52. Charles Wolfe, 'The Poetics and Politics of Nonfiction: Documentary Film', in Tino Balio, ed., *Grand Design: Hollywood as a Modern Business Enterprise, 1930–1939* (New York, NY: Charles Scribner's, 1993), pp. 351–86 (p. 351).

53. Kahana, *Intelligence Work*, pp. 89–90.

54. Cosgrove, *Geography and Vision*, p. 197.

55. See also James Enyeart, *Willard Van Dyke: Changing the World through Photography and Film* (Albuquerque, NM: University of New Mexico Press, 2008), pp. 221–3.

56. Gilles Deleuze, *Cinema 1: The Movement-Image*, trans. Hugh Tomlinson (Minneapolis, MN: University of Minnesota Press, 2003), p. 87.

57. Modern war is 'total', Sven Lindqvist suggests, 'in the sense that it touches the lives and souls of every single citizen in the warring countries. Air bombardment has intensified the concept, since the entire area of the warring country has become a theatre of war'. Sven Lindqvist, *A History of Bombing* (London: Granta, 2002), section 145.

58. Adey, *Aerial Life*, p. 9.

59. The training film documents the US nuclear detonation at Eniwetok Atoll, Marshall Islands.

CHAPTER 9

Invisible Cities, Visible Cinema: Illuminating Shadows in Late Film Noir

TOM GUNNING

The visible, as Maurice Merleau-Ponty has taught us, always involves the invisible; what we see entails a zone of the not-seen.[1] Seventies film theory too frequently thought of cinema as exemplifying the glare (or frenzy) of the visible, devoted to the lure of visual mastery. This led to a simplification of cinema's ideological role as propping up the viewer's investment in a visual image as the product of a gaze. However, such analysis too often celebrated the insight of the analyst over the complicity of the medium, rather than offering a detailed exploration of cinema's complex stylistic interaction within modern visual culture. Cinema also offers an exploration of the vulnerability and limitation of vision. As an art of the visible, film must necessarily become an art of the invisible.

This essay explores the cinematic portrayal of urban space, a theme by now well established in the field of film studies. But by exploring both the style and the thematics of cinematic cities within a dialectic of vision that sees vision as specific, limited, embodied and also shaped by social and histori-cal contexts, I hope to show that the visible city shadows an invisible city, not simply as a formal device, but as an essential structure of our modern environment. The visible winds about the invisible, not only in film style, but in our experience of the modern urban environment and, for that reason, cinema supplies one of the richest means of portraying, exploring and – ultimately – understanding the city.

In the years that stretched from the late 1840s to 1950 new technologies transformed urban spaces and redefined modern visual experience. The invention of photography, the rise of mass media (from newspapers, to film, to television), the visual modes of mass marketing and consumer culture (from the omnipresent advertising posters to the department store show window) all transformed the city into a hyper-visual zone, a daily spectacle. At the same time, the increasingly complex infrastructure of cities, the system of sewers and the delivery of utilities such as water, gas and, eventually, elec-tricity, as well as systems of transportation and communication, created an increasingly hidden, subterranean network, the inverted mirror image of the city, tucked away from view. As Rosalind H. Williams puts it, in the modern city excavation, mining the foundations of the city in the earth became as much a part of daily life as construction.[2]

Invisibility in the modern city goes beyond this realm lurking beneath the surface and offers a mode of existence, or non-existence, for the city dweller. In the big city people can disappear, become lost in an urban throng, in which people do not know their neighbours and rarely examine one another closely. In Edgar Allan Poe's 1842 tale 'The Mystery of Marie Roget', literature's first 'amateur detective', C. Auguste Dupin, claims 'nothing is more vague than impressions of individual identity',[3] adding that Marie, the murdered girl of the tale, may have taken her last walk through the city 'without meeting a single individual whom she knew, or by whom she was known'.[4] In law enforcement, but perhaps even more powerfully in literature, a new figure appeared who engaged this system of invisibility: the detective.[5] The detective's powerful observation of people and scrutiny of clues responds to the threat of urban invisibility with a heightened visual awareness, following traces of identity unknowingly left behind. The modern city stages a *pas de deux* between clarity and obscurity. The double physical structure of the city itself – a shimmering illuminated surface with its constant solicitation of vision, and a subsurface in which darkness, disorientation and lack of grounding overwhelms the intruder – mirrors the duel between the detective's visual acuity and the criminal's desire to disappear into the urban thicket.

John F. Kasson describes two forms of urban representation frequently found in nineteenth-century accounts of the city: the bird's eye view and the mole's eye view, exemplified on the one hand by aerial views of a city showing key landmarks and ordered streets and, on the other, by the exploration of the 'mysteries' or 'secrets' of the big city, the hidden dark corners invisible from an overview.[6] The contrast between the evident and the obscure aspects of city life generated narratives of adventure in which the dark side could be exposed to view. Nineteenth-century publishers offered popular guides to the seamy side of urban pleasures, whose titles often stressed the play of light and shadow the city offered, both in its diurnal round (the official and public bright city of daytime versus the dangerous and fascinating city of night) as well as the opposition between different neighbourhoods (the brightly illuminated and open world of wealth and the hidden world of narrow alleyways found in the slums). Kasson cites such titles as: *New York by Gaslight: With Here and There a Streak of Sunshine*; *Sunshine and Shadow in New York*; *New York by Sunlight and Gaslight*; *Lights and Shadows of New York Life*; *Light and Shadows in San Francisco*; and *Chicago by Gaslight*.[7] The emphasis that these titles place on artificial illumination, as much as on darkness, highlights the era's fascination with a technological exposure of what had previously remained obscure. The bull's eye lantern, with its bulging glass lens designed to focus light in a specific direction, which urban police carried on their nocturnal patrols, offered an image of a form of exploration and even narration, in which not only the detective, but technology itself, pierced the opacity that defined city space. Journalist and reformer Jacob Riis's investigation of 'How the Other Half Lives' used the flash of the magnesium flare (needed for his photographs) to expose slum dwellings and hangouts, presenting illuminated images of previously unseen haunts of crime and poverty that could fascinate and outrage his middle-class readers.[8] Riis also presented the photographic views he obtained as lantern slides projected during his lectures on the need for urban reform.[9]

The spectacle of the modern city seemed to demand new visual forms of representation. Guidebooks were often heavily illustrated, first by drawing and eventually by photographs, while public lectures, whether conceived as slum tours or pleas for reform, were accompanied by projections of lantern slides and eventually motion pictures. For its first decade or so early cinema primarily presented views and actualities and focused nearly as much on city scenes as on the picturesque wonders of nature. These early city films recorded milling urban crowds, while phantom rides (films shot from the fronts of streetcars and buses) dynamically portrayed busy city streets. Overviews also appeared in film, whether Grimoin-Sanson's ambitious plan to film European capitals from an aerial balloon for exhibition at the Parisian 1900 Exposition, or the more modest images of urban crowds taken from rooftops or the tops of double-decker buses. These overhead viewpoints allowed viewers a certain distance from the ghetto pushcart markets or bargain-crazed shoppers crowding into a Lower East Side department store.

As cinema turned towards narrative as its dominant mode in the teens, filmmakers often set the new story films in the heart of the city, generally filming on the streets right outside their urban-based studios. D. W. Griffith's gangster film *The Musketeers of Pig Alley* (1912) and George Loan Tucker's white slavery shocker *Traffic in Souls* (1913) staged the often deadly conflict between criminal subterfuge and violent exposure. Such films provided the prototypes for later gangster and detective films. In Europe, the sensation films of Victorin Jasset and Louis Feuillade in France and, slightly later, Fritz Lang and Joe May in Germany created an urban topography of crime that scrambled over rooftops and descended into sewers. By the middle of the twentieth century the American film noir brought this urban thriller tradition to a cinematic climax. In spite of transformations in urban space and both cinematic and police technology that took place over these decades, films noirs renewed already familiar scenarios of vision and opacity, the effacement and revealing of identity, even as urban space itself began to give way to suburban sprawl.[10] While film noir's exploration of the cityscape is well known, I want to explore the arabesque it traced between light and shadow, transparency and opacity, within the larger history of visual representation of the city in order to demonstrate that film noir offered a meditation on both the tyranny and the contingency of vision, on its power as a disciplinary force, as well as exploring anxieties about its limitations.

The classical film noir of the forties enacted murders for profit and crimes of passion against the background of the city's back alleyways, nightclubs and streets. In the late forties a subgenre of the noir series actually cast the city as a major character (in *City that Never Sleeps*, 'the Voice of Chicago' not only speaks on the soundtrack, but actually plays an embodied role as a semi-supernatural entity). These films often present themselves as panoramic presentations of the urban environment, city symphonies within the noir series. Their opening prologues introduce the city and seem to demonstrate the cinema's power to visualize it as an entity. But as I hope to show, these opening sequences already present a series of contradictions and tensions within the project of seeing the city. The ensuing narratives of the films complicate the possibility of such an overview and descend into a realm of opacity and ambiguous vision. The films I will discuss are Jules Dassin's *Naked City* and Alfred Werker's *He Walked by Night*, both from 1948, and both fairly well known, at least to aficionados of film noir. The third film, rather obscure in every sense of the term, is *City that Never Sleeps*, directed by John H. Auer in 1953.

'Naked City'. The phrase, taken from the title of a famous book of New York images by newspaper photographer WeeGee, pseudonym of Arthur Fellig, announces a dynamic exposé.[11] A naked city implies a city stripped bare, an image both erotic and violent. A naked city is a city with something to hide. Walter Benjamin quoted Goethe as claiming that every man carries around a secret whose revelation would horrify his neighbour.[12] The essence of Baudelairian spleen, as Benjamin observes, lies in its ability 'to expose the passing moment in all its nakedness'.[13] The merciless flash of WeeGee's camera uncovered metropolitan night scenes, as corpses, crimes and disasters took on an obscene visuality. One searches for some filter to mollify these harsh images, just as the arrested suspects WeeGee shot seated in a 'pie wagon' police van rather pathetically sought to veil their faces with handkerchiefs.

However, as film and architectural historian Edward Dimendberg shows (in his recent brilliant discussion of the role of the city in film noir, *Film Noir and the Spaces of Modernity*), Jules Dassin's film, while evoking WeeGee, takes a different tone, simultaneously more human and more conformist. *Naked City* opens with the sort of aerial view of metropolitan space that seems emblematic of many urban films noirs, uniquely marked, however, by a voice-over (spoken by the film's producer Mark Hellinger) that replaces the traditional graphic rendition of the film's credits as words on the screen. Rather than providing a background for screen graphics, this series of mobile aerial views thrusts the city forward, providing an uncluttered view of its grid-work and skyscrapers in bright daylight. The succeeding views of the city shift to night as Hellinger's voice-over describes the diurnal round of urban life as the nocturnal city takes on a different appearance, even if it never goes to sleep entirely.

These opening nocturnal images project a pervasive anomie. Heard in voice-over commentary, night-time workers express a nearly hostile isolation from the public that they supposedly serve. A woman mopping up a bank wonders if the whole world tramped over her floor with their dirty feet. A solitary linotype operator muses ironically on the 'exciting' people he encounters in the newspaper business, while a disc jockey endlessly cycling records on and off the turntable wonders if anyone other than his wife actually listens to his show. As Dimendberg says, 'the film depicts the city as a socially produced set of distances between its inhabitants', a honeycomb of barely communicating niches, rather than an organically communicative community.[14] This opening montage of night-time activities ends with the murder of the young woman whose investigation takes up the rest of the film. Using a cinematic motif familiar from Vertov to Hitchcock, the camera sneaks through a half-opened window to catch a brief struggle, shrouded in darkness, of a woman whose face we will only see clearly on the front page of the newspaper that proclaims her killing the next day. The naked city does not surrender its secrets easily; detectives must uncover both culprits and motivations from beneath an accumulation of daily routines and details of urban life. As in Poe's story of Marie Roget, written a century earlier, the search emphasizes the contingencies of urban identity and the continued possibility of disappearing within the metropolitan wilderness.

Produced in 1948, *Naked City* stands on the threshold of fundamental changes in the Hollywood system and the evolution of the film noir series. The US Federal Courts handed down the Paramount divestment decree in 1948, which would eventually end the studio system, as the major studios were forced to unload their theatres. In 1948 the House Un-American Activities Committee (HUAC) hearings on Communist 'subversion' in Hollywood also began, leading to the imprisonment of *Naked City*'s scriptwriter Albert Maltz and eventually to the blacklist that forced director Dassin to leave Hollywood and work in Europe. After 1948, film noir increasingly followed the lead of *Naked City* and focused on police detectives rather than the hard-boiled private eyes who dominated earlier noir films. These later police-centred films often adopted a semi-documentary style that characterized the series known as the police procedural, as opposed to the more expressionistic treatment of the crimes of passion and *femmes fatales* found in such earlier films noirs as *The Maltese Falcon, Murder My Sweet, Scarlet Street, Out of the Past* or *Gun Crazy*. Even more than *Naked City*, *He Walked by Night* (produced by Eagle Lion, one of the independent studios that emerged from Poverty Row hoping to cash in on the divestment decree's break up of the major studios' control of distribution) exemplified these changes.

For a brief period after the war, films by directors like Dassin and scriptwriters like Maltz promised a new sort of Hollywood film, progressive in political critique and mature in style – a promise snuffed out by the HUAC hearings and the subsequent blacklist. But a film like *He Walked by Night* shows the secondary gain that this repression brought to American cinema of the late forties and fifties – a more deeply cynical and violent style, the product of a divided consciousness, driven to camouflaged protests and pseudonymous scriptwriting. While the audience alignment with the forces of law and order may represent a conformist and reactionary move, the stylistics of the films I discuss nonetheless undercut viewing the focalization on cops as merely an act of disciplinary ideology.

Although Dassin and Maltz claimed that studio or producer intervention blunted its social critique, *Naked City* still projected a critical image of American society, filled with class tension and anomie. Its populist tone, and the avuncular performance by Barry Fitzgerald as the seasoned detective, provided a humanizing touch that may compromise its critique, but also recalls the Popular Front optimism of the Roosevelt era. Shot on a lower budget, *He Walked by Night* anticipates the cynicism and paranoia of the fifties, projecting a nastier, more violent, less comforting, image. Fitzgerald's ethnicity and democratic attitude contrast sharply with the waspish FBI agents in *He Walked by Night* who express irritation when a Chinese man they are interrogating cannot reply in English, and teeter on the edge of violence as they question witnesses. Paranoia and suspicion pervade this film, anticipating the series of rogue cop films (such as Fritz Lang's *The Big Heat* [1953] or Joseph H. Lewis's *The Big Combo* [1955]) that will bring the noir cycle to its end.

He Walked by Night, with its focus on Los Angeles rather than New York, anticipates the major demographic shift from what Dimendberg describes as centripetal cities like New York to the new de-centered, centrifugal cities of the emerging car-based culture, exemplified by Los Angeles. The voice-over that opens *Naked City*, while using the traditional city of contrasts approach, presents New York as an organic if complex whole, endowed with a common pulse. Co-scriptwriter Melvin Wald described the tone of this voice-over (apparently written by Hellinger himself) as indebted to Walt Whitman's paeans to the urban energy of New York a century earlier.[15] In contrast, the voice-over that opens *He Walked by Night* sets up irresolvable dichotomies whose facile reconciliation through booster clichés underscores their essential schizoid nature:

> This is Los Angeles . . . the fastest growing city in the nation. It's been called a bunch of suburbs in search of a city, and it's been called the glamour capital of the world; a Mecca for tourists, a stopover for transients, a target for gangsters, a haven for those fleeing from winter, a home for the hard-working, a city holding the hopes and dreams of over two million people. It sprawls out horizontally over 452 hundred square miles, of valleys and upland, of foothills and beaches. Because of that vast area and because of a population made up of people from every state in the union, LA is the largest police beat in the nation and one of the toughest.

The images that unroll under this commentary also contrast with the panoramic aerial views that open *Naked City*. A montage of unrelated views – from vast vistas of urban sprawl, to the skyscraper-lined streets of downtown, to sunny beaches – represents LA. The opening sequence ends with a tilt down the towering Los Angeles City Hall, the landmark that anchors the opening of a number of other films noirs, such as *Criss Cross* (Robert Siodmak, 1949), housing, as the voice-over informs us, the LA police headquarters. This centre of law and order seems to discipline the city's diversity, as it surveys its expanse like the central tower in a panopticon prison. The film enters police headquarters through its 'Communications Division, the eyes and ears of the police'. Rather than footsore cops like those who covered the neighbourhoods in *Naked City* in search of someone who might recognize their photograph of suspect Garza, the Communications Division's switchboard and its attendants provide a depersonalized and mechanized image of law and order, as police functionaries and women co-workers take in information, and then disseminate it. Technology dominates the investigation in *He Walked by Night*.

In spite of this abrupt change in tone between the two films, *He Walked by Night* renews the dialectic of vision and opacity within the de-centered city. The threat of invisibility deepens in this dispersed topography as the police search for, in the words of the voice-over narration, 'a shadow of a man, hidden away somewhere in the vast city'. If the police seem dominated by a faceless technology, dehumanized (other than bursts of violent frustration), the burglar/murderer they are tracing shares their dependence on technology and anonymous rage. Described as a genius in electronics, Roy Martin initially specializes in stealing electronic equipment. While perfecting his burglary tools, Roy listens (with a George Walker Bush-like smirk) to a police radio monitoring futile attempts to identify him. But the police find no traces left by the perpetrator, no record of him in their archives of information.

Rather than a colourful urban underworld character like Ted de Corsia's Garza in *Naked City*, Richard Basehart's chilling performance as Martin (the first starring role for this fine neglected actor, best known for his role as the Fool in Federico Fellini's *La Strada*) depicts a cipher, a man whose face seems either to convey an odd detachment or to register incommensurable physical impulses of anger, amusement, excitement and panic. Even more chilling than the calm with which he shoots victims who get in his way is the precision with which Martin, after a shootout with cops, methodically operates upon himself to remove a bullet from his side. In looming close-ups, harshly lit from above, cinematographer John Alton (the dean of noir camera stylists) intently delineates Basehart's odd amalgam of intellectual concentration, intense pain and expressions of satisfaction, hinting at masochistic pleasure. Roy remains a contradictory character that the film makes no attempt to explain. Other than the fact that he gained his knowledge of technology and police procedure in the Army Signal Corps as a radio operator and by working within the police force (a 'civilian employee', the police stress, like the many functionaries we see at headquarters managing information), we learn nothing of his past or his motivations. Psychologically he remains a blank.

John Alton's cinematography nearly defines the stylistics of film noir, expressing its subordination of the visible to an overwhelming darkness. While his mastery of shadow with sharp contrasts between zones of light and darkness has been admired, few commentators have noticed how simple his set-ups can be. Instead of a multiplicity of lights, Alton avoids all but a few sources and relies on opaque elements within the set or location to shape shadows for him. The sides of buildings, the frame of a window or a doorway split light and generate shadows, endowing Alton's noir images with something more than atmosphere. Darkness swells up from the city itself and pours shadows onto the streets and its inhabitants.

This literal visual obscurity reaches its climax in this film with the shootout in Roy's final refuge – the storm drains of Los Angeles. The voice-over describes this refuge as a hidden labyrinth, the subterranean network of the city's infrastructure, 'an intricate structure' that supplied the cunning culprit with '700 miles of hidden highway'. Alton's lighting here remains minimalist. In the narrow tunnels a glare from an unseen source scoops out their circular shapes, backlighting Roy into a dark silhouette. Roy's flashlight often supplies the only lighting in the sewer's broader spaces. A nearly dark screen contains recessive quadrangles of alternating light and darkness illuminated by the small swaying light that Roy holds as he runs, zones of light growing ever smaller as he dives into this heart of darkness.

Roy seems to rule his abject underworld, the master and only inhabitant of its solipsistic obscurity. Its invasion by police (as well as the chance blocking off of his route of escape by a police car tyre resting on a manhole cover) produces true panic in this previously untouchable monarch of the depths. As other lights penetrate his refuge of shadows, Roy's attempt to defend his realm becomes overwhelmed by the sound of running water and the unearthly subterranean echoes of gunfire and footsteps. The combatants clash within an abstract space dominated by a harsh geometry that Alton's lights carve out of surrounding obscurity. Light takes on a deadly force as it illuminates the clouds of tear gas that force Roy from his tunnel, greeted by a hail of bullets from the gas-masked police.

The film ends abruptly. Roy tumbles within a sewer, falling face down into the water that the drains seek to remove from the city. The final shot shows the feet and legs of the law officers wading through the water to reach Roy's corpse. A hand reaches down and turns the body over. With an ominous chord on the soundtrack, Roy's face, previously unseen by the police, appears, gazing wide-eyed upward, a slight amusement seeming still to play around the rictus of his mouth. The film ends with this revelation. There is no return to normalcy of everyday life as in the end of *Naked City*, no sense that the diurnal round of city life continues. Rather, we face a confrontation between the obscure and the revealed, a face whose expression cannot be read. In the cloacal depths of the city, lawful vision locates its target and eliminates it, except for this lingering deathly impersonal gaze that seems to mock the off-screen agent of the law. This is perhaps the most noir of noir films, as if in *He Walked by Night* this series of films reaches what William Blake described as 'the limit of opacity'.

My final film noir comes from 1953, five years later, and further develops the city as a zone of visual opacity with a new emphasis on personal vision, spectatorship and surveillance and its emotional resonance. The film takes place during a single night. Cinematographer John L. Russell (who shot Frank Borzage's velvety dark *Moonrise* in 1948, and, most famously, Hitchcock's *Psycho* in 1960) filmed the nocturnal alleyways, garages, basements, EL tracks and abandoned tenements of Chicago in a style that recalls Alton's use of flood lights to create looming shadows and misty auras. Like the other films I have discussed, the protagonist of the film is a cop, John Kelley, but the cop's ambivalence towards his job has become central to the plot, pivoting on his decision whether to leave the force and work for a corrupt business-man (aligning it with the rogue cop series). But while night enwraps this cop's odyssey, a fairly minor – if unforgettable – character gives the theme of vision a new twist, a mechanical man who performs in the window of a strip joint to draw in customers to the show.

The opening of the film recalls my other noir city films. A panoramic shot of the skyline of Chicago (recalling the opening of *Psycho*) appears behind the credits. Then, as a time-lapse shot of the Wrigley building moves from daylight to night-time, a voice-over picks up familiar themes as it literally personifies Chicago:

> I am the city, of, and part of, America. Melting pot of every race, creed, color and religion of humanity, from my famous stockyards to my towering facto-ries, from my tenement district to swank Lake Shore Drive. I am the voice, the heartbeat of this giant, sprawling, sordid and beautiful, poor and magnifi-cent citadel of civilization and this is the story of just one night in this great city. Now, meet my citizens . . .

Although the voice-over will soon introduce the cop hero of the film, it opens by panning from the stately Wrigley building to the marquee of the strip joint and introduces 'Gregg Warren, a mechanical man working in a store window. Once an actor, now he's down to this'. Although Warren is Kelley's rival for the affection of stripper 'Angel Face' Connors (played by the oddly compel-ling Mala Powers), he mainly plays a metaphorical role in this film as an epitome of dehumanized fifties America. Warren attracts customers through the question (endlessly repeated over a loudspeaker to passers-by), 'Is he mechanical or real? Is he a human being or a machine?' as he pantomimes a series of endlessly repeated machine-like gestures. His mechanical role almost too patly symbolizes his repression of anguish over Angel Face's affair with Kelley (he repeats to her the phrases of his recorded sidewalk come-on, 'Am I real or just coils and springs?').

But this simple metaphor takes on a new wrinkle when Warren witnesses a murder while performing in the window. The situation recalls the exploration of spectatorship, the act of witnessing a crime and the vulnerability of vision so often discussed in criticism of Hitchcock's contemporaneous film from 1953, *Rear Window* (that also explores visuality within urban space – although Hitchcock's rear window view dramatically restricts any attempts at a pano-ramic overview). While hardly the tour de force that Hitchcock offers, *City that Never Sleeps* provides a particularly ambiguous image of the limits placed on vision and the act of witnessing (which becomes central in fifties noir – and politics). The murderer shares the general uncertainty over whether Warren is really a mechanical man or simply a human actor and is unsure if he could identify him. When Officer Kelley asks Warren's aid in solving the murder, he expresses his mechanical apathy to his romantic rival, claiming, 'I'm a mechanical man. I don't see, I don't hear, I don't feel.' Warren's role as a commercial spectacle demands a scotomatized perception, a lack of seeing that allows him to endure his alienated labour. When one of the strippers asks him how he can stand performing in the window, endlessly making the same gestures, he explains that he simply pretends he's not there: 'All that time

I'm thinking: I'm not in the window at all.' To admit he has seen the murder would not only mean aiding his rival, but, more painfully, acknowledging the reality of his own situation. He is there to be seen, not to see, the objectified and alienated product of an urban commercial vision. However, when Angel Face confesses her love for him as he does his routine in the window, a looming close-up of his impassive face coated in metallic paint reveals tears running from his eyes.

This sequence stages visibility and invisibility in the urban environment with a complex interaction between spectacle and spectatorship that expresses post-war social and emotional alienation with almost mythic clarity. As the tears pour from Warren's eyes they belie his assumed emotional blindness. Demonstrating to the passers-by that he is indeed human ('Look, the mechanical thing is cryin'!'), he also reveals to the concealed murderer (who watches him from his hiding place) that he did in fact witness the murder. As the murderer, in order to eliminate an incriminating witness, fires at Warren in his illuminated window, he also reveals his own hiding place to the cops who have staked out the night-time street hoping the murderer will reappear, surveying each pedestrian (an earlier cut from a passing rummy making a gesture to the cops shows Warren echoing the same hand movement mechanically). The visual scenography of the sequence pivots on a confrontation between visibility and invisibility that goes beyond Sartre's classic description of the discovered voyeur: Warren on display hoping to attract the murderer; the concealed murderer who hopes to eliminate the person who saw him; the cops hidden themselves on watch for the murderer's revealing action.[16] This dark street is honeycombed with concealed antagonists, who emerge murderously as the human factor suddenly makes an unexpected appearance.

While these films from the late forties and early fifties bring to light the patterns of paranoia and threat that marked the cold war rhetoric of figures like Senator Joseph McCarthy, I don't want to indicate that cinema's engagement with vision only escapes the straitjacket of ideological complicity when it dwells in this dark environment. I therefore want to repopulate the city with people absorbed by the energies of play and fantasy, albeit often of a mysterious and even threatening sort. In closing, therefore, I will discuss perhaps the greatest American city film from this period, the experimental documentary *In the Street*. An extraordinary collaboration between James Agee, Helen Levitt, Janice Loeb and Sidney Meyers, *In the Street* also comes from the key year 1948, but was made entirely outside of the Hollywood system. *In the Street* returns us to the view aesthetic of early cinema, although a new mobility of the film camera allows the filmmakers to interpenetrate the life-world of the city's inhabitants, rather than viewing them from a distance or above, and without having to create a fictional persona or dramatic scenario for them. The film's lack of a synchronized soundtrack seems less an anachronistic return to the silent cinema than a purging of sound, a silence that descends over these images, inviting viewer absorption rather than authorial commentary. The key figure in the making of this film was clearly the street photographer Helen Levitt, whose extraordinary still photographs not only recall the film's images but were often shot simultaneously with the filming. The intertext of these remarkable still photographs (especially those gathered in the book *A Way of Seeing*) highlights the world of motion that this film captures; a whole realm of gesture and physical interaction unfolds here. *In the Street* captures what Walter Benjamin, as emphasized by Miriam Hansen, called the innervation of modernity, the mimesis of adventure and violence of childhood, the flirtation with and performance of pain and excitement.[17] To dismiss this film as simply a picturesque or charming view of childhood blinds one to the dark spaces it also illuminates. In his foreword to *A Way of Seeing*, James Agee said of a photograph of Levitt's:

> Now the forces of beauty and fear in this picture might be suspect, if they drew one to enjoy them for their own sake alone, and it is possible, I realize, to enjoy this and many other of the pictures in this precious, limited and inhuman way. But it seems to me that the super-rational beauty, fear, and mystery, and the plain strength and sadness of the girl, and her particular moment and stance in her own and in universal existence, all powerfully interdepend upon and enhance one another, reverberating like mirrors locked face to face the illimitable energies set up in the paradox formed in the irrefutably actual as perceived by the poetic imagination.[18]

The delight in seeing that this film celebrates has a dark side, and its sense of adventure posits the possibility of vulnerability and pain. Our sympathy and identification with these stolen moments – gestures, expressions and interactions – come through cinema's ability to communicate a vivid sense of physical embodiment, not simple visual mastery and dominance. As Agee indicates, there is a way of seeing that assumes one's shared vulnerability with the subject of the image, while a moving image allows us to mime the thrill of movement witnessed in the spontaneous action of another. Witnessing need not be restricted to objectification or to an investment in an imaginary ego ideal (although it remains the role of criticism to remind us of the danger of these possibilities of reified vision). If there is a mode of perception and representation we associate with the cinema, we need to recognize its ongoing energy, not simply as an expression of modern life, but as a tool in making modern life something more than the nightmare it often seems to be set on becoming. To grasp the cinema's rhythm of the visible and the invisible, the basic flicker that underlies its existence, entails seeing into modernity's play of hiding and seeking, its promise and threat. As *City that Never Sleeps* showed, even a mechanical man can remember how to cry.

Notes

1. Although this is a theme in much of Merleau-Ponty's work it forms the centre of his late unfinished work *The Visible and the Invisible* (Evanston, IL: Northwestern University Press, 1968).
2. Rosalind H. Williams, *Notes on the Underground* (Cambridge, MA: The MIT Press, 1992), p. 52.
3. Edgar Allan Poe, 'The Mystery of Marie Roget', in Patrick F. Quinn, ed., *Poe: Poetry and Tales* (New York, NY: Library of America, 1984), pp. 506–55 (p. 530).
4. *Ibid.*, p. 532.
5. I have discussed the relation of the detective to the city environment in literature and early cinema in my essay 'From Kaleidoscope to the X-Ray: Urban Spectatorship, Poe, Benjamin and *Traffic in Souls* (1913)', *Wide Angle* 19.4 (1997), 25–61.
6. John Kasson, *Rudeness and Civility: Manners in Nineteenth-Century Urban America* (New York, NY: Hill and Wang, 1990), pp. 72–3.
7. *Ibid.*, p. 76.
8. Jacob A. Riis, *How the Other Half Lives* (1890) (New York, NY: Dover, 1971).
9. Maren Stange, *Symbols of Ideal Life: Social Documentary Photography in America 1890–1950* (Cambridge: Cambridge University Press, 1989), especially pp. 1–3.
10. Ed Dimendberg, *Film Noir and the Spaces of Modernity* (Cambridge, MA: Harvard University Press, 2004).
11. WeeGee, *Naked City* (1945) (New York, NY: Da Capo Press, 1985).
12. Walter Benjamin, 'The Paris of the Second Empire in Baudelaire', in Michael W. Jennings, Marcus Bullock, Howard Eiland and Gary Smith, eds, *Selected Writings: 1938–1940*, vol. 4, trans. Harry Zohn (Cambridge, MA: Harvard University Press, 2003), p. 20.
13. *Ibid.*, p. 40.
14. Dimendberg, *Film Noir*, p. 61.
15. *Ibid.*, p. 58.
16. Jean-Paul Sartre, *Being and Nothingness*, trans. Hazel E. Barnes (New York, NY: Washington Square Press, 1966), pp. 347–8.
17. See Miriam Hansen, 'Benjamin and Cinema: Not a One Way Street', *Critical Inquiry* 25.2 (Winter, 1999), 306–43.
18. James Agee, Helen Levitt, *A Way of Seeing* (Durham, NC: Duke University Press, 1989), p. xi.

Part 4

Digital Cinematicity

Cinema, Video, Game: Astonishing Aesthetics and the Cinematic 'Future' of Computer Graphics' Past

LEON GUREVITCH

In an early publication on the possibilities of computer graphics, Robert Goldstein and Roger Nagel described a 'visual simulation technique by which fully computer-generated perspective views of three-dimensional objects may be produced'.[1] Published in 1971 to articulate several years of research at MAGI (Mathematical Applications Group Inc. – the company that went on to form the backbone of Disney's 1982 movie *Tron*), this paper reveals a number of interesting ways in which the future possibilities of computer-generated imagery (CGI) were envisaged. Describing their new process of 'raytracing' (a process still used today in Pixar's *Renderman* software) and its distinguishing difference from the vector-based graphics forms dominant up to that point, one of the most intriguing aspects of Goldstein and Nagel's paper is the negotiation that takes place between computer graphics as a form naturally given to utilizing cathode ray tube (CRT) outputs and the cultural and economic need to appeal to the dominance of celluloid.

Describing raytraced images, Goldstein and Nagel describe the resultant 'pictures' in quotation marks, acknowledging the fact that they have no physically printed existence without further technological transcription. Equally, Goldstein and Nagel describe their new process as a matter of simulating the 'basic ingredients involved in the photographic process', which they identify as 'a source of light, a camera, and the object to be photographed'. With these factors in mind, they claim:

> The simulation approach treats an object as a set of three-dimensional surfaces that reflect light, and it is this reflected light impinging on photographic film [. . .] that forms an image of an object. The result is, therefore, a fully toned picture, closely resembling a photograph of the real object. It is this added degree of realism that makes the simulation approach attractive for many applications.[2]

Notably, then, Goldstein and Nagel's work framed digital imaging in relation to mechanically reproduced indexical counterparts and the processes involved in obtaining such image forms.[3] At the time of publication in 1971, Goldstein and Nagel could not know how deep and far-reaching the transition from analogue to digital imaging, symptomatized by research like theirs, was to be over the coming forty years. Regardless, the telling point lies not in any proclamation of a revolutionary new image form (a claim they did not make) so much as in the careful and modest line they tread between new research, technology and economies of imaging, and old. Such a negotiation did not only manifest itself in the linguistic need to explain a new digital image form in terms comprehensible to an audience more familiar with a previous analogue one. Later in the paper the pair describe the 'picture output' process with which permanent stills can be taken. These, they point out, can take the form of a recording on magnetic tape or a photographic still camera image (or 16 mm camera in single frame exposure mode) taken of the cathode ray screen containing the image.[4] When finally, at the end of the paper, it is time for the authors to describe the potential commercial applications of this technology beyond the university and corporate research lab, they turn unequivocally to the motion picture industry or, as they state, to a potential new form of 'computer generated motion pictures'.[5] The basis for this claim is, they argue in a methodical explication that reads like a passage from Lev Manovich's *Language of New Media* some thirty years in advance, that computer-automated animation techniques could bring economic benefits to an animation industry entirely dependent on costly and labour-intensive manpower. Although they were entirely correct in predicting a computer-generated animation industry, it may have surprised Goldstein and Nagel that it would be another twenty-four years before a feature length computer-animated movie (*Toy Story*, 1995) would emerge. In the meantime they may not have expected computer-generated (CG) imaging to spend the intervening years developing as visual attractions commercially funded via television advertising and brand logos.

I have argued elsewhere that both computer-generated visual effects (VFX) and computer games had early histories remarkably reminiscent of cinema's own emergence as a multiply promotional spectacular commercial form a century before. Such image forms (special effects that operate in both movies and as promotional material for their trailers; visual effects deployed in television advertising; promotional CGI used by modern architectural, aerospace, automotive and electronic industries to secure funding for future projects) constitute an emergent body of digital attractions that I have termed the cinemas of transactions/interactions.[6] In this chapter I shall expand this to argue that gaming and CG imaging have both contained – as interrelated functions of their audiovisual lexicon and as circumstances of their industrial emergence – parallels with the multiple social, cultural and economic forces that informed cinema a century before. In both cases we can see in these emergent forms three broadly common characteristics influencing production and consumption that can be summarized as spectacular, promotional and astonishing.

In this chapter, then, I will consider the emergence of CG image forms in the latter half of the twentieth century not as revolutionary departures from the cinematic (as they have often been treated) but as symptoms of a mediated negotiation with, and expansion of, audiovisual functions that during the twentieth century came to be associated with the cinematic. This argument does not conflict with, or ignore, calls from the gaming studies community to reject a tendency to problematically apply scholarly frameworks devised for other media to the task of explaining emergent gaming and graphics. Rather, the task here is to articulate the paths by which computer graphics and games emerged from, and more importantly reshaped, the attraction that came to be embodied in cinema during the twentieth century but which was moulded by audiovisual functions that preceded cinema, and that show every sign of succeeding it, too.

In other words, in the demand that graphics and games be understood in their own terms – and not within the straitjacket of a scholarly framework inherited from another field of study – there is a danger that crossovers, comparisons and correlations between cinematic attractions and those of games and graphics go unexamined. Significant here is not the identification of cinematic conventions or filmic lexicons that can be traced through emergent graphics and gaming forms: Such studies have already been undertaken in great detail by other theorists,[7] not to mention the body of work now addressing machinima.[8] Instead there is a broader analysis to be undertaken of the shared cultural and economic factors driving the emergence of graphics and games in ways reminiscent of cinema a century before. The interest here, then, is not in making direct comparison of one form to another, or in using one disciplinary language with which to try to reductively understand another. Rather, we can trace patterns of emergent spectacular visual media forms that have anticipated, have been marked by and have shaped the cinematic attraction – games and graphics included. This does not preclude an understanding of games as 'fundamentally processual' as Thomas Malaby argues,[9] but it does seek to recognize continuities in the emergence of gaming and graphics with cultural configurations that also shaped the emergence of earlier visual media forms (deeming them to be astonishing, desirable and, therefore, collectively noteworthy), of which cinema came to be emblematic. From magic lanterns and early Victorian optical toys to later stereoscopic forms and subsequently early cinematic attractions, there have often been shared characteristics that qualified a new visual media form as worthy of public attention. Gaming and computer graphics have been no different. Thus, the drivers that not only preceded cinema and fed into its emergence but that are also succeeding it after the shift away from traditional celluloid technologies can be found shaping many of the developmental processes of contemporary games and graphics.

There is a danger here in seeming to reduce games and graphics to comparisons with the cinematic attraction: Clearly they are many other things besides being attractions. Manovich has suggested in his 'archeology of the screen' that computers and their graphical outputs have more in common with television and the real-time spatial tendencies inherited from the cathode ray tube's origins as a radar technology than with the indexical technology of celluloid.[10] Given this, it could seem reductive to relate gaming and graphics forms to a cinematic culture that, aside from its current transformation to a medium characterized as the 'slave of the computer' is still emerging from a century dominated by celluloid.[11] But this is precisely why relating gaming and graphics forms to cinematic attractions bears fruit. In her examination of emergent 'new' media, *Always Already New*, Lisa Gitelman argues that 'new media emerge as local anomalies that are also deeply embedded within the ongoing discursive formations of their day, within the what, who, how, and why of public memory, public knowledge and public life'.[12] Gitelman's point goes a long way to explaining Goldstein and Nagel's deference to the motion picture industry in general and the technology of celluloid in particular when they were suggesting potential future avenues of growth for their graphics techniques. By contrast with the contemporary shift to a digital media landscape, the discursive formations of Goldstein and Nagel's day upheld cinema and celluloid as the paramount audiovisual form. While the manner and means by which both games and computer graphics were to be most profitably deployed and consumed were not yet clear, Goldstein and Nagel were careful to make a claim for the commercial and industrial appeal of their new form to the motion picture industry.

To give them their due, Goldstein and Nagel do finally turn, at the end of their paper, to an acknowledgement of the potential deployment of graphics techniques in television. Even here, however, they cite another academic, Roger Boyell, almost as an afterthought, briefly repeating his 'basic point' that 'visual simulation is well suited to a TV output format'.[13] Given the technical and technological obstacles at that time to overcoming the media divide between CRT-based computer graphics and celluloid, and given the comparative ease with which such graphics could be transferred directly to television, the fact that Goldstein and Nagel presented the second, more logical, possibility as an afterthought could not make their point more clear: Raytraced graphics were worthy of a place in a media hierarchy that privileges cinema (and that they could be useful in television was merely an added bonus).

Nevertheless, industrial reality meant that, despite occasional Hollywood commissions for movie credit sequences like *The Black Hole* (1979) or a more ambitious feature length one-off such as *Tron* (1982), MAGI and other significant innovators in the computer graphics simulation industries were, for decades, only to find a consistently reliable revenue stream in television advertisements and logos. Despite this, however, as the move of computer graphics into mainstream Hollywood cinema was to eventually demonstrate, Goldstein and Nagel's claims for the cinematic potential of CG visual effects proved prescient. This was perhaps motivated by an understanding on their part that their graphics form, however suited to electronic, video and television distribution and exhibition, also contained a range of features common in the cinematic attraction and its function as a platform for astonishing spectacle.

We must be careful, however, to avoid a conflation of two quite different visual forms. While games and graphics emerged from the same origin within the computer processor, they followed different development paths and were put to different functional and economic uses. In both cases the development paths affected were partly the result of hardware considerations in early computing: namely processing capacity. This in turn influenced the industrial potential of each, and the economic possibilities that followed. While visual effects could call upon many processors or even expensive supercomputing necessary for complex and detailed simulative rendering (because the result, transferred onto celluloid or video, was not dependent upon the presence of a computer in its exhibition phase), computer games could only call upon significantly lower quantities of processing power and for the most part required continual real-time processing. Equally, these constraints reflected in the output at the other end, with one form pre-rendered and non-interactive (once the director and animation team had locked it down for public consumption) and the other preconfigured but rendered anew and in real-time, each and every time. The difference in these development paths meant that the spectacular function of visual effects and computer games took equally differentiated routes.

While initially during the 1950s and 1960s both rudimentary computer graphics and early games were a fascination for their novelty and for the possibilities that they implied, during the 1970s, as commercially deployed CG and domestic gaming developed, the nature of these forms diverged. In expensively rendered and professionally constructed computer graphics, new image forms emerged that functioned as astonishing digital attractions: interesting for their illusory powers alone (to paraphrase Tom Gunning). With games, the nature of a user's fascination was different. Early games were primitive in their graphics capacity, and their appeal was in their interactive function as much as their illusory power. By contrast, and like the cinematic attractions of a century before, early showreels from MAGI, Abel & Associates, Digital Effects, Information International Inc., Digital Productions, Marks & Marks and Pacific Data Images abound with visuals and subject matter intended to perform the function of impressing the audience with the illusory capacities of the silicon chip. With a certain sense of déjà vu for the visual culture enthusiast or historian, many of these graphics demos featured objects rushing out of the screen and toward the viewer (Figure 10.1).

Reminiscent of the oncoming vehicles that dominated early attractions,[14] early computer graphics demos endlessly feature automobile objects from trains, cars, helicopters, planes, boats and spaceships through to anything one can think of that, while not normally automobile, may in computer-animated form be rendered flying through space. Goldstein and Nagel's research paper itself provided multiple examples of this, offering the reader a helicopter, a car and a plane as prime examples of objects that could be rendered with this new technique (Figure 10.2).

These CG demos shared more with early cinematic attractions than just the rendering of oncoming vehicles, however: In early attractions there was also an opening up of potential new cinematic space that the emerging automotive vehicles of modernity facilitated. Ben Singer has argued that this provided an audiovisual accompaniment to what he has described as the hyperstimulus of modernity,[15] while Lynne Kirby has traced the parallels between train track technologies and those of the railed camera dolly in her book *Parallel Tracks.*[16] Like the early filmmakers that placed their cameras on the fronts of trains, trams, planes and cars in order to open up the new spaces and experiences that industrial modernity had to offer, early CG companies similarly situated the 'virtual camera' in entirely new spaces facilitated by the simulative capacities of the computer. While this new, postmodern, ultra-automobile, postindustrial space with its vector line graphics and digital object rendering were of an inherently electronic and cathode ray delivered nature, the content of it also betrayed a preoccupation with the visualization of data-culture and the electronic communications that facilitated it. And yet there was an essential cinematicity to these showreels, too, driven by the same urge to astonish early audiences with new visual attractions that had formed the staple of cinema's emergence. There was even something explicitly fairground about these demo-reel attractions in the plethora of juggling clowns, exotic brightly coloured objects and weird and wonderful new creatures visualized (Figure 10.3).

If we examine the emergence of CG attractions further, we find that

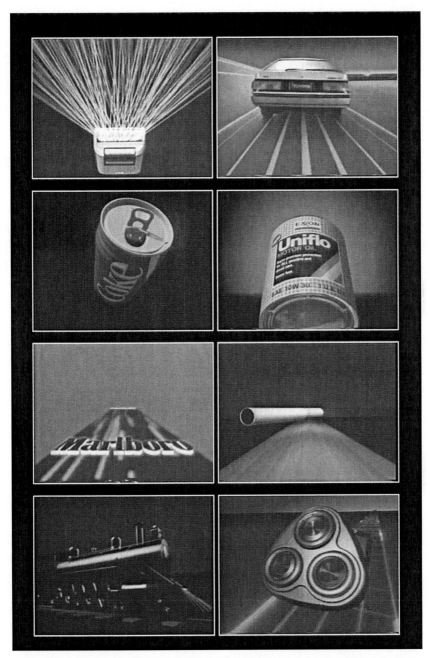

Figure 10.1 *From top left to bottom right, train effects of: Braun Shaver (Abel & Associates, 1981), Toyota Car (Abel & Associates, 1982), Coke Can (Digital Productions, 1984), Exxon Oil (Digital Productions, 1984), Marlboro Logo (Digital Effects Inc., 1980), Advance Cigarette (Information International Inc., 1982), Steam Train (MAGI, 1984), Norelco Shaver (MAGI, 1984).*

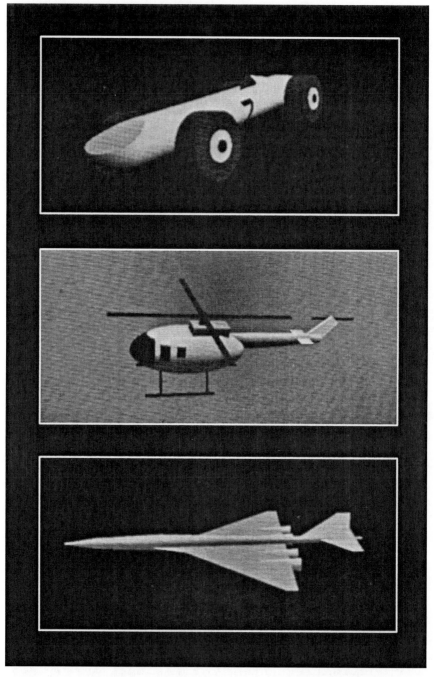

Figure 10.2 *From top to bottom, all three images created by Robert Goldstein and Roger Nagel (MAGI), from '3-D Visual Simulation', Simulation 16 (January 1971), pp. 25–31.*

Figure 10.3 *Clown (MAGI, 1984), Juggling Entertainer (Information International Inc., 1982), Magician (Abel & Associates, 1987).*

their history bears parallels with early cinematic attractions beyond that of their shared function as astonishing amusements. While the technological development of CG imaging was quite different to cinema, the circumstances under which it was subsequently commercially deployed are revealing. Originally used as a means of simulating radiation dispersal during the mid-1960s, MAGI commercialized raytracing animation in the early 1970s. Despite their 1971 paper extolling the cinematic potential of raytracing, MAGI formed SynthaVision in 1972 and quickly found civilian commercial applications for CGI in television advertising, making what has been credited as the first CGI advert for IBM. It is worth recalling, then, that many of the earliest films while functioning as attractions – for audiences less concerned about subject matter than about witnessing the astonishing spectacle of the moving image – also doubled as industrial films, funded by and featuring the products and services of various industrial interests.[17] As 1890s adverts for the likes of Admiral Cigarettes and Dewar's Scotch Whiskey demonstrate, industrial interests realized quickly that the astonishment that cinematic attractions engendered made them an ideal platform on which to deploy a commercial message. Like early cinema, early CG reels contain a plethora of industrial objects visualized anew and commercial services advertised by companies keen to capitalize on the astonishing new aesthetics of computer graphics. Because most of the early CG houses disappeared in the precarious, volatile and rapidly changing industrial landscape they occupied, the highest profile surviving example of this commercial relationship is now Pixar (which began life relatively late, in 1986). Pixar survived on a great many advertising commissions long before it established itself as a producer of feature length CG movies. Perhaps unsurprisingly, many of the animation techniques and philosophies developed through advertising – especially those towards creating ever new astonishing attractions – can now be observed, with a certain sense of continuity, pervading their feature movies.

In his work on early incredulous cinema spectators and what he calls an 'aesthetic of astonishment', Gunning (and later Steven Bottomore) draws upon Méliès's observations of the early audience experience to point out that spectators, when first confronted with the cinema screen, were greatly impressed by footage of what would now seem rather mundane: clouds, ocean waves, leaves rustling in trees or, as Bottomore puts it, 'complex natural motion'.[18] What impressed and pleased spectators most, however, argues Gunning, was 'a vacillation between belief and incredulity', or as Bottomore describes it, a feeling of 'That's it exactly!'[19] Pleasure was derived from the experience of watching phenomena rendered in detail and movement that was technically analogous to the real-life event: rendered 'realistically' yet impossibly on the cinema screen. Despite the pleasure of beholding what was, for these early viewers, the breathtaking realism of such images, they argue that a prerequisite for this pleasure was the simultaneous cognisance that what they were seeing was not, in actual fact, real. Gunning argues that cinema in turn inherited this reflex towards astonished incredulity from earlier visual forms such as *trompe l'oeil* and magic theatre. Indeed, as Gunning asserts, the 'magic theatre laboured to make visual that which it was impossible to believe. Its visual power consisted of a trompe l'oeil play of give-and-take, an obsessive desire to test the limits of an intellectual disavowal – I know, but yet I see'.[20] While Gunning does not expand into contemporary examples of where this might take place, it takes little deduction to see late twentieth-century CG effects (and what I will shortly describe as spectacular computer gaming) as an inheritor of such a dynamic.

As director of *Toy Story*, John Lasseter stated in a revealing description of Pixar's development philosophy:

> At Pixar, we like to think we use our tools to make things look photorealistic, but not try to reproduce reality. We like to take those tools and make something that the audience knows does not exist. Every frame, they know it's a cartoon. So you get that wonderful entertainment of, 'I know this isn't real, but boy it sure looks real'. I think that's part of the fun of what we do.[21]

Notably, while Pixar was not one of the first computer graphics companies, it was an inheritor of many of the CG imaging skills that inevitably arrived from older companies as they went bankrupt or were bought out. In this sense, Lasseter's description is not only symptomatic of Pixar's philosophy but can be observed in the aesthetic of most early visual effects productions. David Price has, for instance, described the 'awestruck' response of an audience of CGI specialists at the SIGGRAPH (Special Interest Group on Graphics and Interactive Techniques) Conference in 1980, when Loren Carpenter exhibited *Vol Libre*, the two-minute film he animated while working for Boeing.[22] In a rerun of the spectacular capacities of the natural world in early cinema, Carpenter's breakthrough was to use fractal algorithms originally discovered by Benoit Mandelbrot to describe mathematical patterns found in the natural world. With these algorithms Carpenter rendered the sides of mountains with what – to the academics and engineers observing – was astonishing, naturalistic realism amidst what was still a synthetic-feeling early computer-generated image culture. The result of this was a prompt offer to Carpenter of a job at Lucas Arts. In twentieth-century special effects culture, then, we see precisely both the 'trompe l'oeil play of give-and-take' and the 'obsessive desire to test the limits of an intellectual disavowal – I know, but yet I see' described by Gunning. From MAGI's raytraced and reflective surfaces to Digital Effects Inc.'s computer-generated images demonstrating their distinctly trompe l'oeil

Figure 10.4   *Trompe l'oeil demonstration, 'Great Northwest Talent' (Digital Effects Inc., 1982).*

capacities (Figure 10.4), visual effects picked up the baton of 'astonishing aesthetics' that had resided within the cinematic apparatus for much of the preceding century.

Beyond its illusory power, however, CG imaging was not only eye catching and novel, it also signified the simulated immaterial futurism with which telecommunications companies, car companies, electronic manufacturers and many others sought to be associated. Thus, the emergence of the digital attraction was similar in nature to the history of the emergence of the cinematic attraction: both characterized by their capacity to astonish, and both deployed as audiovisual forms that simultaneously functioned as promotional vehicles and encapsulated that sense of techno-futurist modernity/post-modernity that the companies featured wanted to convey. The significant difference between the two lies in the fact that CG graphics found their promotional platform on television rather than, as the first audiovisual adverts did, on the cinema screen. This could be seen as a symptom of the technological and industrial difference between CG imaging as a televisual form distinct from the cinematic. However, it would be more accurate to approach this distinction as indicative of cinema's digital and convergent future since, lying in early CG imaging's public televisual output were the seeds of future developments in cinematic production and exhibition.[23] This can be seen again and again in the special effects sequences first trialled in television adverts before finding their way into Hollywood,[24] or the feature length advertisements like *Toy Story 1, 2* and *3* indebted to a two-decade long test bed process in national television advertising spots. In Pixar features, as with their televisual advertisements that made them so appealing to industry, the objects and characters that populate their attractions are integrally related to contemporary practices of industrial product design engineering: creating a situation in which every object on screen is an industrially fabricated, carefully placed product.[25]

Perhaps most reflective of early cinema, CG imaging did not simply visualize new industrial products; such imaging stood directly for a new industrial economy of high precision design, engineering and manufacture. Nearly a century before, the cinematic apparatus had done precisely the same thing in standing for the mass industrial manufacturing methods of modernity. Thus by the late 1970s the 'virtual camera' could now envision and represent the industrial object in new and more intimate ways (like the cinema camera). Equally, this new form of visualization did not need a narrative and it did not need a raison d'être; it was enough that it could render an astonishing industrial spectacle for industrial spectacle's sake. The very creation of such a technologically expensive spectacle was enough to signify industrial prowess and confer it on the company and product being advertised. In this sense, too, CGI betrayed its own inherent cinematicity: in the capacity of the image to represent capital to the point that it becomes spectacle.[26] Small wonder then that Hollywood spotted an opportunity in short order and started to incorporate CG imaging into its special effects culture. Interestingly this was not, as Goldstein and Nagel argued, because it was cheaper and labour saving, but precisely the opposite: because it was expensive. As Bruce Bennett has insightfully argued, the political economy of Hollywood's special effects industry has long dictated that conspicuous waste, excess and expense shape the logic of spectacle.[27] In this sense, CG imaging and the costly technological and labour arms race that it entailed made it an ideal candidate for Hollywood's digital future. Consequently, the promotional function of CG imaging, while nurtured by terrestrial television in its early phase, became a valuable asset to Hollywood with its large budgets and high production values. What was less clear, until the industrial developments of the last decade, was whether video gaming would follow this path, too.

While there are many games platforms creating a vast array of non-spectacular games (not least the rapidly growing mobile platforms that have encouraged a resurgence in the small screen, pre-3D, heavily ludological forms of gaming reminiscent of video games from its early period), the past decade has also seen the rise of what we could call the 'spectacular game'.

With the processing power of modern video consoles far surpassing the supercomputers that MAGI and other CG imaging industrialists used to create CG effects in the early 1980s, large games studios have arisen that often resemble special effects companies and their pipeline products. The 3D game engines that have emerged alongside have not only promised and delivered tools with which to rapidly render a nearly photorealistic space (one that is endlessly referred to by critics as 'cinematic'), they have been incorporated into the working processes of film and VFX studios. At both ends of the production scale, from directors using game engines to pre-visualize their special effects sequences, to low budget 'machinimators' making machine cinema in their bedrooms, the graphics visualization granted by video game culture has rapidly moved into the heart of cinema's present and future. I do not wish to suggest here, however, that games are increasingly 'cinematic'; to do so is to miss the point of the impact of game engines (and visual effects): that games and graphics engines have increasingly become emblems of contemporary cinematicity. With this in mind we can turn to a consideration of the relationship between games, computer graphics and the economy of astonishing aesthetics.

With extreme constraints on processing power in early video consoles and domestic computers, games existed in a different visual context to their vastly more powerfully pre-rendered CG imaged filmic and televisual counterparts. Despite this, video games were still a fascinating visual attraction, but their appeal lay as much if not more in their interactive function as in their illusory power (some game theorists would argue that their appeal lay primarily in their interactive function, but generations of players who grew up content to watch gameplay as well as undertake it suggest that the dynamics of this were more nuanced – certainly the area is ripe for further research). Regardless, the implication that interactivity implies a differentiated path for early games not suitable to cinematic analogy is problematic in suggesting that the interactive function is opposed to the cinematic.

Work on the train effect and early cinema's fabled flinching audiences suggests that even the first viewers were, to some extent, interactive (and keen to be interactive) with the emergent cinema screen. Clearly this interactive potential was limited, as *The Countryman and the Cinematograph,* early cinema's famously self-reflexive account of the limited interactive screen, made a point of highlighting in 1901 – with its subject a naïve country dweller failing to understand the limits of the screen before tearing it down. Nevertheless, even this limited interactivity was enough of a feature of early cinematic experiences to become a staple of exaggerated newspaper accounts about fleeing audiences: a subsequent founding myth of the screen. In an odd but telling remake of *The Countryman and the Cinematograph,* a 1982 Intellivision game

Figure 10.5 *Game console advertisement (Intellivision, 1982).*

console advertisement featured George Plimpton and a wide-eyed country bumpkin confirming that the close encounter with a UFO he had witnessed was precisely the same as the console game on the screen before him (Figure 10.5). While Intellivision's early games may not have been very sophisticated by contemporary standards, their advertising was. In this case their advertisement pokes fun at, and acknowledges, their game's relative graphical limitations while simultaneously asserting that it is better than the competitors'. More broadly, this advertisement and many others in the Intellivision and Atari line up demonstrate that from the inception of the domestic video game market, graphics capability not only mattered but constituted a significant selling point. This was to be a major feature of the video gaming hardware and software industry for the next thirty years (of which more later).

Returning to cinema's founding myth of the flinching audience, early racing video games in particular functioned in some ways like an interactive train effect (elsewhere I have suggested we may call this 'the game effect'). Anyone viewing gamers twisting input controllers as if the angle of incidence affected control of the onscreen object (car, plane or spaceship, for example), or who has seen players physically ducking from virtual oncoming objects will agree that games have taken the flinching audience to a new, albeit individuated, level. Of course in a founding myth of cinema the audience does not merely flinch, it flees. In the case of games no such founding myth took flight, and this may partly have been a function of the fact that video gaming, like early Victorian optical toys a century before, were largely ignored in their cultural significance as children's playthings rather than as symptoms of an emergent new visual culture.[28] In addition to starting life as a children's medium, video games were representationally simplistic, two-dimensional and iconographic. By contrast, cinema started life as an apparatus for conjuring an illusion of overwhelming realism, the extent of which

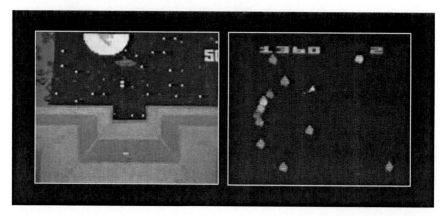

Figure 10.6 Star Strike *advertisement (Intellivision, 1981/2) comparing the 'superior' Star Strike with its 3D graphics and visual effects to Asteroids.*

supposedly overrode an audience's capacity to bear in mind this illusionistic foundation.

Nevertheless, it is notable that even with so little processing power to hand, game designers spent so much time developing new ways of constructing three-dimensional game spaces and improving visual aesthetics (colour range and detail early on, texture mapping and render quality later) to provide a greater degree of what was often termed as 'realism'. As Mark Wolf has described in rich detail, there were varied strategies deployed in computer and video game development for creating 3D-like spatial effects on limited processing power during the 1980s. However, the capacity to create genuine 3D space in gaming was not to come until the mid-1990s.[29] It was not just the game designers that aspired to the 'realism' that 3D space could theoretically provide, however; many of the games advertisements of the time based their sales pitch for new games on their capacity to create a visually realistic and therefore spatially 'immersive' experience. Again we find a revealing sales pitch exemplifying this in an Intellivision advertisement. George Plimpton advises the audience that Intellivision supplies a superior gaming experience, this time because of a combination of both 3D and visual effects. As he explains, '*Star Strike* has moving images, which make the game appear three dimensional, *Asteroids* doesn't. And *Star Strike* features our most exciting visual effect: the total destruction of a planet. This [turning to the other screen showing *Asteroids*] is what the other game offers, which is why after *Star Strike, Asteroids* left me rather flat.' Intriguingly this advertisement appeals to both 3D space and what they tellingly refer to as a 'visual effect'. One would have thought that all the game's graphics constitute a visual effect, but the fact that Plimpton's job here is to single an effect out for specific attention demonstrates a recognition on the part of the developers and advertisers that deploying a sales pitch long used in cinema could also work with games.

The claim here is not that all video games industries headed explicitly towards a cinematic illusionism, however. There are many examples of game development in which they clearly did not. What the games industry did often do, however, was aspire towards a set of game player experiences that can be traced through not only cinema, but the audiovisual apparatus of the screen that preceded cinema and formed its foundation in the first place. These player experiences were the result of the constant attempt to provide aston-ishing aesthetics; at the same time they promised an immersive experience that could engage players in new ways. In this sense the tendency towards 3D in gaming cannot be reductively attributed to the desire for greater cinematic illusionism – after all, renaissance perspective has been a function of our visual culture for centuries and is hardly the sole domain of cinema. And yet, 3D graphical capabilities did stand for the achievement of a cinematic form in the games industry at various points. As Dan Houser (original creator of the infamous *Grand Theft Auto* games and founder of Rockstar Games Studio) aptly summarizes in interview, the simulation of 3D space was initially regarded as a means of achieving 'movie' aesthetics in games. Later, however, 3D space came to function as a means by which a greater level of immersion and involvement than cinema could deliver played a part in a new develop-ment incentive:

> [W]ith those first 3D games, we were trying to make something that had the aspirations to be like a movie [. . .], by GTA [*Grand Theft Auto*] IV, we wanted to try to find something that could be better than movies in a way – more alive and more vibrant. It was time to move on and do our own thing.[30]

The irony here is that while Houser presents this desire to create something 'more alive and more vibrant' than a movie, a very similar drive underpinned the emergence of cinema itself. With this in mind it is notable that the video games market is reaching a state of maturity in which, as William Boddy highlights, television's cinematic large screen and immersive capacities have finally started to match up to the hyperbolic promises made over decades of advertising.[31]

In the contemporary context, games and games consoles are now touted as approaching the photorealistic event horizon so mythically heralded by games developers, players and commentators for decades. The 'obsessive desire to test the limits of an intellectual disavowal – I know, but yet I see' that Gunning talks about has begun to enter the dynamics of game design in earnest. In recent years games such as *Heavy Rain, L.A. Noire, Final Fantasy 13, Modern Warfare, Call of Duty* and many more have emerged to fanfare and

Figure 10.7   L.A. Noire *(Rockstar, 2011)*, Final Fantasy 13 *(Square Enix, 2010)*, Heavy Rain *(Quantic Dream, 2010)*, Call of Duty: Modern Warfare 3 *(Activision, 2011)*.

proclamations from developers and reviewers alike that the fabled, elusive and astonishing photorealist aesthetic has finally been achieved.

Approaching this photorealistic 'milestone' from a less fervent point of view, its arrival is likely to be somewhat more underwhelming than the cultural hype that has circulated around the notion for many years has suggested. After all, audiences have been engaged with photorealistic content for more than a century. Indeed, we could say that the photorealistic milestone for gaming is both already upon us and at the same time will never arrive. For the definition of photorealistic graphics depends greatly (like all aesthetic evaluations) upon what comparative yardstick is used to determine its relative quality. It is quite clear already that games are on the market that closely resemble the 'photorealistic' graphics of Hollywood special effects movies (see Figure 10.7). In both cases these graphics are no less an aesthetic and generic convention than the romantic paintings of a century before that inform them. Here, then, 'photorealism' is and will likely always be a relative and continually shifting stylistic term. The larger question then becomes: Why the obsession?

The promise of contemporary spectacular gaming seems to rest in the implication that photorealism previously only encountered in pre-recorded media will finally be combined with the capacities of modern, powerful central processing units (CPUs) and graphics processing units (GPUs), thus providing real-time narrative and ludological control. The implication, then, is that this will blur the creative and experiential boundaries of gaming and will herald a new stage in its cultural relevance (and even rise to dominance). In other words, gaming will finally be able to enter the (dubious) pantheon of accepted expressive visual arts. This somewhat questionable position has been expressed many times but was perhaps most clearly reiterated recently by Christoph Hartmann, the head of 2K games, when talking about the near-term future of gaming:

> Recreating a *Mission Impossible* experience in gaming is easy; recreating emotions in *Brokeback Mountain* is going to be tough [. . .] It will be very hard to create very deep emotions like sadness or love, things that drive the movies. Until games are photorealistic, it'll be very hard to open up to new genres. We can really only focus on action and shooter titles; those are suitable for consoles now. To dramatically change the industry to where we can insert a whole range of emotions, I feel it will only happen when we reach the point that games are photorealistic; then we will have reached an endpoint and that might be the final console.[32]

In acknowledging that current games have reached a point where they resemble Hollywood action blockbusters and yet have not yet reached the hallowed photorealist finishing line, we witness in Hartmann's statement a perfect example of the way in which discussions of games already act out a somewhat schizophrenic dynamic. Hartmann's declaration presents games as already delivering a cinematic experience, yet at the same time this experience must develop further in order for 'photorealistic' gaming to arrive. In other words, while one cinematic experience is already upon us, cinematic photorealism is still to arrive. Perhaps more telling about Hartmann's statement is his somewhat surprisingly naïve assertion that photorealism is a finishing line both for games ('we will have reached an endpoint') and for games hardware ('that might be the final console'). The implication from this is always that gaming and game design has not yet grown up. It is still pushing on the door of its cinematic big brother's bedroom asking to be allowed to play. The message here is that the moment gaming reaches a 'cinematic' level of photorealism (leaving aside the point that cinematic aesthetics has always been a moving target in its own right anyway) will be the moment when it is not only allowed in to play, but comes to dominate its once mighty cinematic big brother's play space.

There are many obvious problems with this thinking that are too numerous to explore at the end of a chapter. Not only does it focus a great deal of power in the hands of an aesthetic verisimilitude, but it relies upon a mythical moment imagined in 'the future' when gaming will reach its equivalent of the singularity of cinema. Equally, it implies that games are, and have long been on a trajectory of 'progress', the achievement of which can be measured by photorealistic milestones along the way. But rather like IBM Deep Blue's seminal chess winning moment, one wonders whether an obsessive focus on a computer's capacity to cognitively best the viewer/player is really to miss the point that the winning or losing is less important than the fact that computers are now intimately implicated in the game. This brings us full circle. In the early 1970s Goldstein and Nagel insisted on comparing their computer graphics techniques to the simulative equivalent of a photograph. While they could not have known how far reaching the shift to digital media would go in the following forty years, one wonders if this would have surprised them more or less than the residual cultural attachment to notions of the photoreal that they were so careful to pay homage to. Fundamentally, it seems, while gaming is indeed a very different beast to its cinematic predecessor, the cinematicity of astonishing aesthetics in games culture has a long future ahead of it.

ACKNOWLEDGEMENTS

I would like to thank a number of people who were directly and indirectly responsible for this chapter. This includes Stephen McCormick and Sue Irwin for their indispensible editorial comments; Bruce Bennett for his many vital thoughtful inputs to, and discussions of, my work over the years; Mark Bartlett and Suzanne Buchan for their thoughtful encouragement in recent years; and indirectly, Tom Gunning and Lev Manovich for work that has inspired me greatly.

Notes

1. Robert A. Goldstein and Roger Nagel, '3-D Visual Simulation', *Simulation* 16 (January 1971), 25–31 (p. 25).
2. *Ibid.*
3. This strategy is hardly surprising given the manner by which new media forms do not destroy their predecessors so much as remediate them, as Friedrich Kittler (*Gramophone, Film, Typewriter*, trans. Geoffrey Winthrop-Young and Michael Wutz, Stanford, CA: Stanford University Press, 1999), Jay David Bolter and Richard Grusin (*Remediation: Understanding New Media*, London: The MIT Press, 2000) and Lev Manovich (*The Language of New Media*, London: The MIT Press, 2001) and many others have pointed out.
4. Such techniques were not limited to Goldstein and Nagel's experience but appear to have been standard fare at the time, as David Price's description of future Pixar founder Ed Catmull's contemporaneous work demonstrates.

See *The Pixar Touch: The Making of a Company* (New York, NY: Vintage, 2008), p. 14.

5. Goldstein and Nagel, '3-D Visual Simulation', p. 28.

6. For more on this see Leon Gurevitch, 'Problematic Dichotomies: Narrative and Spectacle in Advertising and Film Scholarship', *The Journal of Popular Narrative Media* 2.2 (2009), 143–58; Gurevitch, 'The Cinemas of Transactions: The Exchangeable Currency of the Digital Attraction', *Television and New Media* 11.5 (2010), 367–85; Gurevitch, 'The Cinemas of Interactions: Cinematics and the "Game Effect" in the Age of Digital Attractions', *Senses of Cinema* 57 (December 2010), at: http://www.sensesofcinema.com (accessed 1 January 2013).

7. For some excellent accounts of this see especially: Martin Picard, 'Video Games and Their Relationship with Other Media', in Mark J. P. Wolf, ed., *The Video Game Explosion: A History from Pong to PlayStation and Beyond* (London: Greenwood Press, 2008), pp. 293–300; Mark J. P. Wolf, 'Z-Axis Development in the Video Game', in Wolf and Bernard Perron, eds, *The Video Game Theory Reader 2* (London: Routledge, 2009), pp. 151–68; Michael Nitsche, *Video Game Spaces: Image, Play, and Structure in 3D Worlds* (London: The MIT Press, 2008).

8. For detailed work on machinima, the virtual camera and game spectatorship see: Henry Lowood, 'High Performance Play: the Making of Machinima', in Andy Clarke and Grethe Mitchell, eds, *Videogames and Art* (Bristol: Intellect, 2007), pp. 59–79; Barry Atkins, 'What Are We Really Looking at?: The Future Orientation of Video Game Play', *Games and Culture* 1.2 (April 2006), 127–40; Mike Jones, 'Vanishing Point: Spatial Composition and the Virtual Camera', *Animation: An Interdisciplinary Journal* 2.3 (November 2007), 225–43.

9. Thomas Malaby, 'Beyond Play: A New Approach to Games', *Games and Culture* 2.2 (2007), 95–113 (p. 96). Nor does this suggest that there is a singular 'medium of the computer game', as Espen Aarseth argues in 'Genre Trouble: Narrativism and the Art of Simulation', in Noah Wardrip-Fruin and Pat Harrigan, eds, *First Person: New Media as Story, Performance, and Game* (Cambridge, MA: The MIT Press, 2004), pp. 45–56 (p. 46).

10. Manovich, *Language of New Media,* p. 99. Notably the first primitive computer game (William Higinbotham's 1957 *Tennis for Two* game) adapted a computer's capacity to calculate a ballistic missile trajectory to the task of simulating a tennis ball and functioned on an oscilloscope.

11. Compounding this, theorists such as Sheila Murphy rightly argue that in discussions of computers and video games, television has too often been ignored simply as a medium through which the games or graphics flow. See Sheila Murphy, '"This is Intelligent Television": Early Video Games and Television in the Emergence of the Personal Computer', in Wolf and Perron, pp. 197–212 (p. 198).

12. Lisa Gitelman, *Always Already New: Media, History, and the Data of Culture* (Cambridge, MA: The MIT Press, 2008), p. 29.

13. Goldstein and Nagel, '3-D Visual Simulation', p. 30.

14. See especially Tom Gunning, 'The Cinema of Attractions: Early Film, its

Spectator and the Avant-Garde', in Thomas Elsaesser, ed., *Early Cinema: Space, Frame, Narrative* (London: BFI, 1990), pp. 56–62; Steven Bottomore, 'The Panicking Audience?: Early Cinema and the "Train Effect"', *Historical Journal of Film, Radio, and Television* 19.2 (1999), 177–216; Christa Blümlinger, 'Lumière, the Train and the Avant-Garde', in Wanda Strauven, ed., *The Cinema of Attractions Reloaded* (Amsterdam: Amsterdam University Press, 2006), pp. 245–64.

15. Ben Singer, 'Modernity, Hyperstimulus, and the Rise of Popular Sensationalism', in Leo Charney and Vanessa Schwartz, eds, *Cinema and the Invention of Modern Life* (Berkeley, CA: University of California Press, 1995), pp. 72–102.

16. Lynne Kirby, *Parallel Tracks: The Railroad and Silent Cinema* (Durham, NC: Duke University Press, 1997).

17. For example, Edison Manufacturing's *Blacksmithing Scene* (1894), the Lumières' *Workers Leaving the Factory* (1895), Edison's *Black Diamond Express* (1896), Biograph's US postal system series including *Throwing Mail into Bags* (1903), and finally Westinghouse Works' car and turbine production films of 1904. For more detail on this see: Charles Musser, *The Emergence of Cinema: The American Screen to 1907* (New York, NY: Macmillan, 1990); Kerry Segrave, *Product Placement in Hollywood Films: A History* (London: McFarland, 2004); Gurevitch, 'Problematic Dichotomies' and 'The Cinemas of Transactions'.

18. Bottomore, 'The Panicking Audience?', p. 212.

19. Tom Gunning, 'An Aesthetic of Astonishment: Early Film and the (In)credulous Spectator', in Leo Braudy and Marshall Cohen, eds, *Film Theory and Criticism: Introductory Readings* (New York, NY: Oxford University Press, 1999), pp. 818–32 (p. 823).

20. *Ibid.*, p. 821.

21. Jonathan Ross and John Lasseter, 'Welcome to My World' (Interview with John Lasseter), *The Guardian,* 23 November 2001; at: http://www.guardian.co.uk/culture/2001/nov/23/artsfeatures7 (accessed 15 January 2013).

22. Price, p. 37.

23. For more details, see: Yvonne Spielmann, 'Expanding Film into Digital Media', *Screen* 40.2 (1999), 131–45; also Laura Mulvey, 'Passing Time: Reflections on Cinema from a New Technological Age', *Screen* 45.2 (2004), 142–55.

24. See Gurevitch, 'The Cinemas of Transactions'.

25. See Leon Gurevitch, 'Computer Generated Animation as Product Design Engineered Culture or Buzz Lightyear to the Sales Floor: To the Checkout and Beyond!', *Animation: An Interdisciplinary Journal* 7.2 (2012), 131–49.

26. Guy Debord, *The Society of the Spectacle*, trans. Donald Nicholson-Smith (New York, NY: Zone Books, 1995).

27. Bruce Bennett, 'Towards a General Economics of Cinema', in Susan Bruce and Valeria Wagner, eds, *Fiction and Economy* (New York, NY: Palgrave, 2007), pp. 167–86.

28. For an excellent account of this, see Nicolas Dulac and André Gaudreault, 'Circularity and Repetition at the Heart of the Attraction: Optical Toys and the Emergence of a New Cultural Series', in Wanda Strauven, ed., *The Cinema*

of Attractions Reloaded (Amsterdam: Amsterdam University Press, 2006), pp. 227–44.

29. Wolf, 'Z-Axis Development'.
30. Keith Stewart, 'How Dan Houser Helped Turn Grand Theft Auto into a Cultural Phenomenon', *The Guardian*, 18 November 2012; at: http://www.guardian. co.uk/media/2012/nov/18/dan-houser-grand-theft-auto?INTCMP=SRCH (accessed 15 January 2013).
31. See William Boddy, *New Media and Popular Imagination: Launching Radio, Television, and Digital Media in the United States* (Oxford: Oxford University Press, 2004).
32. Quoted in James Brightman, 'Games Must Achieve Photorealism in Order to Open Up New Genres Says 2K', *Games Industry International*, 1 August 2012; at: http://www.gamesindustry.biz/articles/2012-08-01-games-must-achieve-photorealism-in-order-to-open-up-new-genres-says-2k (accessed 20 January 2013).

CHAPTER 11

Miniature Pleasures:
On Watching Films on an iPhone

MARTINE BEUGNET

'Thus the minuscule, a narrow gate, opens up an entire world.'
Gaston Bachelard, *La Poétique de l'espace*[1]

If one of the distinctive characteristics of the cinematic experience in the age of 'remediation' and 'media convergence' is the collective viewing of a film shown on a large screen, then the smartphone, as the smallest portable and personal screening device, represents its very antinomy. With its diminutive screen and set of earphones, the smartphone as screening device encourages the kind of individual and intimate viewing that appears, on the one hand, typical of spectatorial habits in the age of the digital and, on the other, more evocative of the kinetoscope's peephole apparatus than of the film theatre.

As what was initially designed as a communication implement was turned into a screen on which users could stream and watch mobile images, viewers started to engage with miniature versions of complex sequences of moving images, including film images, whose intricate compositions and variations were originally intended for the cinema screen. Hence in public spaces as well as private, domestic ones – whether in the busy carriage of a commuter train or lying in the cosy surroundings of the bedroom – smartphone owners hunched over miniature, self-contained wonderlands like modern-day Alices have become a familiar sight.

In what follows, I propose to go beyond the debate about the 'proper' ways of screening films to concentrate instead on the specific characteristics of watching film images on very small screens. I will therefore look at issues of mobility, manipulability and distracted-versus-attentive viewing only briefly, before I focus on the effect of miniaturization on the film image. Indeed, I choose to focus on the more diminutive screens, those that can be held in one's hand, for only the very small-size moving image elicits the sense of magic and fascination that I wish to evoke here. Rather than pertaining to cinema per se, the phenomenon partakes in a diffuse sense of 'cinematic-ity' and, as such, it calls for its own set of terms and references. Drawing on haptic theories of visuality, as well as on the aesthetics of miniature art forms and the curio, I will explore the effects of reduction on the moving image, from the intensification of the colour fields and of movement, to the miniaturization of moving figures, and more specifically, of the human figure. I will suggest that, through the experience of miniaturized, intimate viewing that it offers even in the midst of the bustle of public spaces, as a screening device the smartphone arguably creates, to paraphrase Laura Mulvey, its own type of possessive spectator.[2]

POCKET-SIZE CINEMA?

Where small screen viewing is concerned, Apple was at the leading edge.[3] Indeed from the start, the iPhone's distinctive qualities as a viewing device, suitable to watch even images intended for the cinema, was a key aspect of its success.[4] These specific qualities were duly highlighted when the device was launched in 2007.[5] At the Apple *grand messe* where he first presented his revolutionary touch-based device, Steve Jobs emphasized the iPhone's unique design: Compared to other mobile phones, Apple's iPhone was immediately recognizable through its lack of a hard keyboard. As a result, whereas other mobile phones only afforded square, stamp-size screens, with its retractable, touch keyboard, the iPhone not only offered a comparatively expansive screen space framed by a case whose 'clean' non-intrusive design would become its trademark, but, in addition, a screen that could be held length-wise. At the same time, the iPhone could still be held in the palm of one's hand, and could easily fit in one's pocket.

In his 2007 presentation of the new device, Jobs thus pointed out that, for the first time, it would become enjoyable to not only watch mobile images on one's phone, but to watch images originally created for the cinema. Indeed, Jobs's choice of film as the prop for his demonstration is telling: The sequence of images selected to illustrate the iPhone's superior qualities as a screening device were extracted from *Pirates of the Caribbean: Dead Man's Chest* (2006, dir. Gore Verbinski) – a high production value costume drama, boasting not only a star-studded cast but elaborate sets, costumes, large numbers of extras, expansive seascapes and spectacular battle scenes. From the start, the expectation was that in spite of the small screen, viewers would not shy away from watching images that rely on a wealth of detail and that may require sustained attention – if not at the narrative level, at least where the visual composition was concerned.[6] Indeed, Jobs further pointed to two specifications that suggested that cinephiles, as well as occasional, distracted viewers, would use the device to watch films: the 'pinching' application, allowing the user to zoom into the image by applying tactile pressure, and a cinemascope option ensuring that the images would not be automatically 'boxed' and have their content cropped.

Pelle Snickars and Patrick Vonderau's introduction to *Moving Data: The iPhone and the Future of Media*, begins with an account of Jobs walking the red carpet at the 2010 Oscar ceremony, a strong indicator, the authors remark, of Apple's growing interest in the cinema business.[7] As several of the essays contained in *Moving Data* emphasize, however, in practice access to films – in their integral, unaltered form, that is – remains an issue. The online streaming and downloading of movies is tightly regulated; storage space and battery power are a concern when downloading and watching a feature film; and it remains to be seen whether so-called cloud-based providers of moving-image based art and entertainment such as Ultraviolet will at some point in the future allow viewers to select and access the films that they want to watch anywhere, at any time, and at an acceptable cost.[8] The by-product of this situation is that the major modes of access to films on small portable screening devices like smartphones are television channels and video-hosting websites such as YouTube. The impact on the quality of the viewing experience is unquestionable, whether in terms of the integrity of a film work (that is, the possibility of watching a film devoid of gaps, glitches and re-edits involving the removing and reordering of sequences as well as the insertion of advertisement breaks) or of the resolution of its images and soundtrack.

As far as the quality of the image is concerned, however, the compactness of the smallest screening devices, where the imperfections due to low resolution are less tangible, is a definite advantage. Moreover, the technical improvements sought and implemented since 2007, and in particular the willingness to provide the best possible image rendition, indicate a belief in the continuing, growing use of such devices for watching moving images, including films (that is, features or shorts, shot in analogue or digital format, but initially intended for theatrical release). For instance, Apple rapidly developed the so-called Retina display for the iPhone – a liquid-crystal display (LCD) screen that boasts a high pixel density enhanced by the small size of the screen, its high pixel resolution being squeezed into a 3.5 inch screen.[9] Thus even in the face of restricted access to a limited number of titles, film viewing was, from the start, one of the iPhone's selling assets (and other smartphone manufacturers soon followed suit and copied the iPhone design); with the iPhone came the promise that users would carry with them their own 'pocket size cinema' and watch films wherever and whenever they wished.

'EXISTENTIAL BUBBLES'

To most cinephiles, such an assertion is, of course, an anathema. The arguments against the kind of media convergence epitomized in the streaming and watching of films on portable digital platforms and the effect it has on the cinematic experience are sufficiently well known to have become topics of tongue-in-cheek debate among YouTube viewers. A spoof of an iPhone commercial, posted in 2008 and based on the clever remix of audiovisual footage from extras of a special edition of an *Inland Empire* DVD release, has in effect become a classic in relation to the debate over the cinematic apparatus.[10] It features a furious rant by filmmaker David Lynch warning viewers against the abomination of watching films on iPhones.[11] Interestingly, the hundreds of bloggers who commented were not particularly interested in determining whether or not this was a fake, and if so who the author was, nor did they discuss its achievements as an iPhone advertisement. Reviewers were primarily interested in talking about the maverick director himself (and the irony of Lynch, the master creator of warped fictional worlds, asking us to 'get real' was not lost on the commentators). There were also heated exchanges about the message of the fake advertisement: on the acceptability of watching actual feature films on such a tiny screen, with reduced audio span. Out of the remarks emerge familiar concerns: As viewers, as well as missing the rituals associated with communal viewing and shared experience, we lose out on the large screen projection experience with all it entails in terms of audiovisual quality. Only within the film theatre's enfolding darkness, secluded from the outside world, can we surrender to the sense of suspended time while we sit – spellbound and immobile – among a crowd of strangers, immersing ourselves in the vast expanse of the image projected on the cinema screen. Here, and in spite of the usual observations on the alleged added 'freedom' ('anywhere, anytime') brought to the user by mobile technology, the bloggers' ambivalent comments often mirrored those of academic observers. For many a film theorist, the possibility of experiencing a film projected in a theatre at least once is precisely what continues to define cinema; it remains cinema's unique prerogative in an era of remediation and media convergence, where films are turned into (mere) data so as to be redistributed in a multitude of formats and shifted between a growing number of platforms and screens of all sizes. Probably because of its long tradition of art-house cinema and cine-club-bound cinephilia, francophone film theory offers particularly polarized points of view. Serge Daney's classic advice in favour of watching films on television, and Roger Odin's advocacy for the development of a 'communication space' where the frontiers between watching and making films becomes blurred, however, remain the exception.[12] From Jacques Aumont to

Raymond Bellour and Eric de Kuyper,[13] Jean-Luc Godard's classic aphorism, echoed by Chris Marker, still holds:

> Cinema is larger than us; you should have to raise your eyes to the cinema screen. When you start lowering your eyes on a smaller display, cinema loses its essence [. . .] On television, you see the shadow of a film, the nostalgic memory of a film, its echo – never a film.[14]

In the introduction to his recently published *La Querelle des dispositifs: cinéma – installations, expositions*, Raymond Bellour summarizes the argument eloquently:

> *To experience the projection of a film in a cinema, in the dark, as part of an audience – large or reduced – has become, and remains, the condition of a unique experience of perception and memory that will be transformed, to a lesser or greater extent, in any other viewing situation. This and only this deserves to be called 'cinema'.*[15]

Media historians interested in the longer view, however, tend to take a more relativist stance. Hence in the aptly called *In Broad Daylight*, Gabriele Pedulla echoes many 'new media' theorists when he states:

> In the brief history of moving image systems, the movie theatre's absolutism was only a brief parenthesis [. . .] a brief encounter that today we are all the more inclined to remember nostalgically for its transience.[16]

In the past few decades, the emergence in the field of media studies of a media archaeology approach that looks at the evolution of cinema as part of a broader, non-linear and ongoing history of technology[17] has contributed to this tendency to revaluate the importance of the actual cinema-going experience epitomized by Pedulla's quote. Here, the question of the multiple origins and genealogies of the medium of the moving image comes into play, calling for a re-contextualization of cinema in relation to a broad range of modes of experiencing films, including the individual viewing of small-scale film images. As part of an archaeological approach to media, connections can be drawn, for instance, between today's small mobile screens and early forms of exhibition that did not involve public projection, such as peephole viewing (the kinetoscope) or the zoetrope that depended on the viewing of small scale images by one or a few spectators at a time. Similarly the flipbook, or kineograph, involved the kind of manipulation that could be compared to the gesture-based activity of using palm-size mobile media, such as iPhones.

Given the mongrel origins of the medium of the moving image and of its apparatus, therefore, and acknowledging that cinema has, so far, survived the digital onslaught that was meant to annihilate the very notion of cinema as we know it, a number of film and visual studies historians see no reason to equate media convergence, and the possibility of viewing film on a variety of platforms, with its imminent death. Writing as part of the aforementioned *Moving*

Data collection, Francesco Casetti and Sara Sampietro thus argue, in contrast with Bellour's quote cited earlier, that 'if it is true that media are no longer tied to an exclusive platform or technology, it is also true that they continue to possess their own identities'.[18] For Casetti and Sampietro, cinema possesses a distinctive way of involving us as well as a distinctive way of reflecting on our relation to the world, which they summarize, in a Bazin-inspired fashion, as 'the ability to simultaneously restore the world to us while creating a new one, thus reconnecting the real to the possible'. Crucially, the technology that grants us this characteristic media experience, they argue, is significant, but not decisive.[19] To the terms 'remediation' and 'media convergence' they therefore prefer the term 'relocation', because 'media are "worlds" that can be shifted elsewhere'.[20]

Casetti and Sampietro emphasize, however, that there are specific conditions to the successful relocation of the film-viewing experience via a technology such as the small, portable screen. The first condition, they argue, is a successful pre-existing relocation (Casetti and Sampietro call this the 'two-step condition').[21] In the case of film, this was done thanks to television and, later, the computer, through which we have grown used to watching movies in small frames such as on Quicktime, Vimeo or YouTube.[22]

The second, key condition is dependent on the ability to create what Casetti and Sampietro call an effective 'existential bubble', that is, the capacity for a subject to isolate herself or himself within collective environments (although, as mentioned before, you may well elect to watch your iPhone in the privacy of a domestic space). Although the authors do not address this particular aspect of the creation of 'existential bubbles', one can expect sound to take on – to a certain extent at least – the function traditionally assumed by darkness in a cinema-going experience: The sound received through earphones allows the individual sitting among a crowd to seclude him- or herself and engage in what Casetti and Sampietro describe as an intimate and 'exclusive relationship with the text'.[23] The 'intimate experience' rendered possible by the creation of an 'existential bubble' is to be distinguished from the 'multifocalized' and 'epidermal' modes of viewing, where the viewer exercises not an attentive but a dispersive gaze, switching between several objects, or privileges interaction with the technology itself, leading to a superficial, inattentive and highly discontinuous gaze. In these latter cases, as with web platforms such as YouTube where films appear in fragmented, manipulated forms, and abridged to 'pill-size doses', cinema does indeed, Casetti and Sampietro remark, 'un-*cinematize* itself'.[24]

It is not the attempt at asserting cinema's uncertain 'relocation' via the iPhone that is of interest here, but, rather, the way in which Casetti and Sampietro's analysis points to the possibility of a different encounter with the moving image – one that goes beyond what Bellour calls a 'degraded vision' of film[25] and calls forth the small screen's own, intriguing, mode of spectatorial engagement.

It is the so-called 'intimate experience' that I will therefore implicitly assume as the basis of my further exploration of the specific pleasures associated with small screen film viewing. The viewer that I am now picturing is an attentive one. It is probably a viewer whose cinema-going habits are not altered by the possession of a portable screen. It is one who is likely to prefer to watch a given film at least once on a large screen, without fragmenting it, before seeing it via miniaturized media. At the same time, however, she or he will also routinely elect to watch, and re-watch, a particular moment or scene on her or his smartphone. By extension, size of screen notwithstanding, it is a viewer who is susceptible to becoming immersed in the world of the film, whether it is a narrative feature or non-narrative work. In effect, the issue of continuity (as in narrative continuity or simply in viewing a work in its entirety) versus fragmentation is not necessarily crucial here: The viewer sensitive to the attractions of the miniaturized image may well be one who appreciates miniaturization in temporal terms as well as in scale – finding pleasure in watching brief, self-contained extracts, non-narrative and short films. However, what interests me most here is the involvement with the material, tactile aspects of the experience of watching moving images on a very small screen rather than questions of narrative formats. I want to suggest that the attraction of viewing high-quality film images on a small screen has less to do with the much advertised freedom to watch the latest mainstream feature anywhere at any time, than with the effect of image reduction itself.

Hence to consider the specific enjoyment afforded by small screen viewing is not, by any means, to suggest the possibility of one mode of viewing emulating, let alone replacing, the experience of the film projected in a cinema, but rather to explore the ways that diverse or complementary modes of experiencing film may coexist and offer different pleasures. Clearly, even if it is possible to effectively create an existential 'bubble' allowing for an intimate relation to the film that one is watching on one's iPhone, this has little in common with the experience of cinema-going. Even if, as Casetti and Sampietro suggest, the cinema experience could be successfully 'relocated', iPhone viewing would still imply a highly distinctive relation to the medium of the moving image – one that is undeniably bound to the change of scale and the experience of the miniature.

SCALE AND MAGIC

Scale has always been a key component of the magic of cinema: Where analogue, nitrate or celluloid film is concerned in particular, the magic comes not only from the immersion of the viewer within the world represented on a gigantic screen, but also from the projection, that is, the capacity to transform, through the power of light, an image that is tiny – the miniature picture contained in each of the film strip's individual frames – so as to render it on a massive scale.

When watching on a mobile phone screen the effect is reversed, but the magic remains (and Jobs is well aware of this, using the term 'magic' repeatedly in his presentation). In a sense, iPhone viewing can remind us of the wonder of looking at the miniature photographic world that is enclosed and repeated within sequences of single analogue film frames.

Daniel Szöllösi plays on this association in his 2012 'untitled', a short film that was awarded first prize in the Amsterdam EYE Museum 'celluloid remix' competition, and for which he used a series of mobile phones laid out next to one another so that they evoked photograms on a film strip.[26] Following the rules of the competition, Szöllösi used found footage from the museum's early film collection from which he selected shots of camera operators of the silent period at work, as well as amateur footage of a man, woman and child awkwardly acting up and laughing in front of the camera. Part of the footage showed at the end of the film is badly decayed – to the point where the photographic content becomes entirely obscured. Szöllösi inserted split-screens and freeze frames, and remixed and looped various sequences before playing them on three iPhones placed side by side. He then reshot this pocket-size installation work from above – the three screens contained within one frame. At first, his hands (and the hand is, in Susan Stewart words, 'the measure of the miniature')[27] appear in the frame to switch the three devices on, and as the images start to unravel on each of the small screens in turn, the soundtrack fills with the noise of an old-fashioned projector, soon mixed with the sound of a woman laughing. At one point, Szöllösi's hand reappears, lays a fourth phone on top of one of the iPhones already on display, wherein this new device seems to pick up a sequence of images as if by contagion. Little by little, both the sound of the projector and the display of images become more erratic. Parasite noise – static, buzzing and whistling – invades the soundtrack and the images start to flick by at an irregular speed, only then to decompose and vanish, as when analogue footage jams and combusts during a projection: It is as if the small electronic devices had become inhabited with the malevolent spirit of an old, dysfunctional projector. This uncanny cohabitation of the obsolete with the new is further emphasized by the author's 'signature shot' at the end, when Szöllösi switches the central device into video mode, so that his own image appears, framed by footage of a silent film cameraman briefly displayed on either side. The repeated involvement of the filmmaker (first coming into sight as a pair of giant hands and then as a small silhouette enclosed within one of the frames) as both a *deus ex machina* and a kind of Alice in Wonderland emphasizes the small size as well as the touch-based, intimate interface offered by the iPhone. It also brings out the sense of enchantment that the meeting, across time and scale, of diverse moving image technologies can elicit.

Indeed the miniature, as Gaston Bachelard reminds us in *La Poétique de l'espace*, belongs first and foremost to the land of fairy tales, and is never far from the world of children and their toys.[28] If, to paraphrase Casetti and Sampietro, films are 'worlds' that can be shifted elsewhere, then in this case, to enter them through an iPhone screen is to engage with an experience of viewing that arguably has something in common with the fairytale and with childhood. The iPhone is, after all, a kind of toy, albeit a very expensive toy that relies on the latest technology.

In *On Longing: Narratives of the Miniature, the Gigantic, the Souvenir, the Collection*, Susan Stewart stresses the ambiguous relation between miniaturiza-tion and technology: While the development of new technologies has allowed for the miniaturization of data of all kinds, including audiovisual data, the miniature also harks back to traditional forms of craftsmanship celebrated for their capacity to create images and replicate the world in as tiny a scale and as completely as possible, while maintaining proportion.[29]

'Unlike the gigantic, which celebrates quantity over quality',[30] the art of the miniature insists on proportional perfection and detail.[31] If one of the main attractions and wonders of miniature representation is born out of the kind of association of tininess with exactness, it calls for a distinctive form of gaze. For the reduction in scale induces a commensurate concentration of details – in the case of complex film images, with compositions saturated with visual information and transformations, one might even talk, as Stewart notes, of a 'hallucination of details'.[32] As such, the iPhone as a screening device arguably encourages us not only to interface in a tactile way through our fingers, but also to exercise our tactile gaze. In her seminal books *Touch* and *The Skin of Film*, Laura Marks has emphasized how, in a culture that has privileged the distanced, optical gaze over the haptic one, we need to be reminded that vision is also a form of contact. Among the types of haptic images that encourage us to exercise our haptic or tactile gaze, she mentions diverse 'traditions that involve intimate, detailed images that invite a small, caressing gaze'.[33] It is to film and video that Marks devotes her study of tactile vision, but in so doing, she relates the medium of the moving image to other traditions such as weaving and embroidery, and to older media such as medieval illuminated manuscripts, which require us to direct our attention to the surface of the image, its textures, contrasts, colours, minutiae and details.[34] In the case of the iPhone, the high resolution and soft glow of the Retina LCD screen and the condensation of contrasts and colours as well as figures arguably yields the same visual attraction that the *enlumineurs* once sought to create, with their insistence on the luminosity and vivid hues and contrasts of their tiny paintings.

As suggested earlier, however, the gaze of today's user of tiny mobile media platforms is sustained by a distinctive relation to the soundtrack that accompanies or provides a counterpoint to the film images. In his chapter on the miniature in *La Poétique de l'espace*, Bachelard mentions a '*miniature du son*'.[35] At that point Bachelard is talking about Tom Thumb climbing inside a horse's ear, and his remarks, oddly evocative of a discussion on the functions of the earbud type of audio device, may help to give a poetic spin to the often banal depiction of the role of this kind of auditory prosthetic. In effect, as my slightly off-kilter rapprochement suggests, in Bachelard's literary account, as with the technology concerned here, a synaesthetic or tactile quality is associated with the kind of sound delivered in the close, intimate mode that characterizes the 'auditory miniature':

> Tom Thumb is at home inside the ear, at the entrance of the natural sound cavity. He is an ear within an ear. [. . .] He has settled there in order to speak softly, that is, to command loudly, with a voice that no-one could hear except the one who should 'listen'.[36]

The wording of this passage evokes the kind of excluding perception that immersion in the microcosm presented on an iPhone's small screen can induce – a highly individualized mode of viewing and hearing that yields a specific relation to its object in terms of intimacy but also in terms of control and possessiveness. If the device effectively draws the viewer into the world that unravels on its screen and via its earbuds or headphones, the sense of possession ultimately lies, however, with the viewer as 'user'.

Indeed, if the minuscule invites us to surrender our sense of height to penetrate its microcosms, and while the haptic gaze is, for Laura Marks, a mode of vision that encourages us to 'yield into the image', smallness and tactility also play into forms of ownership and mastery. In *Death 24x a Second*, Laura Mulvey suggests that technologies such as the VCR and the DVD with their ability to still the moving image, contribute to the creation of new kinds of spectators, among which she posits the 'possessive' spectator. In using a small, individual media platform such as an iPhone to watch films, the viewer arguably develops an even greater sense of control – for here, the spectator is also the sole 'user' and owner of a device that he carries himself. Intimacy thus yields into possessiveness: She carries her screen in her pocket and holds it in the palm of her hand. She can select a frame ratio, rewind, fast-forward and still the image, but can also 'pinch' or zoom into the screen image to try to discover its mysteries. In the case of the iPhone, it is not when the image is stilled, however, that the greater sense of mastery comes into play, but when the image moves. Suddenly, actors and actresses, stars as well as less known figures, are reduced to the size of Tom Thumb, moving through miniaturized sets and landscapes. As they run around this reduced space, seemingly imprisoned in the tight confines of the diminutive frame, and their movements rendered more hysterical by their miniaturization, the distant observer may well compare the owner of the iPhone to a kind of entomologist, or a distant heir of the gigantic blue humanoids of René Laloux and Roland Topor's *La Planète Sauvage* (1973) who entertain themselves with the spectacle of the insect-sized humans they capture or purchase.[37]

And thus, by extension, we are also reminded that the art of the miniature has always been an art form favoured by the collector. As Stewart reminds us, to carry a miniature picture of a loved one was always a way of keeping them close, their portrait secured in a locket and often kept against one's skin; by extension, however, miniature representations are related to specific patterns of possession and collection that would later feed into the forms of commodification of the body that the advertisement came to epitomize.[38]

CONCLUSION

Rather than a radical loss of the cinema effect, there arguably is a strange metamorphosis as well as a doubling of it in the experience of watching moving images on the diminutive, portable screen of a smartphone: The viewer's immersion in the world of the film is, simultaneously, an immersion in a miniature universe whose gate opens in the palm of one's hand. However, the mix of intimacy and possession that such viewing entails effortlessly yields to patterns of possession and consumption where the smallness of the image, the reduction of the human figure as well as its environment, becomes part and parcel of the device's functioning as a commodity form. To a certain extent, therefore, to emphasize the connections that exist between such a mode of viewing and a diverse range of historical, literary, poetic and artistic precedents is to attempt to re-appropriate it, away from the technological fetishism and commodifying discourses that often dominate the advertising as well as critical studies of new technologies. For there is, undoubtedly, a distinctive beauty and fascination in the spectacle of extremely complex moving images rendered in such diminutive, yet perfect, fashion; the captivation exercised by the shifting glow that the small images cast against their surroundings testifies to this, as does the irrepressible need, in the bustle of public transport, to peer over the shoulder of the absorbed fellow traveller who holds the miniature screen in her hand.

Notes

1. Gaston Bachelard, *La Poétique de l'espace* (Paris: PUF, 2011 [1958]), p. 148; see also *The Poetics of Space*, trans. Maria Jolas (Boston, MA: Beacon Press, 1994), p. 155.
2. See Laura Mulvey, *Death 24x a Second* (London: Reaktion Books, 2006), p. 161.
3. Coincidentally, in his chapter on the miniature in *La Poétique se l'espace*, Bachelard quotes from Cyrano de Bergerac a passage where Cyrano describes the apple as 'un petit univers à soi même, dont le pépin plus chaud que les autres parties, répand autour se soi la chaleur conservatrice de son globe' ('a little universe in itself, the seed of which, being hotter than the other parts, gives out the conservative heat of its globe'). Edmond Rostan, *Cyrano de Bergerac* (1897), quoted in La *Poétique de l'espace*, p. 142; see also *The Poetics of Space*, p. 151.
4. Hence, if, in spite of the fierce competition, we still tend to associate touch phone technology with Apple's iPhone, it is not the communication aspect *per se* that has turned the iPhone into such an emblematic artefact of the digital era – an 'ideal-type commodity form' as media theorists would have it. As a telephone proper, Apple's iPhone was never rated among the best. It is other functions, including that of a screening device, which take precedence.
5. See Steve Jobs's introductory presentation of the iPhone, at: <www.youtube.com/watch?v=6uW-E496FXg and www.youtube.com/watch?v=Vququ7x8gnw> (accessed 1 January 2013).
6. A strange effect of shifting scales is created, however, by the fact that Jobs's presentation, taking place in a vast cinema-like auditorium, is supported by *giant* images of the iPhone displayed on a large screen.
7. Pelle Snickars and Patrick Vonderau, eds, *Moving Data: The iPhone and the Future of Media* (New York, NY: Columbia University Press, 2012), p. 1.
8. Alisa Perren and Karen Petruska, 'Big Hollywood, Small Screens', in Snickars and Vonderau, eds, *Moving Data*, pp. 104–24; Chuck Tryon, 'Pushing the (Red) Envelope: Portable Video, Platform Mobility and Pay-Per-View Culture', in Snickars and Vonderau, eds, *Moving Data*, pp. 124–39; Jennifer Holt, 'Platforms, Pipelines, and Politics: The iPhone and Regulatory Hangover', in Snickars and Vonderau, eds, *Moving Data*, pp. 140–55.
9. The Retina display has four times the number of pixels as previous iPhones. See, for instance, Chris Brandrick, 'The iPhone 4's Retina Display Explained', *TechHive*, at: <http://www.pcworld.com/article/198201/iPhone_4s_retina_display_explained.html> (accessed 15 February 2013).
10. See Roger Odin, 'Spectator, Film and the Mobile Phone', in Ian Christie, ed., *Audiences* (Amsterdam: Amsterdam University Press, 2012), p. 155.

11. This fake advertisement features on a number of sites. See, for example, <www. youtube.com/watch?v=wKiIroiCvZ0> (accessed 1 February 2013).

12. Odin, 'Spectator, Film and the Mobile Phone', pp. 156–8. In effect, Daney's comments are but an extension of his defence of the unique experience that cinema represents (in its traditional format, both as practice and as viewing experience). Serge Daney, 'The Zapper's Salary', trans. Hemlata Agarwal Beck, in Jacques Kermabon and Kumar Shahani, eds, *Cinema And Television: Fifty Years Of Reflection In France* (Bombay: Orient Longman, 1991), pp. 237–47.

13. See Jacques Aumont, 'Que reste-t-il du cinéma ?', *Trafic* 79 (September 2011), 95–107; Raymond Bellour, 'The Cinema Spectator: A Special Memory', in Christie, ed., *Audiences*, pp. 206–18; Bellour, 'La Querelle des dispositifs', *Art Press* 262 (Novembre 2000), 48–52, and Bellour, *La Querelle des dispositifs: cinéma – expositions, installations* (Paris: POL, 2012), pp. 13–47. Eric De Kuyper, 'L'autre Histoire du Cinéma, ou la perte du spectacle: Qui gagne, qui perd ?', in Francesco Casetti, Jane Gaines and Valentine Re, eds, *In the Very Beginning, at the Very End: Film Theories in Perspective* (Udine: Forum, 2010), pp. 143–51. See also Dudley Andrew, *What Cinema Is!* (Oxford: Wiley-Blackwell, 2010), in particular pp. 66–79.

14. 'Le cinéma, c'est ce qui est plus grand que nous, sur quoi il faut lever les yeux. En passant dans un objet plus petit et sur quoi on baisse les yeux, le cinéma perd son essence. [. . .] On peut voir à la télé l'ombre d'un film, le regret d'un film, la nostalgie, l'écho d'un film, jamais un film'. Jean-Luc Godard, quoted in Chris Marker, 'Cinéma zone', in *Immemory* (CD-ROM, Paris: Yves Gevaert Editeur/ Centre Georges Pompidou, 1997); my translation.

15. '*La projection vécue d'un film en salle, dans le noir, le temps prescrit d'une séance plus ou moins collective, est devenue et reste la condition d'une expérience unique de perception et de mémoire, définissant son spectateur et que toute situation autre de vision altère plus ou moins. Et cela seul vaut d'être appelé « cinéma »*'. Bellour, *La Querelle des dispositifs*, p. 14. Italics in original; my translation. By the same token, Bellour rebuffs claims by art historians that cinema's future lies with the galleries and museums. See pp. 30–7.

16. Gabriele Pedulla, *In Broad Daylight: Movies and Spectators after the Cinema* (London: Verso, 2012), p. 79.

17. See Thomas Elsaesser, 'The New Film History as Media Archaeology', *Cinémas: Journal of Film Studies*, 14.2–3 (2004), 75–117.

18. Whereas Bellour's argument posits a precise definition of what the term 'cinema' designates (cinema's identity having become, in the course of time, inseparable from specific conditions of viewing that involve public projection), Casetti and Sampietro's analysis rests on the overlapping use of a set of loosely defined terms ('media', 'cinema' and 'film'). See Francesco Casetti and Sara Sampietro, 'With Eyes, with Hands: The Relocation of Cinema into the iPhone', in Snickars and Vonderau, eds, *Moving Data*, pp. 19–33 (p. 20). Bellour, *La Querelle des dispositifs*, pp. 14–15.

19. Casetti and Sampietro, p. 20.

20. *Ibid.*, p. 21.

21. *Ibid.*, p. 22.
22. On this topic, see Vivian Sobchack's 'Nostalgia for a Digital Object: Regrets on the Quickening of *Quicktime*', *Millennium Film Journal* 34 (1999), 4–23. See also Lev Manovich, 'Little Movies', at: <http://www.manovich.net/little-movies/> (accessed 15 January 2013).
23. Casetti and Sampietro, in *Moving Data*, p. 28.
24. *Ibid.*, pp. 26–7 (italics in original).
25. Bellour, 'La vision dégradée du film de cinéma', *La Querelle des dispositifs*, p. 14.
26. The film can be viewed at: <celluloidremix.openbeelden.nl/media/125755/Untitled> (accessed 15 January 2013).
27. Susan Stewart, *On Longing: Narratives of the Miniature, the Gigantic, the Souvenir, the Collection* (Durham NC: Duke University Press, 1993), p. 46.
28. Bachelard, *La Poétique de l'espace*, p. 140; also *The Poetics of Space*, p. 148.
29. Stewart, *On Longing*, p. 46. Miniaturization thus belongs to the latest technology and to the pre-industrial and early industrial worlds still connected to manual craft and to which it often nostalgically refers, as in Szöllösi's piece, with its restaging of archive footage and its insistence on the presence of the hand.
30. *Ibid.*, p. 112.
31. Both Stewart and Bachelard, in their respective explorations of the miniature, offer examples drawn from literature as well as painting, including the classic description of Tom Thumb sleeping in his walnut shell, a description that celebrates the beauty of smallness associated with perfect proportions. See Stewart, *On Longing*, p. 46; Bachelard, *La Poétique de l'espace*, p. 154; also *The Poetics of Space*, p. 166.
32. Stewart, *On Longing*, p. 112.
33. Laura U. Marks, *The Skin of the Film: Intercultural Cinema, Embodiment, and the Senses* (Durham, NC: Duke University Press, 2000), p. 169.
34. *Ibid.*
35. Bachelard, *La Poétique de l'espace*, p. 154; *The Poetics of Space*, p. 166.
36. See Bachelard, *The Poetics of Space*, pp. 165–6. 'Le Petit Poucet est chez lui dans l'espace d'une oreille, à l'entrée de la cavité naturelle du son. Il est une oreille dans une oreille. [. . .] Il s'[y] est installé pour parler bas, c'est-à-dire commander fort, d'une voix que personne n'entend sauf celui qui doit « écouter »'. *La Poétique de l'espace*, p. 154.
37. In effect, this sense of mastery may well extend to the diegetic world of the film as a whole, and, as such, function as a reprieve – a counterpoint to the sense of powerlessness experienced by one living in the era of global uncertainty. In the following quote, Bachelard, writing in 1957, is talking about philosophy as a discursive practice, and the unattainable ambitions of the metaphysician, rather than discourses of globalization. However, the passage quoted below has a contemporary resonance in the way that it emphasizes the exercise of reduction as a form of mastery and as a means to fight the sense of loss one experiences when confronted with the complexity of the world at large: 'In fact, I feel more

at home in miniature worlds, which, for me, are dominated worlds. [. . .] To have experienced miniature sincerely detaches me from the surrounding world, and helps me to resist dissolution of the surrounding atmosphere' (*The Poetics of Space*, p. 165). 'Je suis plus à mon aise dans le monde de la miniature. Ce sont pour moi des mondes dominés. [. . .] La miniature sincèrement vécue me détache du monde ambiant, elle m'aide à résister à la dissolution de l'ambiance' (*La Poétique de l'espace*, pp. 149–50).

38. Stewart, *On Longing*, p. 125.

while they can't easily produce the analytical diagrams such as the one created by Eisenstein (figure 12.1), they can do other things that would be very hard or very time-consuming for a human observer.

One of Vertov's key concepts was Kino-Eye (*Kino-Glaz* in Russian), which received its best realization in *The Man with a Movie Camera* (many other equally radical film plans of Vertov's remained unrealized). In a 1924 article, 'The Birth of Kino-Eye', he writes:

> Kino-Eye is understood as 'that which the eye does not see',
> as the microscope and telescope of time,
> as the negative of time,
> as the possibility of seeing without limits and distances,
> as the remote control of movie cameras,
> as tele-eye,
> as X-ray eye,
> as 'life caught unawares', etc., etc.
> [. . .]
> Kino-Eye as the possibility of making the invisible visible.[7]

Today, data visualization designers often use the same phrase, 'making the invisible visible', to describe how visualization can reveal patterns in the data. For Vertov, this goal called for new cinematographic, editing and logistic techniques. The visualizations presented in this project aim to reverse *kino-eye*, pointing it at Vertov's films.

I wrote the code to create all visualizations in this chapter using ImageJ, a popular open-source image processing software used in live sciences, astronomy, geography and other fields of science.[8] In my lab we also developed a number of other tools for the computational analysis and visualization of image and video collections; they are available for download at our website.[9]

The digital copies of the films were provided by The Austrian Film Museum (Vienna). I am grateful to film researcher and Austrian Film Museum staff member Adelheid Heftberger for initiating and making possible this project in 2009, and providing detailed feedback on the work as it developed. Some of the visualizations use her manually created lists of shots in Vertov's films. While we did use shot detection software in other projects, in this case we relied on manual annotations of the shots. This method is more accurate in recording many very short shots, which are characteristic of Vertov's films. Some of the visualizations appeared previously as supplementary material on the DVD of two Vertov films published by Austrian Film Institute;[10] others appear here for the first time.

Figure 12.5   The Eleventh Year *(Vertov, 1928): average amount of visual change in every shot. The length of a bar corresponds to the average amount of visual change in the shot (details on the method for this calculation can be found in Section III, below). The second frame of a shot is placed above the bar.*
Top image: the complete visualization of the whole film.
Second image: a close-up of the visualization.
Bottom image: a tighter close-up showing the pattern of gradual changes in the shots' average amount of visual change.[11]

I. Average amount of visual change in each shot

This visualization uses a very simple algorithm (described below) to calculate the average amount of visual change in each shot in Vertov's *The Eleventh Year*. Each column corresponds to one shot. The second (from the beginning) frame of a shot is above; the bar representing the measurement of the average amount of visual change in this shot is below. For a shot where little changes, the bar will be short; a shot with lots of changes (be they movements of a camera, or the subjects, or both) has a long bar. A static shot of two people talking is an example of the former; a shot filmed from a rapidly moving vehicle is an example of the latter.

Visualization of these measurements reveals both the patterns that we might expect, as well as patterns that are quite surprising. The close-up from

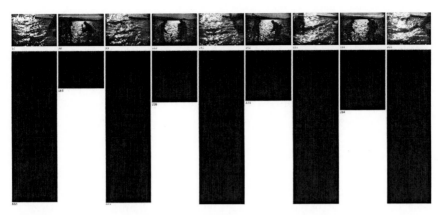

Figure 12.6   The Eleventh Year: *close-up from the visualization of the complete film.*

Figure 12.7   The Eleventh Year: *a different close-up from the visualization.*

the visualization of the complete film shown (Figure 12.6) illustrates a pattern that we may anticipate in a cross-cutting sequence: two short shots alternating back and forth, each with its own level of visual activity.

This next close-up (Figure 12.7) demonstrates a different pattern that seems to completely contradict our expectations of montage in film: The average amount of visual change in each shot at first gradually decreases and then gradually increases. This pattern of gradual increase/decrease in the amount of activity occurs a number of times throughout the film.

Vertov and a number of other Russian filmmakers (Lev Kuleshov, Sergei Eisenstein and Vsevolod Pudovkin) advocated *montage* as the key organizational principle of cinema. While they proposed a number of alternative theories of montage, common to these theories and their films was the idea of a collision between shots – that is, generation of meaning and emotional effects through juxtaposition rather than continuity. (In contrast, in normal film editing the progression of shots serves the primary purpose of advancing the narrative.)

However, as the example above shows, opposition and continuity are not always enemies. In this example, the alternating close-ups and medium shots oppose one another graphically. At the same time, the amount of visual change in each shot gradually decreases and then increases over time.

Were Vertov and his collaborators Mikhail Kaufman and Yelizaveta Svilova aware of this subtle pattern? The fact that the shots in a sequence follow a pattern is not surprising. The Russian montage theorists advocated that shots should be arranged in a sequence following some system (for example, Eisenstein distinguished between 'metric montage', 'rhythmic montage', 'intellectual montage', and so forth). However, since they did not have computational tools, they could not analyze precisely all visual changes from frame to frame, or from shot to shot, and thus systematically plan subtle patterns of change in dimensions such as 'the average amount of visual change per shot' used in our visualization. This would not have prevented Vertov and his collaborators from creating such patterns 'by hand', however – even though they could not be graphed and named until now.

II. Details

In this Vertov film, there is no correlation between shots' lengths and average amount of visual change, as measured by our method described below (correlation = -0.06). While in general lots of things can result in 'visual change' (think of twentieth-century experimental films or contemporary motion graphics), in Vertov's films, visual changes between frames are due to the movements (of objects, people, shadows, camera or lens changes, or of some combination of these). If we use this substitution, we can state that the amount of movement in shots and the shot lengths do not have any connection to one another. (This is comparable to the general finding of James Cutting and his collaborators for the Hollywood films of 1935 to 1960 that they studied.)[12]

Time series analysis (autocorrelation and partial autocorrelation calculated using software available at: <http://www.wessa.net/rwasp_autocorrelation.wasp>)[13] of the shot lengths data and shot movements data both show strong structures (that is, the opposite of randomness). This means that both values change systematically in a significant proportion of the films' shots.

Comparatively, the shot lengths data has more structure than average amount of movement in shots data (as I measured it – see below). This makes sense: While Vertov could plan the exact length of every shot, he did not have the means to do the same for movement. Examining the graphs visually, we also see that the proportion of the film that has systematically varying shot lengths is larger than that which has systematic movement patterns.

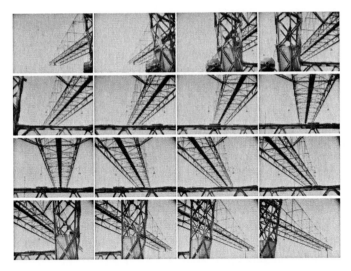

Figure 12.13 The Eleventh Year: *montage of the shot, every twenty-first frame; the frames are arranged in order from left to right, top to bottom.*

V. Frame by frame: anatomy of a shot

This section analyzes a shot from *The Eleventh Year* (see the video clip at: <http://www.youtube.com/watch?v=_0bE9suAIDQ&feature=share&list=UUQYMh3afEnBHnwcJ8y-e9Mg>). In Figure 12.13, the illustration shows sampled frames from this shot.

The Russian montage school privileged the shot as the basic unit of cinema. However, if we look at their films as opposed to theoretical texts and manifestos, we find that the reality does not always correspond to the theory. *The Eleventh Year* contains many short shots that are static (or almost static) tableaux. They contain a single 'burst' of information, presented on the screen just long enough for a viewer to absorb it, and then are replaced by the next burst. The film also contains longer dynamic shots that show some activity that follows a cycle. In addition to communicating semantic information (a human or a machine performing some action), such shots also communicate the larger theme of *work* central to the film. Because they feature movement, they don't just signify 'work' – instead, they are motivating the viewers to join the workers they see on the screen. We can also find a third type of longer shots that do not contain repetitions; instead, new information is communicated as the shot unfolds. (Some of these shots are filmed from a train; as the train moves forward, we see new parts of the landscape, or new objects passing by.)

How can we visualize the development of a single shot? As our example, I selected a shot that exemplifies Vertov's aesthetics in a pure way: moving geometric machine forms. In 'WE: A Variant of a Manifesto', Vertov categorically states:

> The machine makes us ashamed of man's inability to control himself,
> [. . .]
> *For his inability to control his movements, WE temporarily exclude man as a subject for film.*[16]

This adoration of machines was typical of the aesthetic programs of various avant-garde groups in the 1910s and the 1920s, groups that included visual artists, poets, architects, photographers and graphic designers. Vertov adapts this general program of the European avant-garde to the medium of cinema. What he takes from machines is the precision and regularity of their movements. (Vertov was apparently unaware of the time-study methods of Frederick Winslow Taylor and the motion studies by the Gilbreths already developed in the 1920s. These methods were used to standardize and rationalize workers' movements, fine tuning them to achieve the ideal of machine-like precision. In Russia, the ideas of Taylor became popular in the early 1920s.)

The shot I've selected lasts one hundred and sixty-seven frames, and contains no human beings. Instead, the camera tracks along a long crane that extends perpendicular to it. The unfolding geometry contains a horizontal part of the crane that occupies the same section of the frames in which it appears, also two vertical crane parts that rapidly cross frames one to fifty and then again frames one hundred to one hundred and sixty-seven, and the long part of the crane which is perpendicular to the camera. Because the camera pans, the position of this part continuously changes throughout the whole shot.

Here are some possible ways to visualize a shot (many others are also possible). In the first visualization below (Figure 12.14), all frames in the shot were averaged together, pixel by pixel. In this visualization, the objects that appear in the shot only briefly are no longer visible. The objects that appear in the same position for periods of time show up as dark and sharp outlines (for example, a dark line in the bottom). What about moving objects? In this shot, the camera pans to show a long crane part that extends perpendicular to it. Because of the pan, the position of the part continuously changes throughout the shot. In the visualization, this movement is translated into the blurred triangle-like form; the faster the movement, the more blurred is its representation.

Instead of adding all frames, we can instead add subsets of frames, generating a number of images. In the next visualization (Figure 12.15), each image is the result of adding ten subsequent frames. This visualization allows us to see more clearly the changing speed of the relative movement of the crane (I

Figure 12.16 The Eleventh Year: *three selected difference images generated by subtracting subsequent frames from the shot. From top to bottom: difference images for frames 37–8, 77–8, 133–4.*

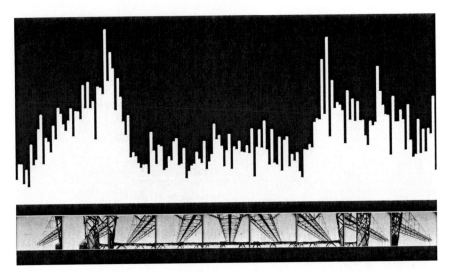

Figure 12.17   The Eleventh Year: *graph of the frame differences. The measure of the difference between subsequent frames used is the Raw Integrated Density of a difference image. Note the occasional irregular spikes in the graph. The reason for these relates to the jumps between certain frames, which are artefacts in the original film recording. If the same shot were recorded with a recent camera, these spikes would disappear.*

The same holds for all other visual dimensions of a shot. Unless we are dealing with an extremely 'structural' shot where visual change is confined to a single parameter (think of Hans Richter's *Rhythmus 21* [1921] or parts of Michael Snow's *Wavelength* [1967]), no single graph can capture all of the changes you can see with your eyes. While we can construct graphs that show patterns of many separate dimensions in a single shot, they may still not capture the overall gestalt that we experience in watching the shot.

However, graphs have their own advantage: By representing changes in distinct visual dimensions with lines and curves, they give us a visual language to talk about temporal patterns. In the graph above, we see two peaks (at about frame 37 and frame 137) that correspond to the moments as the two vertical parts of the crane pass the frame. We can also see that the sweeping movement of the long perpendicular crane part (the part between the two peaks) is translated into approximately the same rate of visual change. The graph also confirms that the rate of change of the first part of the shot (frames zero to thirty-seven) is larger than in the last part (frames one hundred and thirty-seven to one hundred and sixty-eight). (The occasional jumps in value from frame to frame reflect the artefacts in the film recording.)

Figure 12.18 The Man with a Movie Camera: *frames from three consecutive shots. The length of each original shot is ninety-four frames, one hundred and fifteen frames and one hundred and thirty-eight frames, from top to bottom. The montage shows every twenty-first frame of this sequence.*

VI. Visualizing movement

This section analyzes three shots from *Man with a Movie Camera* (you can see the video clip with these shots online at: <http://www.youtube.com/watch?v=PV-FzvHi0lk&feature=share&list=UUQYMh3afEnBHnwcJ8y-e9Mg>).

Figure 12.18 shows sampled frames from these shots. In the manifesto 'WE', quoted at the beginning of this chapter, the young Vertov defines his distinctive cinema (still to be fully created) as the art of organizing movements:

> *Kinochestvo is the art of organizing the necessary movements of objects in space as a rhythmic artistic whole,*
>
> [...]
>
> Cinema is, as well, the *art of inventing movements* of things in space in response to the demands of science.[17]

Did the practice, which came later, fit these statements made much earlier? Looking at films such as *The Eleventh Year* and *Man with a Movie Camera*, we find that only some parts of the films use objects' movements in space as the organizing principle. Other parts contain sequences of still-like shots, or shots with little or slow movement.

This impression is confirmed if we analyze the films. Adelheid Heftberger has manually annotated motion information in each shot in these films using a number of tags. In *The Eleventh Year*, she tagged only seven per cent of shots as having 'fast motion'; she assigned a 'no motion' tag to twenty-two per cent. As we may expect from viewing the two films, in *Man with a Movie Camera* the percentage of shots tagged as 'fast motion' was much higher (thirty per cent) – but this still only represents one-third of the film.

Nevertheless, Vertov's initial idea of film as an organization of 'movements of things in space' is important. We can find this technique used later in numerous twentieth-century films, beyond its existence in key parts of Vertov's own films. But in order to study movements more precisely and on a large scale, we need automatic techniques for movement tracking, analysis and visualization. Where do we start?

In the Introduction, I noted that the development of visual recording media in the nineteenth century went hand in hand with inventing techniques to capture movements for the analyses of Marey, the Gilbreths and others. In the twentieth century, rotoscoping – manual tracing of filmed movements of actors – became a major technique in the animation industry. In the last decades of the century, more methods for automatic *motion capture* and analysis using computers and expanding on the original techniques of Marey and the Gilbreths were developed and adopted in many fields. These fields range from sports and video games production to surveillance and automatic car navigation. Given the ubiquity of inexpensive video cameras, detection, tracking and identification of movement-based activity (including behaviour analysis) using video recording has become a particularly large area of research in computer science.

Computer scientists have developed a number of techniques for automatic motion estimation and movement tracking, and these techniques are built into most basic digital media technologies. For example, MPEG (Moving Picture Experts Group) video codecs use automatic motion estimation to compress video.

Most of the software for animation, compositing and visual effects also offer a number of techniques that use automatic or manual methods or their combination.[18] All animated characters in video games and feature films today use motion and face capture of live actors. Films and commercials also rely on the tracking of movements of objects and camera in video footage in order to combine live action footage and computer graphics. In fact, *motion tracking and motion capture may be as fundamental to early twenty-first century cinema and video production as the development of editing was a hundred years ago.* (In this respect,

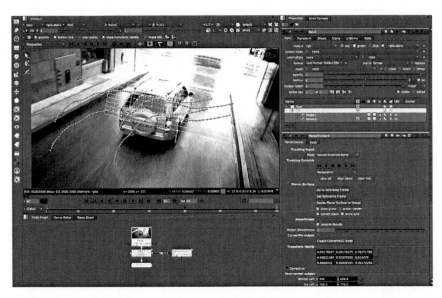

Figure 12.19   *Planar tracker in NUKE 6.3, one of the most popular software used in cinema and television production for motion tracking.*

the idea of cinema as the art of inventing the movement of things in space put forward by Vertov in his twenties anticipated both the major technology of early-twenty first century cinema and the aesthetics of many fantasy and action films made possible by this technology. Imagine what Vertov would have done if he had access to these technologies in his time!)

Typically in professional film and video production today, tracking movements within a single shot requires some time, and the quality of the results and the time required depend on the type of the shot.[19] However, the most challenging issue in using any method to analyze movements in Vertov's films, or any other director for that matter, is not technical but theoretical. Let's imagine that we managed to track every movement of every object in a complete film across hundreds or thousands of shots: How do we visualize, analyze and interpret this data? In the case of calculating average shot lengths (ASL), the data existed in one dimension (a sequence of numbers representing the lengths of shots in a sequence) – but now, we may have hundreds of numbers for every second, representing movements of potentially dozens of objects in every shot.

To illustrate this conceptual challenge, I will use an extremely simple 'toy method' for visualizing movement that already appeared in Figure 12.14: averaging all frames in a shot together. This method works only partially, but it is sufficient for an illustration. Here are averages of three shots from the clip shown above (Figure 12.18) created using the method described in Section V.

As I explained earlier, when we apply this technique to map a shot into a single image, the objects that appear in the shot that only briefly or quickly move through space disappear; the objects that move more slowly for longer periods of time are translated into blurred parts of the image.

Figure 12.20   The Man with a Movie Camera: *visualizations of movement in three shots using frame averaging techniques. A video of the shots is online at: http://www.youtube.com/watch?v=PV-FzvHi0lk&* *feature=share&list=UUQYMh3afEnBHnwcJ8y-e9Mg*

In the visualization of the first shot (Figure 12.20, left), the main movement of the tram is well represented. In the visualization of the second shot (Figure 12.20, centre), the results are less successful: The arc movement of the tram is preserved, but the faster moving car almost disappears. In the visualization of the third shot (12.20, right), all we can tell is that some movements occurred where the image is blurred, but we can't conclude anything more.

In all, the technique is partially successful in making visible 'large' movements that have simple geometry (here, moving trams), but most of the 'small' movements (here, people in the street, or the hands of the typist) are not preserved. I take their lack of visibility in these images as a metaphor for the conceptual challenge of describing them. What would we do with the tracks of all people in the first two shots if we could obtain them? It is not easy to describe conceptually – and yet I think they are as important to these shots as the larger scale movements of the trams. (Gilles Deleuze's verbal descriptions of different types of cinematic movements in his *Cinema 1: The Movement-Image* are both fascinating and frustrating to read, as we witness his struggle to express linguistically the variety of the movements in the cinema universe.)[20]

This chapter has illustrated only some of the many other possible ways to visualize cinema. New film languages and new cinematic forms that develop from the middle of the 1990s as the result of the adoption of software tools and digital workflow call for their own visualization techniques. *Motion graphics* videos, which often do not have discrete objects or representational content, allow for particularly interesting visualization approaches (that I will describe in a future article). As movement is even more crucial for motion graphics (as the name itself implies) than for feature films, developing adequate techniques for visualization of movement in these works should allow us to reuse these techniques with Vertov's films. Ideally, we will go beyond his desire for 'graphic symbols of movement', creating more precise, expressive and rich visualization and analytical tools that will allow us to see cinema in new ways.

Notes

1. Dziga Vertov, 'WE: Variant of a Manifesto' (1922), in Vertov, *Kino-Eye: The Writings of Dziga Vertov*, ed. Annette Michelson, trans. Kevin O'Brien (Berkeley, CA: University of California Press, 1984), pp. 5–9 (p. 9).
2. See Lev Manovich, 'What is Visualization?', *Visual Studies* 26.1 (2011), 36–49, at: http://lab.softwarestudies.com/2010/10/new-article-is-visualization.html (accessed 1 December 2012).
3. For the analysis and other examples of the application of some of the visualization techniques we developed, see Lev Manovich, 'Media Visualization: Visual Techniques for Exploring Large Media Collections', *Media Studies Futures*, ed. Kelly Gates (Oxford: Wiley-Blackwell, forthcoming), at: http://softwarestudies.com/cultural_analytics/Manovich.Media_Visualization.web.2012.v2.doc (accessed 1 December 2012).
4. See Software Studies Initiative at: http://lab.softwarestudies.com/p/research_14.html (accessed 1 December 2012).
5. High-resolution versions of all visualizations appearing in this text are available on Flickr, at: http://www.flickr.com/photos/culturevis/sets/72157632441192048/with/8349174610/ (accessed 1 December 2012).
6. See Manovich, 'Peter Kubelka's *Arnulf Rainer*: The Film as a Visualization', at: http://lab.softwarestudies.com/2012/11/peter-kubelkas-arnulf-rainer-film-as.html (accessed 1 December 2012).
7. Dziga Vertov, 'The Birth of Kino-Eye' (1924), in Vertov, pp. 40–2 (p. 41).
8. See ImageJ: Image Processing and Analysis in Java, at: http://rsbweb.nih.gov/ij/ (accessed 1 December 2012).
9. See Software Studies Initiative: Software for Digital Humanities, at: http://lab.softwarestudies.com/p/software-for-digital-humanities.html (accessed 1 December 2012).
10. Dziga Vertov, *A Sixth Part of the World* (1926) / *The Eleventh Year* (1928) [*Sestaja čast' mira / Odinnadcatyj*], DVD (Edition Filmmuseum, 2009).
11. See full resolution visualization (60,000 pixels wide) on Flickr, at: http://www.flickr.com/photos/culturevis/4117658480/in/set-72157632441192048 (accessed 1 December 2012).
12. James Cutting, Kaitlin Brunick, Jordan DeLong, Catalina Iricinschi and Ayse Candan, 'Quicker, Faster, Darker: Changes in Hollywood Film Over 75 Years', *i-Perception* 2 (2011), 569–76; full text at: http://people.psych.cornell.edu/~jec7/pubs/iperception.pdf (accessed 1 December 2012). The details of the method

Lev Manovich

are described in Cutting, DeLong and Brunick, 'Visual Activity in Hollywood Film: 1935 to 2005 and Beyond', *Psychology of Aesthetics, Creativity, and the Arts* 5.2 (May 2011), 115–25.

13. Full software citation is P. Wessa (2013), Free Statistics Software, Office for Research Development and Education, version 1.1.23-r7, at: http://www.wessa.net/ (accessed 1 December 2012).
14. Cutting, *et al.*, 'Quicker, Faster, Darker'.
15. Gary Chinga Carrasco, Image CorrelationJ, at: http://www.gcsca.net/IJ/ImageCorrelationJ.html (accessed 1 December 2012).
16. Vertov, *Kino-Eye*, p. 7; italics in original.
17. *Ibid.*, p. 9, italics in original.
18. A comprehensive overview of related concepts, technologies and their applications can be found in this set of Wikipedia articles: 'Match Moving', at: http://en.wikipedia.org/wiki/Camera_tracking and http://en.wikipedia.org/wiki/Match_moving; 'Motion Estimation', at: http://en.wikipedia.org/wiki/Motion_estimation; and 'Motion Capture', at: http://en.wikipedia.org/wiki/Motion_capture (all accessed 1 December 2012).
19. For a partial history of tracking in visual effects production up to 2004 see Mike Seymour, 'Art of Tracking Part 1: History of Tracking', *fxguide*, 24 August 2004, at: http://www.fxguide.com/featured/art_of_tracking_part_1_history_of_tracking/ (accessed 1 December 2012).
20. Gilles Deleuze, *Cinema 1: The Movement-Image*, trans. Hugh Tomlinson (Minneapolis, MN: University of Minnesota Press, 1986).

Select Bibliography

Acland, Charles R., ed., *Residual Media* (Minneapolis, MN: University of Minnesota Press, 2007).

Adey, Peter, *Aerial Life: Spaces, Mobilities, Affects* (Oxford: Wiley-Blackwell, 2010).

Albera, François and Maria Tortejada, eds, *Cinema Beyond Film: Media Epistemology in the Modern Era* (Amsterdam: Amsterdam University Press, 2010).

Albersmeier, Franz-Josef, Kirsten Hagen and Claudia Hoffmann, eds, *Intermedia* (Bonn: Romanistischer Verlag, 2007).

Allen, Steven and Laura Hubner, eds, *Framing Film: Cinema and the Visual Arts* (Bristol: Intellect, 2012).

Andriopoulos, Stefan, 'Kant's Magic Lantern: Historical Epistemology and Media Archaeology', *Representations* 115 (Summer, 2011), 42–70.

Bellour, Raymond, *La Querelle des dispositifs: cinéma – installations, expositions* (Paris: POL, 2012).

Benjamin, Walter, *Charles Baudelaire: A Lyric Poet in the Era of High Capitalism*, trans. Harry Zohn (London: Verso, 1973).

Boddy, William, *New Media and Popular Imagination: Launching Radio, Television, and Digital Media in the United States* (Oxford: Oxford University Press, 2004).

Bolter, Jay David and Richard Grusin, *Remediation: Understanding New Media* (Cambridge, MA: The MIT Press, 1999).

Bruno, Giuliana, *Atlas of Emotion: Journeys in Art, Architecture, and Film* (London: Verso, 2002).

Burnett, Ron, *Cultures of Vision: Images, Media, and the Imaginary* (Bloomington, IN: Indiana University Press, 1995).

Chapman, Jane, *Comparative Media History: An Introduction – 1789 to the Present* (Cambridge: Polity Press, 2005).

Charney, Leo and Vanessa R. Schwartz, eds, *Cinema and the Invention of Modern Life* (Berkeley, CA: University of California Press, 1995).

Christie, Ian, *The Last Machine: Early Cinema and the Birth of the Modern World* (London: BBC Educational Projects/British Film Institute, 1994).

Chun, Wendy Hui Kyong and Thomas Keenan, eds, *New Media, Old Media: A History and Theory Reader* (New York, NY: Routledge, 2006).

Crary, Jonathan, *Techniques of the Observer: On Vision and Modernity in the Nineteenth Century* (Cambridge, MA: The MIT Press, 1990).

Crary, Jonathan, *Suspensions of Perception: Attention, Spectacle, and Modern Culture* (Cambridge, MA: The MIT Press, 1999).

Deleuze, Gilles, *Cinema 1: The Movement-Image*, trans. Hugh Tomlinson (London: The Athlone Press, 1986).

Deleuze, Gilles, *Cinema 2: The Time-Image*, trans. Hugh Tomlinson and Robert Galeta (London: The Athlone Press, 1989).

Elsaesser, Thomas, 'The New Film History as Media Archaeology', *Cinémas: Journal of Film Studies* 4.2–3 (2004), 75–117.

Elsaesser, Thomas, ed., *Early Cinema: Space, Frame, Narrative* (London: BFI, 1990).

Fell, John R., ed., *Film before Griffith* (Cambridge, MA: Harvard University Press, 1983).

Friedberg, Anne, *Window Shopping: Cinema and the Postmodern* (Berkeley, CA: University of California Press, 1993).

Fullerton, John and Jan Olsson, *Allegories of Communication: Intermedial Concerns from Cinema to the Digital* (Rome: John Libbey, 2004).

Gaudreault, André, *From Plato to Lumière: Narration and Monstration in Literature and Cinema*, trans. Timothy Barnard, with a Preface by Paul Ricoeur and a Preface to the English Language edition by Tom Gunning (Toronto: University of Toronto Press, 2009).

Gaut, Berys, *A Philosophy of Cinematic Art* (Cambridge: Cambridge University Press, 2010).

Gumbrecht, Hans Ulrich, 'Why Intermediality – if at all?', *intermédialités: histoire et théorie des arts des lettres et des techniques* 2 (automne, 2003), 173–8.

Gitelman, Lisa, *Always Already New: Media, History, and the Data of Culture* (Cambridge, MA: The MIT Press, 2006).

Gitelman, Lisa and Geoffrey Pingree, eds, *New Media 1740–1915* (Cambridge, MA: The MIT Press, 2004).

Gunning, Tom, 'The Cinema of Attractions: Early Cinema, Its Spectator and the Avant Garde', in Thomas Elsaesser, ed., *Early Cinema: Space, Frame, Narrative* (London: British Film Institute, 1990), pp. 56–62.

Gunning, Tom, 'An Aesthetic of Astonishment: Early Film and the (In)Credulous Spectator', in Linda Williams, ed., *Viewing Positions: Ways of Seeing Film* (New Brunswick, NJ: Rutgers University Press, 1994), pp. 114–33.

Gunning, Tom, 'Heard over the Phone: *The Lonely Villa* and the de Lorde Tradition of the Terrors of Technology', in Annette Kuhn and Jackie Stacey, eds, *Screen Histories: A Screen Reader* (Oxford: Clarendon Press, 1998), pp. 216–27.

Hake, Sabine, *The Cinema's Third Machine: Writing on Film in Germany, 1907–1933* (Lincoln, NE: University of Nebraska Press, 1993).

Heath, Stephen, *Questions of Cinema* (Bloomington, IN: Indiana University Press, 1981).

Heinrichs, Jürgen, and Yvonne Spielmann, eds, *Convergence* 8.4 (Winter, 1999), special issue on 'What is Intermedia'.

Higgins, Dick, *Horizons: The Poetics and Theory of the Intermedia* (Carbondale, IL: Southern Illinois University Press, 1984).

Higgins, Dick, 'Intermedia' (1981), *Leonardo, the Journal of the International Society for the Arts, Sciences and Technology* 34.1 (2001), 49–54.

Huhtamo, Erkki and Jussi Parikka, eds, *Media Archaeology: Approaches, Applications, and Implications* (Berkeley, CA: University of California Press, 2011).

Hutcheon, Linda, *A Theory of Adaptation* (New York, NY: Routledge, 2006).

Jenkins, Henry, *Convergence Culture: Where Old and New Media Collide* (New York, NY: New York University Press, 2006).

Kaes, Anton, ed., *Kino-Debatte. Texte zum Verhältnis von Literatur und Film 1909–1929* (Tübingen: Max Niemayer, 1978).

Kember, Joe, 'Productive Intermediality and the Expert Audiences of Magic Theatre and Early Film', *Early Popular Visual Culture* 8.1 (2010), 31–46.

Kirby, Lynne, *Parallel Tracks: The Railroad and Silent Cinema* (Durham, NC: Duke University Press, 1997).

Kittler, Friedrich A., *Discourse Networks, 1800/1900*, trans. Michael Metteer with Chris Cullens (Stanford, CA: Stanford University Press, 1990).

Kittler, Friedrich A., *Gramaphone, Film, Typewriter*, trans. and intro. Geoffrey Winthrop-Young and Michael Wutz (Stanford, CA: Stanford University Press, 1999).

Kittler, Friedrich A., *Literature, Media, Information Systems: Essays* (Amsterdam: Overseas Publishers Association, 1997).

Kittler, Friedrich A., *Optical Media* (Cambridge: Polity Press, 2009).

Kooijman, Japp, Patricia Pisters and Wanda Strauven, eds, *Mind the Screen: Media Concepts According to Thomas Elsaesser* (Amsterdam: Amsterdam University Press, 2008).

Kracauer, Siegfried, *Theory of Film: The Redemption of Physical Reality*, intro. Miriam Bratu Hansen (Princeton, NJ: Princeton University Press, 1960, repr. 1997).

Kracauer, Siegfried, 'The Cult of Distraction: On Berlin's Picture Palaces' (1926), trans. Thomas Y. Levin, *New German Critique* 40 (Winter, 1987), 91–6.

Lagerroth, Ulla Britta, Hans Lund and Erik Hedling, eds, *Interart Poetics: Essays on the Interrelations of the Arts and Media* (Amsterdam: Rodopi, 1997).

Levi, Pavle, *Cinema by Other Means* (New York, NY: Oxford University Press, 2012).

Lister, Martin, Jon Dovey, Seth Giddings, Iain Grant and Kieran Kelly, *New Media: A Critical Introduction* (London and New York, NY: Routledge, 2008, 2nd edn).

Lyons, James and John Plunkett, eds, *Multimedia Histories: From the Magic Lantern to the Internet* (Exeter: University of Exeter Press, 2007).

Mannoni, Laurent, Werner Nekes and Marina Warner, eds, *Eyes, Lies and Illusions* (London: Hayward Gallery, 2005).

Manovich, Lev, *The Language of New Media* (Cambridge, MA: The MIT Press, 2001).

Marks, Laura U., *The Skin of the Film: Intercultural Cinema, Embodiment, and the Senses* (Durham, NC: Duke University Press, 2000).

Marks, Laura U., *Touch: Sensuous Theory and Multisensory Media* (Minneapolis, MN: University of Minnesota Press, 2002).

McLuhan, Marshall, *The Gutenberg Galaxy: The Making of Typographic Man* (London: Routledge, 1962).

McLuhan, Marshall, *Understanding Media: The Extensions of Man* (London: Routledge, 1964).

Mecke, Jochen and Volker Roloff, eds, *Kino-/(Ro)Mania: Intermedialität zwischen Film und Literatur* (Tübingen: Stauffenburg, 1999).

Merleau-Ponty, Maurice, *The Visible and the Invisible* (Evanston, IL: Northwestern University Press, 1968).

Metz, Christian, *Language and Cinema* (The Hague: Mouton de Gruyter, 1974).

Mirzoeff, Nicholas, ed., *The Visual Culture Reader* (New York, NY: Routledge, 2002).

Mulvey, Laura, *Death 24x a Second: Stillness and the Moving Image* (London: Reaktion, 2006).

Odin, Roger, 'Spectator, Film and the Mobile Phone', in Ian Christie, ed., *Audiences* (Amsterdam: Amsterdam University Press, 2012), pp. 155–70.

Packer, Randal and Ken Jordan, eds, *Multimedia. From Wagner to Virtual Reality* (New York, NY: W.W. Norton, 2001).

Paech, Joachim and Jens Schröter, eds, *Intermedialität – Analog /Digital. Theorien – Methoden – Analysen* (München: Wilhelm Fink, 2008).

Pedulla, Gabriele, *In Broad Daylight: Movies and Spectators after the Cinema* (London: Verso, 2012).

Popple, Simon and Vanessa Toulmin, eds, *Visual Delights: Essays on the Popular and Projected Image in the Nineteenth Century* (Trowbridge: Flicks Books, 2000).

Rajewsky, Irina O., 'Intermediality, Intertextuality, and Remediation: A Literary Perspective on Intermediality', *intermédialités: histoire et théorie des arts des lettres et des techniques* 6 (automne, 2005), 43–64.

Rieser, Martin and Andrea Zapp, eds, *The New Screen Media: Cinema/Art/Narrative* (London: British Film Institute, 2008).

Robillard, Valerie and Els Jongeneel, eds, *Pictures Into Words: Theoretical and Descriptive Approaches to Ekphrasis* (Amsterdam: VU University Press, 1998).

Rodowick, D. N., *The Virtual Life of Film* (Cambridge, MA: Harvard University Press, 2007).

Roloff, Volker, 'Film und Literatur: Zur Theorie und Praxis intermedialer Analyse am Beispiel von Buñuel, Truffaut, Godard und Antonioni', in Peter Zima, ed., *Literatur intermedial: Musik-Malerei-Photographie-Film* (Darmstadt: Turnshare, 1995), pp. 269–309.

Sconce, Jeffrey, *Haunted Media: Electronic Presence from Telegraphy to Television* (Durham, NC: Duke University Press, 2000).

Shail, Andrew, 'Reading the Cinematograph: Short Fiction and the Intermedial Spheres of Early Cinema', *Early Popular Visual Culture* 8.1 (2010), 47–62.

Sobchack, Vivian, *The Address of the Eye: The Phenomenology of Film Experience* (Princeton, NJ: Princeton University Press, 1992).

Sobchack, Vivian, *Meta-morphing: Visual Transformation and the Culture of Quick-change* (Minneapolis, MN: University of Minnesota Press, 2000).

Sobchack, Vivian, *Carnal Thoughts: Embodiment and Moving Image Culture* (Berkeley, CA: University of California Press, 2004).

Snickars, Pelle and Patrick Vonderau, eds, *Moving Data: The iPhone and the Future of Media* (New York, NY: Columbia University Press, 2012).

Stewart, Susan, *On Longing: Narratives of the Miniature, the Gigantic, the Souvenir, the Collection* (Durham, NC: Duke University Press, 1993, repr. 2007).

Strauven, Wanda, ed., *The Cinema of Attractions Reloaded* (Amsterdam: Amsterdam University Press, 2007).

Sumich, Julianne S., 'Conceptual Fusion: Coleridge, Higgins, and the Intermedium' (2007), at: <http://www.intermedia.ac.nz/pdfs/ConceptualFusionISBN.pdf>.

Thorburn, David and Henry Jenkins, eds, *Rethinking Media Change: The Aesthetics of Transition* (Cambridge, MA: The MIT Press, 2003).

Tryon, Chuck, *Reinventing Cinema: Movies in the Age of Media Convergence* (New Brunswick, NJ: Rutgers University Press, 2009).

Tsivian, Yuri, *Early Cinema in Russia and Its Cultural Reception*, trans. Alan Bodger (Chicago, IL: University of Chicago Press, 1994).

Valiaho, Pasi, *Mapping the Moving Image: Gesture, Thought and Cinema circa 1900* (Amsterdam: Amsterdam University Press, 2010).

Vertov, Dziga, *Kino-Eye: The Writings of Dziga Vertov*, ed. Annette Michelson, trans. Kevin O'Brien (Berkeley, CA: University of California Press, 1985).

Vieira, Célia, *Inter Media: Littérature, cinéma et intermédialité* (Paris: Harmattan, 2011).

Wagner, Hans-Peter, ed., *Icons – Texts – Iconotexts: Essays on Ekphrasis and Intermediality* (Berlin and New York, NY: Walter de Gruyter, 1996).

Warner, Marina, *Phantasmagoria: Spirit Visions, Metaphors, and Media into the Twenty-First Century* (Oxford: Oxford University Press, 2006).

Willis, Sharon, 'Lost Objects: The Museum of Cinema', in Paul Smith, ed., *The Renewal of Cultural Studies* (Philadelphia, PA: Temple University Press, 2011), pp. 93–102.

Winthrop-Young, Geoffrey and Michael Wutz, eds, *Configurations: A Journal of Literature, Science, and Technology* 10.1 (Winter, 2002), special issue on 'Media, Materiality, Memory: Aspects of Intermediality'.

Young, Paul, 'Telling Descriptions: Frank Norris's Kinetoscopic Naturalism and the Future of the Novel, 1899', *Modernism/Modernity* 14.4 (November 2007), 645–68.

Young, Paul, 'Film Genre Theory and Contemporary Media: Description, Interpretation, Intermediality', in Robert Kolker ed., *The Oxford Handbook of Film and Media Studies* (Oxford: Oxford University Press, 2008).

Youngblood, Gene, *Expanded Cinema*, intro. R. Buckminster Fuller (New York, NY: P. Dutton, 1970).

Zielinski, Siegfried, *Deep Time of the Media: Towards an Archaeology of Hearing and Seeing by Technical Means* (Cambridge, MA: The MIT Press, 2006).

Zima, Peter, *Literatur intermedial. Musik–Malerei–Photographie–Film* (Darmstadt: Turnshare, 1995).

Index